WITTGENSTEIN'S
PHILOSOPHICAL INVESTIGATIONS

IDENTITY
AS
PARADOX

BART KEEGAN

Wittgenstein's *Philosophical Investigations*: Identity as Paradox
© 2025 Bart Keegan

trabkeegan@talktalk.net
b1omediaworx.com/bartkeegan

ISBN (hardcover): 978-1-7364497-9-0
ISBN (paperback): 978-1-7364497-3-8
ISBN (Amazon paperback): 979-8-2944182-3-6
ISBN (ebook, all formats): 978-1-7364497-8-3

Published by
B1o Mediaworx
P.O. Box 1233
Liberty, MO 64069
U.S.A.

All rights reserved. Without limiting the rights under copyright reserved above, no part of this publication may be reproduced, stored in or introduced into a retrieval system, or transmitted, in any form, or by any means (electronic, mechanical, photocopying, recording, or otherwise) without the prior written permission of both the copyright owner and the above publisher of this book.

WORKS

- *Diary of Atonement: The case for good and evil*

- *Poems & Prose of Atonement*

- *Wittgenstein's* Philosophical Investigations: *Identity as Paradox*

WORKS

CONTENTS

INTRODUCTION	1
PHILOSOPHICAL INVESTIGATIONS	3
BIBLIOGRAPHY	311
ABOUT THE AUTHOR	313

INTRODUCTION

This book targets philosophers and their students, not the ordinary reader.

The present volume will be referred to as the IAP work – the *Identity as Paradox* work. IAP treats with Remarks 201-693 inclusive in Part 1 of Wittgenstein's *Philosophical Investigations* (PI) work. IAP offers the perspective that the PI thesis is this: that, concerning the law of identity signed by A = A, and contrary to monistic tradition whereby the law is of identity as a onefold-only sense of consistency signed by A as itself, the law is instead of a threefold sense of identity-as-paradox (signed by ' = ') and identical paradox faces (signed by the A/A cases); hence, per this thesis, where the law states of identity that *it is itself,* identity is signified neither by *it* nor by *itself* but by *is* cf. Remark 216. By implication of such thesis, western philosophy is to be re-written – its entire thinking to be understood anew.

Throughout IAP, frequent reference is made to a Remark locating outside the 201-693 corpus, viz., PI 43 which remarks that the meaning of a word is its use in a language.

For IAP, identity-as-paradox is spoken of as the rule, the law of which is spoken of as the grammar – it is the threefold case of paradox + faces (and variants) i.e. paradox + its mutually eclipsing opposite cases. In this regard, two analogies are offered: the drabbit + duck/rabbit faces case (see at PI 201), also the ladder + its way-up/way-down aspects case.

The PI work nowhere states identity law to be other than threefold in its being paradox + faces qua threefold as neither member of paired opposites

+ paired opposites. From which, per the IAP perspective, for Jones to ask "Who or what am I?" would be to answer "I am as the weather – betimes or always either in storm or in sunshine". Here, in variant terms, one would live either objectively happily or objectively unhappily but in either case would be to live objectively. It is, so to say, in objectivity that one soars aloft as freedom.

IAP presents its content in terms of each PI remark being italicised to distinguish it from its treatment, followed by its non-italicised threefold treatment thus: Thesis-rehearsal statement + Comment + Games-talk, bespeaking the proposed PI thesis of IAP. On occasion, the Comment/Games parts are combined. The combination cases aside, any departures from this four-part presentation per each PI remark such as, say, the remark not being fully italicised, are errata. Throughout the entirety of the near-500 PI texts treated with in the IAP work, each PI remark thus presented is given clear and crisply concise treatment.

PHILOSOPHICAL INVESTIGATIONS

201. This was our paradox: no course of action could be determined by a rule, because every course of action can be brought into accord with the rule. The answer was: if every course of action can be brought into accord with the rule, then it can also be brought into conflict with it. And so there would be neither accord nor conflict here.

*That there is a misunderstanding here is shown by the mere fact that in this chain of reasoning we place one interpretation behind another, as if each one contented us at least for a moment, until we thought of yet another lying behind it. For what we thereby show is that there is a way of grasping a rule which is **not** an interpretation, but which, from case to case of application, is exhibited in what we call "following the rule" and "going against it".*

That's why there is an inclination to say: every action according to a rule is an interpretation. But one should speak of interpretation only when one expression of a rule is substituted for another.

DRABBIT

RULE, IDENTITY, PARADOX

DUCK   RABBIT

COURSES OF ACTION, IDENTICAL CASES, PARADOX FACES

Proposal: PI 201 serves as the thesis of the *Investigations* philosophy, the thesis that identity is paradox.

Comment. Per PI 201: no course of action (rule-interpretation, paradox face) can be decisively the case (not because competing interpretations are contradictories but) because competing cases eclipse and are eclipsed by one another (are accordant and conflicting, or are substituting-for and substituted-by, or are rule-following and going-against-the-rule, with respect to one another); hence, identity-as-paradox, here as rule, is neither of its competing aspects but as their coincidence exists by turns as each.

Games: paradox + faces; rule + interpretations (courses of action); mutual eclipse + mutually eclipsing participants; per identity law, stating of identity that *it is itself,* is + *it/itself* cases; per PI 216, identity + identical cases; per analogies, ladder + up/down aspects, drabbit + duck/rabbit faces.

202. *That's why 'following a rule' is a practice. And to **think** one is following a rule is not to follow a rule. And that's why it's not possible to follow a rule 'privately'; otherwise, thinking one was following a rule would be the same thing as following it.*

To rehearse. The (PI 201) thesis of the *Investigations* is that identity is paradox, called the rule, as neither of opposite cases + existing as both qua either.

Comment. Per PI 202: the text reads grammatically (lawfully) as follows; by PI 201, a course of action (here, thinking, a private case) is rule-accordant, also rule-discordant; it cannot be the one twin alone; as grammatically (not logically, not empirically) both twins, it is rule-accordant and rule-discordant but not instead of rule-accordant but as well as rule accordant.

Games: paradox + (mutually eclipsing) faces; practice + practice/practice, verb-sense/noun-sense, practising/practised – cases; per PI 43, word + meaning/use – cf. thinking/speaking – courses of action; per analogies, ladder + up/down aspects, drabbit + duck/rabbit faces.

*203. Language is a labyrinth of paths. You approach from **one** side and know your way about; you approach the same place from another side and no longer know your way about.*

To rehearse. The (PI 201) thesis of the *Investigations* is that identity is paradox, called the rule, as neither of opposite cases + existing as both qua either.

Comment. Per PI 203: a metaphor for language is labyrinth; the labyrinth comprises two side-approaches, not one-only side-approach; the two paths lead to a same place; one approach is familiar, the other unfamiliar; from which, paradox (in a grammar qua law) is to faces; as same-place (in a labyrinth) is to unfamiliar/familiar approaches; as per PI 43, word (in a language) is to meaning/use – cf. private/public – cases.

Games: paradox + faces; same place + approaches; word (language) + meaning/use (private/public) cases; per PI 215, sameness + same/same cases; per analogies, ladder + up/down aspects, drabbit + duck/rabbit faces.

204. As things are, I can, for example, invent a game that is never played by anyone. – But would the following be possible too: mankind has never played any games; once though, someone invented a game – which, however, was never played?

To rehearse. The (PI 201) thesis of the *Investigations* is that identity is paradox, called the rule, as neither of opposite cases + existing as both qua either.

Comment. Per PI 204: grammatically (lawfully), the gaming case is to its private/public, invented/customary, cases; as the humankind case is to its gaming/non-gaming cases; as a paradox is to its faces.

Games: paradox + faces; gaming case + inventor/populace cases; humankind + gaming/non-gaming – inventor/otherwise – cases; per analogies, ladder + up/down aspects, drabbit + duck/abbot faces.

*205. "But that is just what is remarkable about **intention**, about the mental process, that the existence of a custom, of a technique, is not necessary to it. That, for example, it is imaginable that two people should play a game of chess, or even only the beginning of a game of chess, in a world in which otherwise no games existed – and then be interrupted."*

But isn't chess defined by its rules? And how are these rules present in the mind of someone who intends to play chess?

To rehearse. The (PI 201) thesis of the *Investigations* is that identity is paradox, called the rule, as neither of opposite cases + existing as both qua either.

Comment. Per PI 205: whatsoever the logical or empirical sense of (say) chess as an intention case, it is grammatically (lawfully) it meaning as paradoxically its play, its intending aspect as paradoxically its intended aspect.

Games: paradox + faces; rule + courses of action; intention + intending/intended – intentional/move-played, mind/behaviour – cases; gaming + verb/ noun senses; per analogies, ladder + up/down aspects, drabbit + duck/rabbit faces.

*206. Following a rule is analogous to obeying an order. One is trained to do so, and one reacts to an order in a particular way. But what if one person reacts to the order and training **thus**, and another **otherwise**? Who is right, then?*

Suppose you came as an explorer to an unknown country with a language quite unknown to you. In what circumstances would you say that the people there gave orders, understood them, obeyed them, rebelled against them, and so on?

Shared human behaviour is the system of reference by means of which we interpret an unknown language.

To rehearse. The (PI 201) thesis of the *Investigations* is that identity is paradox, called the rule, as neither of opposite cases + existing as both qua either.

Comment. Per PI 206: the logical and empirical talk translates grammatically (lawfully) as follows; rule + interpretations; paradox + faces; order + reactions; human behaviour + cultures; whatever the threefold language game, the paradox-face cases are mutually eclipsing – right-or-wrong/wrong-or-right – cases.

Games: paradox + faces; rule + interpretations; order + reactions; per PI 43, word + meaning/use cases; life + language/deed cases; human language + cultures; per analogies, ladder + up/down ways, drabbit + duck/rabbit faces.

207. Let's imagine that the people in that country carried on usual human activities and in the course of them employed, apparently, an articulate language. If we watch their activities, we find them intelligible, they seem 'logical'. But when we try to learn their language, we find it impossible to do so. For there is no regular connection between what they say, the sounds they make, and their activities; but still these sounds are not superfluous, for if, for example, we gag one of these people, this has the same consequences as with us: without those sounds their actions fall into confusion – as I feel like putting it.

Are we to say that these people have a language: orders, reports, and so on?

There is not enough regularity for us to call it "language".

To rehearse. The (PI 201) thesis of the *Investigations* is that identity is paradox, called the rule, as neither of opposite cases + existing as both qua either.

Comment. Per PI 207: by the threefold grammar (law), paradox is to faces; as human life is to language/deed cases; as per PI 43, language (word) is to meaning/use cases; from which, the meaning/use cases, like the language/deed cases, are) connected regularly qua paradoxically, not regularly qua logically necessarily (see PI 208 next, on regularity as paradox).

Games: paradox + faces cf. regularity + regularly connected cases; human culture + language/activities cases; per analogies, ladder + up/down aspects, drabbit + duck/rabbit faces.

208. Then am I explaining what "order" and "rule" mean in terms of "regularity"? – How do I explain the meaning of "regular", "uniform", "same" to anyone? – I'll explain these words to someone who, say, speaks only French by means of the corresponding French words. But if a person has not yet got the **concepts**, I'll teach him to use the words by means of **examples** and by **exercises**. – And when I do this, I do not communicate less to him than I know myself.

In the course of this teaching, I'll show him the same colours, the same lengths, the same shapes; I'll make him find them and produce them; and so on. For example, I'll teach him to continue an ornamental pattern 'uniformly' when told to do so. – And also, to continue progressions. That is, for example, when given: ... to go on: ... .

I do it, he does it after me; and I influence him by expressions of agreement, rejection, expectation, encouragement. I let him go his way, or hold him back; and so on.

Imagine witnessing such teaching. None of the words would be explained by means of itself; there would be no logical circle.

The expressions "and so on", "and so on ad infinitum", are also explained in this teaching. A gesture, among other things, might serve this purpose. The gesture that means "go on like this" or "and so on" has a function comparable to that of pointing to an object or a place.

A distinction is to be drawn between the "and so on" which is and the "and so on" which **is not** an abbreviated notation. "And so on ad inf." is **not** such an abbreviation. The fact that we cannot write down all the digits of π is not a human shortcoming, as mathematicians sometimes think.

Teaching which is not meant to apply to anything but the examples given is different from that which '**points beyond**' them.

To rehearse. The (PI 201) thesis of the *Investigations* is that identity is paradox, called the rule, as neither of opposite cases + existing as both qua either.

Comment. Per PI 208: paradox = identity = rule = order = regularity = sameness = uniformity; these cases are grammatical (lawful) equivalents, featuring in assorted language games; for examples, paradox is to faces; as and-so-one *ad infinitum* is to and-so-one examples; as reach-beyond is to reaching-beyond/reached-beyond cases.

Games: per grammar i.e. by law, assorted games play out as follows; paradox + faces; identity + identical cases (see PI 216); rule + interpretations; order + reactions; regularity + regularly connected cases; sameness + same/same cases (see PI 215) cf. pert analogy, drabbit + duck/rabbit faces; uniformity + uniform/uniform – cf. same/same – cases; teaching qua training + teacher-qua-trainer/learner-qua-trainee cases; language + exemplifying/practice – cf. thinking/practice and pre-conceptual demonstrating/copying – cases; per PI 43, word + meaning/use cases; and-so-one *ad infinitum* + and-so-one examples; reach-beyond + reaching-beyond/reached-beyond cases; per analogies, ladder + up/down aspects, drabbit + duck/rabbit faces.

209. "But then doesn't our understanding reach beyond all examples?" – A very curious expression, and a quite natural one!

*But is that **all**? Isn't there a deeper explanation; or at least, mustn't the **understanding** of the explanation be deeper? – Well, have I myself a deeper understanding? Have I **got** more than I give in the explanation? – But then, whence the feeling that I have more?*

Is it like the case where I interpret what is not limited as a length that reaches beyond every length?

To rehearse. The (PI 201) thesis of the *Investigations* is that identity is paradox, called the rule, as neither of opposite cases + existing as both qua either.

Comment. Per PI 209: from PI 208, the and-so-one *ad infinitum* case is to and-so-one examples; as the reach-beyond case is to reaching-beyond/

reached-beyond – cf. deep/surface, not-limited/limited – cases; from which, nothing is problematical, mysterious, deep, passing beyond all ken other than it being paradoxically opposite cf. per PI 43, meaning is paradoxically use, language is paradoxically deed cf. per PI 304 whereby nothing is to Nothing/Something, as paradox is to faces; in sum, such are assorted language games qua grammar cases qua cases of law.

Games: paradox + faces; reach-beyond + reaching-beyond/reached-beyond – depth/surface, unlimited-length/every-length – cases; mutual understanding + teacher/learner cases of understanding; per analogies, ladder + up/down aspects, drabbit + duck/rabbit faces.

*210. "But do you really explain to the other person what you yourself understand? Don't you leave it to him to **guess** the essential thing? You give him examples – but he has to guess their drift, to guess your intention." – Every explanation which I can give myself I give to him too. – "He guesses what I intend" would amount to: "various interpretations of my explanation come to his mind, and he picks one of them". So in this case he could ask; and I could and would answer him.*

To rehearse. The (PI 201) thesis of the *Investigations* is that identity is paradox, called the rule, as neither of opposite cases + existing as both qua either.

Comment. Per PI 210: grammatically (lawfully, hence neither logically nor empirically), the text translates as follow; teacher-understanding/learner-understanding cases are connected not accidentally by guesswork but grammatically as mutually eclipsing paradox faces, with understanding as the paradox case.

Games: paradox + faces; understanding + teacher/learner cases cf. question/answer cases; understanding (teacher or learner) + verb/noun senses; per analogies, ladder + up/down aspects, drabbit + duck/rabbit faces.

*211. "No matter how you instruct him in continuing the ornamental pattern, how can he **know** how he is to continue it by himself?" – Well, how do **I** know? – If that means "Have I reasons?", the answer is: my reasons will soon give out. And then I shall act, without reasons.*

To rehearse. The (PI 201) thesis of the *Investigations* is that identity is paradox, called the rule, as neither of opposite cases + existing as both qua either.

Comment. Per PI 211: reading the text grammatically (lawfully), knowing is doing cf. duck face is rabbit face; one knows how to perform by performing; here, paradox is to faces; as knowing is to verb/noun senses; as knowledge is to knowing-how/know-how cases.

Games: paradox + faces; task + know-how/enactment cases cf. per PI 43, word + meaning/use cases; per analogies, ladder + up/down aspects, drabbit + duck/rabbit faces.

212. When someone of whom I am afraid orders me to continue a series, I act quickly, with perfect assurance, and the lack of reasons does not trouble me.

To rehearse. The (PI 201) thesis of the *Investigations* is that identity is paradox, called the rule, as neither of opposite cases + existing as both qua either.

Comment. Per PI 212: a fright case (here, an order) as a paradox case has for its faces the fearing/reaction cases; here, grammatically (lawfully), the faces bond with immediacy cf. per analogy, the up/down aspects of a ladder; per grammar sense, the fear and reason cases occur as distinct assorted games-talk cases, each bespeaking identity as paradox (see Games, next).

Games: paradox + faces; order + fear-factor/behavioural-reaction cases; fear + verb/noun senses; reason + verb/noun senses; per analogies, ladder + up/down aspects, drabbit + duck/rabbit faces.

*213. "But this initial segment of a series could obviously be variously interpreted (for example, by means of algebraic expressions), so you must first have chosen **one** such interpretation." – Not at all! A doubt was possible in certain circumstances. But that is not to say that I did doubt, or even could doubt. (What is to be said about the psychological 'atmosphere' of a process is connected with that.)*

*Only intuition could have removed this doubt? – If intuition is an inner voice – how do I know **how** I am to follow it? And how do I know that it doesn't mislead me? For if it can guide me right, it can also guide me wrong.*

((Intuition an unnecessary evasion.))

To rehearse. The (PI 201) thesis of the *Investigations* is that identity is paradox, called the rule, as neither of opposite cases + existing as both qua either.

Comment. Per PI 213: doubt pertains to logic or empiricism (cf. psychology, intuition), not to grammar qua law other than as raw material for grammatical rendering.

Games: paradox + faces (each face as its right/wrong, eclipsing/eclipsed, accordant/discordant, functions); rule + interpretations; initial segment + knowing-how/enactment cases; choice + verb/noun senses; intuition + inner – intuiting/outer-intuited cases; per analogies, ladder + up/down aspects, drabbit + duck/rabbit faces.

214. If an intuition is necessary for continuing the series 1234 ..., then also for continuing the series 2222 ...

To rehearse. The (PI 201) thesis of the *Investigations* is that identity is paradox, called the rule, as neither of opposite cases + existing as both qua either.

Comment. Per PI 214: grammatically (lawfully), hence neither logically not empirically, and in terms of a threefold intuition/intuition/intuition grammar as a threefold face/paradox/face grammar, if the inner voice of intuition is necessary for the enactment of one of the text's series, it thereby is so for the other series.

Games: paradox + faces; either of the text's series as an intuition case + intuition/intuition – inner-voice/enactment – cases; per analogies, ladder + up/down aspects, drabbit + duck/rabbit faces.

*215. But isn't at least the same **the same**?*

For identity we seem to have an infallible paradigm: namely, in the identity of a thing with itself. I feel like saying: "Here at any rate there can't be different interpretations. If someone sees a thing, he sees identity too."

*Then are two things the same when they are what **one** thing is? And how am I to apply what the one thing shows me to the case of two things?*

To rehearse. The (PI 201) thesis of the *Investigations* is that identity is paradox, called the rule, as neither of opposite cases + existing as both qua either.

Comment. Per PI 215: from PI 208, sameness talk is paradox talk; sameness is to same/same cases; as, per analogy, ladder is to up/down cases; as paradox is to faces; by which, grammatically qua lawfully, per each threefold game, the three members live in one another.

Games: paradox + faces; sameness + same/same cases; unity qua sameness + difference qua different or distinct same/same cases; one thing qua coincidence + two things qua coincidental distinct cases; per PI 216 (see next), identity qua identicality or coincidence + identical cases, per analogies, ladder + up/down ways, drabbit + duck/rabbit faces.

216. "A thing is identical with itself." – There is no finer example of a useless sentence, which nevertheless is connected with a certain play of the imagination. It is as if in our imagination we put a thing into its own shape and saw that it fitted.

We might also say: "Every thing fits into itself." — Or again: "Every thing fits into its own shape." While saying this, one looks at a thing and imagines that there was a space left for it and that now it fits into it exactly.

Does this spot ▲ *'**fit**' into its white surrounding? — **But that is just how it would look** if there had at first been a hole in its place and it then fitted into the hole. So when we say "it fits", we are describing not simply this picture, not simply this **situation**.*

"Every coloured patch fits exactly into its surrounding" is a somewhat specialized form of the law of identity.

To rehearse. The (PI 201) thesis of the *Investigations* is that identity is paradox, called the rule, as neither of opposite cases + existing as both qua either.

Comment. Per 216: picture talk is identity-as-paradox talk; per PI 216, also per identity law stating of an identity that *it is itself*, a thing – an it – is identical with itself (cf. per imagination, an it, a spot, a colour patch – poured into its own shape, space, surrounding, hole, and fitting exactly cf. per analogy drabbit + duck/rabbit faces).

Games: identity-as-paradox + identical paradox faces (and imaginative-talk parallel cases; per identity law, *is* + *it/itself cases* cf. per PI 215, sameness + same/same cases; per analogies, ladder + up/down aspects, drabbit + duck/rabbit faces.

*217. "How am I able to follow a rule?" — If this is not a question about causes, then it is about the justification for my acting in **this** way in complying with the rule.*

Once I have exhausted the justifications, I have reached bedrock, and my spade is turned. Then I am inclined to say: "This is simply what I do."

(Remember that we sometimes demand explanations for the sake not of their content, but of their form. Our requirement is an architectural one; the explanation a kind of sham corbel that supports nothing.)

To rehearse. The (PI 201) thesis of the *Investigations* is that identity is paradox, called the rule, as neither of opposite cases + existing as both qua either.

Comment. Per PI 217: from PI 201, per grammar qua law, each paradox face is rule following (eclipsing), also not rule following (eclipsed); by which, a face is paradoxically a counterpart face; logic is action; thinking is doing; a this-way case is a that-way case; whatever the games-talk case, each of the paired opposites justifies qua warrants the other being the case in that the pair are each other cf. per analogy, the up/down ladder aspects; either of the pair in the absence of a counterpart is sham, ungrammatical, unlawful.

Games: paradox + faces; rule +interpretations; per analogies, ladder + up/down aspects, drabbit + duck/rabbit faces.

218. Whence the idea that the beginning of a series is a visible section of rails invisibly laid to infinity? Well, we might imagine rails instead of a rule. And infinitely long rails correspond to the unlimited application of a rule.

To rehearse. The (PI 201) thesis of the *Investigations* is that identity is paradox, called the rule, as neither of opposite cases + existing as both qua either.

Comment. Per PI 218: grammatically (lawfully), per paradox, face is to counterpart face; as per rule, application is to variant application; as per series or rail-track, finite and visible is to infinite and invisible; as per PI 43, word (language) is to use/meaning (public/private) cases.

Games: paradox + faces; rule + applications; mutual-eclipse activity + mutually eclipsing participants; series or rail-track + beginning/ongoing – cf. finite/infinite, visible/invisible – cases; word (language) + use/meaning (public/private) cases; per analogies, ladder + up/down aspects, drabbit + duck/rabbit faces.

219. *"All the steps are really already taken" means: I no longer have any choice. The rule, once stamped with a particular meaning, traces the lines along which it is to be followed through the whole of space. – But if something of this sort really were the case, how would it help me?*

No; my description made sense only if it was to be understood symbolically. – I should say: **This is how it strikes me***.*

When I follow the rule, I do not choose.

I follow the rule **blindly***.*

To rehearse. The (PI 201) thesis of the *Investigations* is that identity is paradox, called the rule, as neither of opposite cases + existing as both qua either.

Comment. Per PI 219: it is not grammatically (lawfully) the case that identity as the rule cf. drabbit is onefold, offering no choice but to be understood blindly as categorical; rather, however, it only appears (strikes on as being) a consistently monistic identity; symbolically understood, its grammar is indeed that of a onefold case but this as a rule-interpretation case qua paradox face only, functioning as a rule-accordant or paradox-face-eclipsing case cf. drabbit is not really a duck but merely appears to be a duck.

Games: paradox + face i.e. rule + courses-of-action – each face (action) as symbolically drabbit (rule); per analogies, ladder + up/down aspects drabbit + duck/rabbit faces.

220. *But what is the purpose of that symbolical sentence? It was supposed to highlight a difference between causal and logical dependence.*

To rehearse. The (PI 201) thesis of the *Investigations* is that identity is paradox, called the rule, as neither of opposite cases + existing as both qua either.

Comment. Per PI 220: PI 219 employed logical talk to imply rule following to be necessitated by the rule as a onefold identity of consistency as well as employed empirical talk of this idea of monistic identity as psychologically impacting; the symbolic talk is grammatical talk by which rule following pertains to the rule qua an identity as paradox, with rule following as a paradox face, a rule interpretation.

Games: paradox + faces; per PI 43, word + meaning/use – cf. logical/empirical – cases; per analogies, ladder + up/done aspects, drabbit + duck/rabbit faces.

221. My symbolical expression was really a mythological description of the use of a rule.

To rehearse. The (PI 201) thesis of the *Investigations* is that identity is paradox, called the rule, as neither of opposite cases + existing as both qua either.

Comment. Per PI 221: further to PI 220, and as grammatical qua lawful talk, word-use as paradoxically word-meaning thereby is the case of a symbol qua mythological description qua face-only (interpretation-only) of identity-as-paradox (identity-as-rule), hence is not the identity itself, the rule itself.

Games: paradox + faces; per PI 43, word + meaning/use cases; rule + interpretations; per analogies, ladder + up/done aspects, drabbit + duck/rabbit faces.

222. "The line intimates to me the way I am to go." – But that is, of course, only a picture. And if I judged that it intimated this or that, as it were, irresponsibly, I wouldn't say that I was following it like a rule.

To rehearse. The (PI 201) thesis of the *Investigations* is that identity is paradox, called the rule, as neither of opposite cases + existing as both qua either.

Comment. Per PI 222: pertaining to grammar (law), line qua intimation is to this/that – intimating/intimated – cases; as paradox is to faces; as rule is to interpretations; as picture is to out-pictures; from which variant threefold games, each paradox-face case is eclipsing (responsible rule following), also eclipsed (irresponsible non-rule-following).

Games: paradox + faces; rule + interpretations; picture + out-pictures; intimation + this/that – intimating/intimated – cases; per analogies, ladder + up/down aspects, drabbit + duck/rabbit faces.

223. One does not feel that one has always got to wait upon the nod (the prompt) of the rule. On the contrary, we are not on tenterhooks about what it will tell us next, but it always tells us the same, and we do what it tells us.

One might say to the person one was training: "Look, I always do the same thing: I..."

To rehearse. The (PI 201) thesis of the *Investigations* is that identity is paradox, called the rule, as neither of opposite cases + existing as both qua either.

Comment. Per PI 223: from PI 215, considered grammatically (lawfully), the case of paradox + faces, like the case of rule + interpretations, is the case of a sameness + different same/same cases cf. the up/down ladder aspects; to teach the case of a rule is to teach the case of a sameness; whatever the threefold language game, its three members interrelate with immediacy in that all three reside in one another cf. drabbit + duck/rabbit faces.

Games: paradox + faces; sameness + same/same cases; rule-as-paradox + telling/ doing cases cf. PI 43, word + meaning/use cases; task-performance + teacher/ learner cases; coincidence qua immediacy of connection + distinct coincidental cases; per analogies, ladder + up/down aspects, drabbit + duck/rabbit faces.

*224. The word "accord" and the word "rule" are **related** to one another; they are cousins. If I teach anyone the use of the one word, he learns the use of the other with it.*

To rehearse. The (PI 201) thesis of the *Investigations* is that identity is paradox, called the rule, as neither of opposite cases + existing as both qua either.

Comment. Per PI 224: grammatically (lawfully), paradox is to faces, each face as an eclipsing/eclipsed functionality; as rule is to interpretations (courses of action), each as accordant/discordant functionality; from which, the rule/accord cases are indirectly co-referenced – by metaphor, cousins.

Games: paradox + faces; rule + actions; per analogies, ladder + up/down aspects, drabbit + duck/rabbit faces.

225. The use of the word "rule" and the use of the word "same" are interwoven. (As are the use of "proposition" and the use of "true".)

To rehearse. The (PI 201) thesis of the *Investigations* is that identity is paradox, called the rule, as neither of opposite cases + existing as both qua either.

Comment. Per PI 225: in terms of grammar (law), the meaning of a word (rule, same, proposition, true) is its use; by which, the word-uses are interwoven, each within its own threefold language game with the other two members of that game, also interwoven each with the others as parallel-sense word-uses locating in parallel-sense assorted games, each game bespeaking identity as paradox.

Games: paradox + faces; word + meaning/use cases; per analogies, ladder + up/down aspects, drabbit + duck/rabbit faces.

226. Suppose someone continues the sequence 1, 3, 5, 7, ... in expanding the series 2x – 1. And now he asks himself, "But am I always doing the same thing, or something different every time?"

If, from one day to the next, someone promises: "Tomorrow I'll come to see you" – is he saying the same thing every day, or every day something different?

To rehearse. The (PI 201) thesis of the *Investigations* is that identity is paradox, called the rule, as neither of opposite cases + existing as both qua either.

Comment. Per PI 226: grammatically (lawfully), from PI 215, sameness is to different same/same cases; as (per analogy) ladder is to up/down ways; as paradox is to faces; as rule is to actions; as same formula – like same promise – is to repeated performances.

Games: paradox + faces; sameness + difference qua different same/same cases; per analogies, ladder + up/down aspects, drabbit + duck/rabbit faces.

227. Would it make sense to say: "If he did something **different** every time, we wouldn't say he was following a rule"? That makes **no** sense.

To rehearse. The (PI 201) thesis of the *Investigations* is that identity is paradox, called the rule, as neither of opposite cases + existing as both qua either.

Comment. Per PI 227: here, the case of it being sound sense to say that same is difference is warranted by the threefold games talk of paradox + faces, and variants; hence, it makes sound grammatical (lawful) sense – not consistency sense – to say that same is difference, and vice versa. So, see PI 226.

Games: paradox + faces; per PI 215, sameness + different qua distinct same/same cases cf. ladder + up/down ways; per analogies, ladder + up/down aspects, drabbit + duck/rabbit faces.

228. "A series presents us with **one** face!" – All right, but which one? Well, surely, the algebraic one, with a segment of the expansion. Or does it have yet another face? – "But surely everything is already contained in this one!" – But that is not an observation about the segment of the series, or about anything that we notice in it; it gives expression to the fact that all we do is read the lips of the rule and **act**, without appealing to anything else for guidance.

To rehearse. The (PI 201) thesis of the *Investigations* is that identity is paradox, called the rule, as neither of opposite cases + existing as both qua either.

Comment. Per PI 228: continuing the theme of rule + course of action qua paradox + faces qua sameness + difference, the PI 228 talk is of any one-face + all-contained-faces cf. the analogy of drabbet's eclipsing face + all other faces hidden therein; whatever the threefold language game, it suffices as the entirety of the grammar qua law of an identity-as-paradox qua rule by which meaning is paradoxically its employment.

Games: paradox + faces; rule-as-paradox + interpretations; per PI 43, word + meaning/use cases; per PI 215, sameness + different cases; series + segments; rule-as-paradox + lip-reading/action – understanding/enactment – cases; per analogies, ladder + up/down aspects, drabbit + duck/ rabbit faces.

229. I believe that I faintly perceive a pattern in the segment of the series, a characteristic feature, which needs only an "and so on" in order to reach to infinity.

To rehearse. The (PI 201) thesis of the *Investigations* is that identity is paradox, called the rule, as neither of opposite cases + existing as both qua either.

Comment. Per PI 229: the threefold cases of grammar (law) are these; a series of pattern segments is to a series of paradox faces; as the faintly perceived pattern qua characteristic feature locating in the segments is to the indirectly evidenced paradox case locating in the faces; as the and-so-on activity to repeat in the segments to infinity is to the endless mutual-eclipse activity of the faces.

Games: paradox + faces; pattern + segments; per analogies, ladder + up/down aspects, drabbit + duck/rabbit faces.

*230. "The line intimates to me the way I'm to go" is only a paraphrase of: it is my **final** court of appeal for the way I'm to go.*

22   IDENTITY AS PARADOX

To rehearse. The (PI 201) thesis of the *Investigations* is that identity is paradox, called the rule, as neither of opposite cases + existing as both qua either.

Comment. Per PI 230: the grammar talk (law talk) is of intimation + intimating/intimated cases; to rehearse: whatever the threefold language game, it suffices as – is the final court of appeal for – the grammar of identity as paradox whereby meaning is paradoxically its enactment.

Games: paradox + faces; line + directions; intimation + intimating/intimated cases; per analogies, ladder + up/down aspects, drabbit + duck/rabbit faces.

231. "But surely you can see …!" That's precisely the characteristic exclamation of someone who is compelled by a rule.

To rehearse. The (PI 201) thesis of the *Investigations* is that identity is paradox, called the rule, as neither of opposite cases + existing as both qua either.

Comment. Per PI 231: the logical-sense talk, like the empirical-sense talk, translates grammatically (lawfully) as follows; the surely seen case is to the unsurely seen case; as compulsion is to none; as characteristic exclamation is to none; as paradox eclipsing face is to counterpart eclipsed face.

Games: paradox + eclipsing/eclipsed faces; rule + accordant/conflicting interpretations; what-is-the-case + surely-seen/unsurely-seen cases; per analogies, ladder + up/down aspects, drabbit + duck/rabbit faces.

*232. Suppose that a rule intimates to me how I'm to follow it; that is, as my eye travels along the line, an inner voice tells me "Draw **this** way!" – What's the difference between this process of following a kind of inspiration and that of following a rule? For they surely aren't the same. In the case of inspiration, I **await** direction. I won't be able to teach anyone else my 'technique' of following the line. Unless, indeed, I teach him some way of listening, some kind of receptivity. But then, of course, I can't expect him to follow the line in the same way as I do.*

These aren't the experiences I have gained from acting from inspiration and from acting according to a rule; they're grammatical remarks.

To rehearse. The (PI 201) thesis of the *Investigations* is that identity is paradox, called the rule, as neither of opposite cases + existing as both qua either.

Comment. Per PI 232: in terms of converting logical talk or empirical talk to grammatical (lawful) talk, the threefold case of inspiration + guidance/enactment temporal cases are the threefold case of paradox + faces qua rule + interpretations.

Games: paradox + faces; rule + interpretations; inspiration + inner-inspiring/inspired cases; intimation + intimating/intimated cases; per analogies, ladder + up/down ways, drabbit + duck/rabbit faces.

233. One might also imagine such instruction in a certain kind of arithmetic. Children could then calculate, each in their own way – as long as they listened to their inner voice and followed it. Calculating in this way would resemble a sort of composing.

To rehearse. The (PI 201) thesis of the *Investigations* is that identity is paradox, called the rule, as neither of opposite cases + existing as both qua either.

Comment. Per PI 233: grammatically (lawfully), the threefold case of paradox + faces is that of composition cf. inspiration + inner-voice/outer-enactment cases, also calculation by common agreement + calculating/calculated cases i.e. agreement + agreeing/agreed cases.

Games: paradox + faces; rule + interpretations; calculation + private-guidance/public-expression cases cf. per PI 43, word (language) + meaning/use (private/public) cases; music + inspiration/playing case i.e. composing/ composed cases; per analogies, ladder + up/down aspects, drabbit + duck/rabbit faces.

234. Wouldn't it be possible for us, however, to calculate as we actually do (all agreeing, and so on), and still at every step to have a feeling of being guided by the rules as by a spell, astonished perhaps at the fact that we agreed? (Perhaps giving thanks to the Deity for this agreement.)

To rehearse. The (PI 201) thesis of the *Investigations* is that identity is paradox, called the rule, as neither of opposite cases + existing as both qua either.

Comment. PI 234: for its grammar (law) the text presents assorted language games, viz., calculation + calculating/calculated cases, enchantment + spell-bound/activity cases, inspiration + divine-guiding/guided-human cases.

Gomes: paradox + faces; rule + interpretations; calculation + private/public cases cf. per PI 43, word (language) + meaning/use (private/public) cases; agreement + agreed cases; per analogies, ladder + up/down aspects, drabbit + duck/rabbit faces.

235. From this you can see how much there is to the physiognomy of what we call "following a rule" in everyday life.

To rehearse. The (PI 201) thesis of the *Investigations* is that identity is paradox, called the rule, as neither of opposite cases + existing as both qua either.

Comment. Per PI 235: grammatically (lawfully), an eclipsing/eclipsed – rule-following/going-against-the-rule – paradox face is by analogy a physiognomy qua case of changing facial features.

Games: paradox + faces – each face eclipsing/eclipsed in function; rule + interpretations – each interpretation accordant/discordant in function; per analogies, ladder + up/down aspects, drabbit + duck/rabbit faces.

236. Calculating prodigies who arrive at the correct result but can't say how. Are we to say that they do not calculate? (A family of cases.)

To rehearse. The (PI 201) thesis of the *Investigations* is that identity is paradox, called the rule, as neither of opposite cases + existing as both qua either.

Comment. Per PI 236: grammatically (lawfully), whether the empirical case is that of a prodigy or not, calculation is to its verb/noun senses; as paradox is to faces.

Games: paradox + faces; calculation + calculating/calculated cases; per analogies, ladder + up/down aspects, drabbit + duck/rabbit faces.

*237. Imagine someone following a line that serves him as a rule in this way: he holds a pair of compasses, and guides one of its points along the line that is the 'rule', while the other one draws the line that follows the rule. And while he moves along the rule, he alters the opening of the compasses, apparently with great precision, looking at the rule the whole time as if it determined what he did. And watching him, we see no regularity of any kind in this opening and shutting of the compasses. We can't learn his way of following the line from him. Here perhaps we really would say: "The original seems to **intimate** to him how he has to go. But it is not a rule."*

To rehearse. The (PI 201) thesis of the *Investigations* is that identity is paradox, called the rule, as neither of opposite cases + existing as both qua either.

Comment. Per PI 237: the grammar sense (law sense) is this; line qua rule qua paradox is to segments qua interpretations qua faces; as intimation is to verb/noun senses; as original case is to ways to go; as per PI 208, regularity is to different regular/regular cases i.e. irregularity cases; as per PI 215, sameness is to different same/same cases cf. drabbit + duck/rabbit faces.

Games: paradox + faces; rule + interpretations; line + segments; per analogies, ladder + up/down aspects; drabbit + duck/rabbit faces.

*238. The rule can only seem to me to produce all its consequences in advance if I draw them as **a matter of course**. As much as it is a matter of course for me to call this colour "blue". (Criteria for 'its being a matter of course' for me.)*

To rehearse. The (PI 201) thesis of the *Investigations* is that identity is paradox, called the rule, as neither of opposite cases + existing as both qua either.

Comment. Per PI 238: the case of a matter of course qua case of the threefold grammar (law) is exemplified by paradox + faces qua rule + consequences as the threefold case of blue + calling/expression cases – cf. per PI 43, word + meaning/use cases.

Games: paradox + faces; rule + interpretations; blue + calling/expression cases; per analogies, ladder + up/down aspects, drabbit + duck/rabbit faces.

239. How is he to know what colour he is to pick out when he hears "red"? – Quite simple: he is to take the colour whose image occurs to him when he hears the word. – But how is he to know which colour it is 'whose image occurs to him'? Is a further criterion needed for that? (There is indeed such a procedure as choosing the colour which occurs to one when one hears the word "...".)

*"'Red' means the colour that occurs to me when I hear the word 'red'" – would be a **definition**. Not an explanation of what signifying something by a word **essentially** is.*

To rehearse. The (PI 201) thesis of the *Investigations* is that identity is paradox, called the rule, as neither of opposite cases + existing as both qua either.

Comment. Per PI 239: knowing the heard-word 'red' is paradoxically pointing to it; its meaning as a knowing case (or as an imaging or as a mentally-occurring case) is paradoxically its enactment case as a pointed-at case; all such talk is grammar talk qua law talk as descriptive talk, not logical or empirical talk as definitional or explanatory talk.

Games: paradox + faces; per PI 43, red as a word + meaning/use – essence/expression, knowing/selecting, mental-process/natural-expression – cases; knowledge + knowing-how/enactment cases; par analogies, ladder + up/down ways, drabbit + duck/rabbit faces.

240. Disputes do not break out (among mathematicians, say) over the question of whether or not a rule has been followed. People don't come to blows over it, for example. This belongs to the scaffolding from which our language operates (for example, yields descriptions).

To rehearse. The (PI 201) thesis of the *Investigations* is that identity is paradox, called the rule, as neither of opposite cases + existing as both qua either.

Comment. Per PI 240: this text grammatically qua lawfully translates thus; paradoxical cases are not contradictories (for they are complementary mutually eclipsing faces of paradox); the threefold scaffolding is the language game, games talk, or grammar talk qua law talk, or description talk, of identity-as-paradox + identical faces cf. drabbit + duck/rabbit faces.

Games: paradox + faces; rule + interpretations; agreement + verb/noun senses; per analogies, ladder + up/down aspects, drabbit + duck/rabbit faces.

*241. "So you are saying that human agreement decides what is true and what is false?" – What is true or false is what human beings **say**; and it is in their **language** that human beings agree. This is agreement not in opinions, but rather in form of life.*

To rehearse. The (PI 201) thesis of the *Investigations* is that identity is paradox, called the rule, as neither of opposite cases + existing as both qua either.

Comment. Per PI 241: the true/false cases, also the case of that which is true or false, belong to the threefold paradox + faces grammar (law) of identity + identical cases – where the identity case is the human form of life; concerning agreement, it is not a matter of opinion that – per analogy – the way-up/way-down rungs of a ladder agree (coincide); rather the coincidence cannot be otherwise than grammatical (lawful).

Games: paradox + faces; rule + interpretations; agreement + agreeing/agreed cases; per PI 43, word (language) + meaning/use cases; that which is true or false + true/false cases; per human life, coincidence + saying/doing cases; per analogies, ladder + up/down aspects, drabbit + duck/rabbit faces.

242. It is not only agreement in definitions, but also (odd as it may sound) agreement in judgements that is required for communication by means of language. This seems to abolish logic, but does not do so. – It is one thing to describe methods of measurement, and another to obtain and state results of measurement. But what we call "measuring" is in part determined by a certain constancy in results of measurement.

To rehearse. The (PI 201) thesis of the *Investigations* is that identity is paradox, called the rule, as neither of opposite cases + existing as both qua either.

Comment. Per PI 242: grammatical (lawful) equivalents are these: paradox = judgement = agreement = communication = sameness; for these (and added) cases, see Games, next.

Games: paradox + faces; agreement + agreeing/agreed cases; per PI 43, word + meaning/use cases; judgement + judgement/judgement – logical/empirical, definition/practice – cases; measurement + measuring/measured – obtaining/stating – cases; per PI 215, sameness + same/same – consistency/consistency, correct/correct, constancy/constancy – cases; language + thinking/speaking cases; communication + communicating-to/communicated-to cases; culture + language/deed cases; life + culture/culture cases; per analogies, ladder + up/down aspects, drabbit + duck/rabbit faces.

243. A human being can encourage himself, give himself orders, obey, blame and punish himself; he can ask himself a question and answer it. So one could imagine human beings who spoke only in monologue, who accompanied their activities by talking to themselves. – An explorer who watched them and listened to their talk might succeed in translating their language into ours. (This would enable him to predict these people's actions correctly, for he also hears them making resolutions and decisions.)

But is it also conceivable that there be a language in which a person could write down or give voice to his inner experiences – his feelings, moods, and so on – for his own use? – Well, can't we do so in our ordinary language? – But that is not what I mean. The words of this language are to refer to what only the speaker can know – to his immediate private sensations. So another person cannot understand the language.

To rehearse. The (PI 201) thesis of the *Investigations* is that identity is paradox, called the rule, as neither of opposite cases + existing as both qua either.

Comment. Per PI 243: for language to be either a private case or a public case grammatically qua lawfully requires that they be referenced to one another for they are paradox-face cases, where language is the paradox case; the man who seemingly talks to himself but not in any way referenced to a public language is not involving in any private language – his is an ungrammatical case cf. per analogy, a one way ladder – such case is not that of a ladder.

Games: paradox + faces; per PI 43, word (language) + meaning/use (private/public) cases; per analogies, ladder + up/down aspects, drabbit + duck/rabbit faces cases.

*244. How do words **refer** to sensations? – There doesn't seem to be any problem here; don't we talk about sensations every day, and name them? But how is the connection between the name and the thing named set up? This question is the same as: How does a human being learn the meaning of names of sensations? For example, of the word "pain". Here is one possibility: words are connected with the primitive, natural, expressions of sensation and used in their place. A* child has hurt himself and he cries; then adults talk to him and teach him exclamations and, later, sentences. They teach the child new pain-behaviour.

"So, you are saying that the word 'pain' really means crying?" – On the contrary: the verbal expression of pain replaces crying; it does not describe it.

To rehearse. The (PI 201) thesis of the *Investigations* is that identity is paradox, called the rule, as neither of opposite cases + existing as both qua either.

Comment. Per PI 244: the variant threefold grammar cases (law cases) are as follows; sensation is to sensation/sensation – sensing/sensed – cases; as pain is to pain/pain – feeling/felt – cases; as paradox is to faces; as word is to meaning/use cases; as refer-to (reference-to) is to referring-to/referred-to (referencing-to/referenced-to) cases; as cry-out is to crying-out/cried-out cases.

Games: paradox + faces; per PI 43, word + meaning/use cases; sense (like pain, like cry, like refer) + verb/noun cases; per analogies, ladder + up/down aspects, drabbit + duck/rabbit faces. cases.

245. *How can I even attempt to interpose language between the expression of pain and the pain?*

To rehearse. The (PI 201) thesis of the *Investigations* is that identity is paradox, called the rule, as neither of opposite cases + existing as both qua either.

Comment. Per PI 245: grammatically (lawfully), a paradox case is interposed between its corresponding paradox-face cases; as a word is between its meaning and use cases; as the word 'pain' is interposed between its feeling case and its expression case; as drabbit is interposed between its duck and rabbit faces.

Games: paradox + faces; per PI 43, word + meaning/use cases; pain + feeling/expression cases; coincidence + coincidental distinct cases; per analogies, ladder + up/down aspects, drabbit + duck/rabbit faces.

246. In what sense are my sensations **private**? — Well, only I can know whether I am really in pain; another person can only surmise it. — In one way this is false, and in another nonsense. If we are using the word "know" as it is normally used (and how else are we to use it?), then other people very often know if I'm in pain. — Yes, but all the same, not with the certainty with which I know it myself! — It can't be said of me at all (except perhaps as a joke) that I **know** I'm in pain. What is it supposed to mean — except perhaps that I **am** in pain?

Other people cannot be said to learn of my sensations **only** from my behaviour — for I cannot be said to learn of them. I **have** them.

This much is true: it makes sense to say about other people that they doubt whether I am in pain; but not to say it about myself.

To rehearse. The (PI 201) thesis of the *Investigations* is that identity is paradox, called the rule, as neither of opposite cases + existing as both qua either.

Comment. Per PI 246: to say that the private case of feeling/felt pain is contradictorily distinct from the public case of witnessed/surmised case is grammatically (lawfully) as falser as it is foolish unless the cases are complementary distinct cases as paradox faces where the paradox case as their coincidence is the pain language case.

Games: paradox + faces; per PI 43, word (say, pain) + meaning/use cases; pain language + private/public cases; pain + feeling/felt – feeling/behaviour – cases; pain + witnessing/surmised – cf. learning/learned, knowing/known, doubting/doubted – cases; per analogies, ladder + up/down aspects, drabbit + duck/rabbit faces.

247. "Only you can know if you had that intention." One might tell someone this when explaining the meaning of the word "intention" to him. For then it means: **that** is how we use it.

(And here "know" means that the expression of uncertainty is senseless.)

To rehearse. The (PI 201) thesis of the *Investigations* is that identity is paradox, called the rule, as neither of opposite cases + existing as both qua either.

Comment. Per PI 247: the threefold case of paradox + faces, as the threefold case of (per PI 43) word + meaning/use cases, and here as the intention + intending/intended case, is the case of threefold grammar (law) where all three members of the case coincide – compare the threefold case of ladder + up/down ways; such coincidence leaves no room for doubting the existence of any of the three members per threefold case, given that one is the case, the others thereby are the case.; all three members per grammar case are inter-connected as the identity-grammar case; such no-uncertainty talk is accounted knowledge talk.

Games: paradox + faces; intention as a word case + meaning/use cases; per analogies, ladder + up/down aspects, drabbit + duck/rabbit faces.

248. The sentence "Sensations are private" is comparable to "One plays patience by oneself".

To rehearse. The (PI 201) thesis of the *Investigations* is that identity is paradox, called the rule, as neither of opposite cases + existing as both qua either.

Comment. Per PI 248: the playing aspect personalised as the player aspect of the patience game is the player-behaviour aspect cf. PI 43, the meaning of the word is its use; the feeling aspect of a sensation is its natural expression; the private aspect of language is its public aspect; such is the grammar qua law of identity-as-paradox.

Games: paradox + faces; language + private/public cases; sensation + feeling/expression – feeling/felt, feeling/behaviour – cases; word + meaning/use cases; patience + thinking/enactment cases; per analogies, ladder + up/down aspects, drabbit + duck/rabbit faces.

249. Are we perhaps over-hasty in our assumption that the smile of a baby is not pretence? – And on what experience is our assumption based?

(Lying is a language-game that needs to be learned like any other one.)

To rehearse. The (PI 201) thesis of the *Investigations* is that identity is paradox, called the rule, as neither of opposite cases + existing as both qua either.

Comment. Per PI 249: by empirical experience, one knows that the baby is innocent of pretence in that it has not yet learned of its possibility – pretence being a learned, not a generic, behaviour; grammatically qua lawfully, however, innocence (cf. truth-telling) connects paradoxically with pretence (lying).

Games: paradox + faces; per PI 43, word + meaning/use cases; smile + innocence/guile cases; per analogies, ladder + up/down aspects, drabbit + duck/rabbit faces.

250. Why can't a dog simulate pain? Is it too honest? Could one teach a dog to simulate pain? Perhaps it is possible to teach it to howl on particular occasions as if it were in pain, even when it isn't. But the right surroundings for this behaviour to be real simulation would still be missing.

To rehearse. The (PI 201) thesis of the *Investigations* is that identity is paradox, called the rule, as neither of opposite cases + existing as both qua either.

Comment. Per PI 250: in terms not of empirical-sense talk or logical-sense talk but grammatical-sense talk qua lawful-sense talk, the cases are these; per dog, training is to verb/noun senses; as paradox is to faces; as per human, simulation (say, pain) is to verb/moon senses; as per PI 43, word is to meaning/use cases; as culture is to language/deed cases; as human life is to cultures.

Games: paradox + faces (and variants, as per Comment); per analogies, ladder + up/down aspects, drabbit + duck/rabbit faces.

251. What does it mean when we say, "I can't imagine the opposite of this" or "What would it be like if it were otherwise?" – For example, when someone has said that my mental images are private; or that only I myself can know whether I am feeling pain; and so forth.

Of course, here "I can't imagine the opposite" doesn't mean: my powers of imagination are unequal to the task. We use these words to fend off something whose form produces the illusion of being an empirical proposition, but which is really a grammatical one.

But why do I say: "I can't imagine the opposite"? Why not: "I can't imagine what you say"?

*Example: "Every rod has a length." That means something like: we call something (or **this**) "the length of a rod" – but nothing "the length of a sphere". Now can I imagine 'every rod having a length'? Well, I just imagine a rod; and that is all. Only this picture, in connection with this proposition, has a quite different role from one used in connection with the proposition "This table has the same length as the one over there". For here I understand what it means to have a picture of the opposite (and it doesn't have to be a mental picture either).*

But the picture that goes together with the grammatical proposition could only show, say, what is called "the length of a rod". And what should the opposite picture be?

((Remark about the negation of an a priori proposition.))

To rehearse. The (PI 201) thesis of the *Investigations* is that identity is paradox, called the rule, as neither of opposite cases + existing as both qua either.

Comment. Per PI 251: by law qua grammar, imagination is to opposite cases; as private-is-public (qua language) is to private-is-no-public (qua distinct cases); as rod-is-length (qua **this**) is to rod-is-not-length (qua distinct cases); as paradox is to faces; as per PI 215, sameness is to different same/same cases cf. as drabbit is to duck/rabbit faces; as per PI 216, identity is to identical cases cf. as ladder is to up/down aspects; as per PI 43, pain, say, as word (language) is to meaning/use (private/public) cases; as *a priori* proposition per identity-law statement 'A is A', 'is'(qua A-as-A affirmation case) is to A-as-not-A (qua distinct cases negation cases).

Games: paradox + faces (and variants, as per Comment); per analogies, ladder + up/down aspects, drabbit + duck/rabbit faces.

252. *"This body has extension."* To these words we could respond by saying: *"Nonsense!"* – but are inclined to reply *"Of course!"* – Why?

To rehearse. The (PI 201) thesis of the *Investigations* is that identity is paradox, called the rule, as neither of opposite cases + existing as both qua either.

Comment. Per PI 252: by law qua grammar, proposition is to opposite cases; as body-is-extension (qua object) is to body/extension cases (qua distinct cases); as paradox is to faces; as per PI 215, sameness is to different same/same cases cf. per PI 216, as identity is to identical cases cf. per analogy, as drabbit is to duck/rabbi. faces; as per PI 43, word is to meaning/use cases; as coincidence is to distinct cases; as *a priori* proposition per identity-law statement 'A is A', 'is' (qua A-as-A affirmation case cf. "Of course") is to A-as-not-A (qua distinct cases, negation cases cf. "Nonsense").

Games: paradox + faces; word + meaning/use cases; identity + identical cases; this case + extension/body – qualitative/quantitative – cases; sameness + same/same cases; object + extension/extension – cf. body/body – cases; per analogies, ladder + ascent/descent cases, drabbit + duck/rabbit faces.

253. *"Another person can't have my pains."* – **My** *pains – what pains are they? What counts as a criterion of identity here? Consider what makes it possible in the case of physical objects to speak of "two exactly the same": for example, to say, "This chair is not the one you saw here yesterday, but is exactly the same as it".*

*In so far as it makes **sense** to say that my pain is the same as his, it is also possible for us both to have the same pain. (And it would also be conceivable* that two people feel pain in the same – not just the corresponding – place. That might be the case with Siamese twins, for instance.)

I have seen a person in a discussion on this subject strike himself on the breast and say: "But surely another person can't have THIS pain!" – The answer to this is that one does not define a criterion of identity by emphatically enunciating the word "this". Rather, the emphasis merely creates the illusion of a case in which we are conversant with such a criterion of identity, but have to be reminded of it.

To rehearse. The (PI 201) thesis of the *Investigations* is that identity is paradox, called the rule, as neither of opposite cases + existing as both qua either.

Comment. Per PI 253: by law (grammar), paradox is to faces; as per PI 43, a word is to its meaning/use cases; as, per PI 216, identity is to its identical cases; as THIS (pain) is to own/his cases; as chair is to then/now cases; as Siamese case is to twins cases.

Games: paradox + faces (and variants, as per Comment); per analogies, ladder + ascent/descent cases, drabbit + duck/rabbit faces.

254. The substitution of "identical" for "the same" (for example) is another typical expedient in philosophy. As if we were talking about shades of meaning, and all that were in question were to find words to hit on the correct nuance. And that is in question in philosophy only where we have to give a psychologically accurate account of the temptation to use a particular mode of expression. What we are 'tempted to say' in such a case is, of course, not philosophy; but it is its raw material. So, for example, what a mathematician is inclined to say about the objectivity and reality of mathematical facts is not a philosophy of mathematics, but something for philosophical **treatment**.

To rehearse. The (201) thesis of the *Investigations* is that identity is paradox, called the rule, as neither of opposite cases + existing as both qua either.

Comment. Per PI 254: to say – whether in everyday discourse, or in the academic language of such as psychology or mathematics – that a case A is the same as or is identical with a case B, and in order to give exactness of sense to case A, is a talk serving as raw material for philosophical grammatical (lawful) treatment; such treatment would be that to say of case A that it is the same as or identical with case B is to say that the same/same cases qua identical/identical cases qua A/B cases are paradoxically – not consistently – one another; they make for a paradox case, not a onefold-only sense; so see PI 215, also PI 216.

Games: paradox + faces; per PI 215, sameness + same/same cases cf. ladder + way-up/way-down cases; per PI 216, identity + identical/identical cases; per analogies, ladder + up/down cases, drabbit + duck/rabbit faces.

255. The philosopher treats a question; like an illness.

To rehearse. The (PI 201) thesis of the *Investigations* is that identity is paradox, called the rule, as neither of opposite cases + existing as both qua either.

Comment. Per PI 255: philosophy for the received mind-set takes inconsistency to be contradiction; grammatically (lawfully), the *Investigations* questions this by taking inconsistency to be the dualism of distinct onefold/onefold – distinct consistency/consistency – complementary paradox faces, coinciding as the identity-as-paradox case; from which, received philosophy is by analogy an illness, as the raw material treated with by the *Investigations* to render its sense as grammatically (lawfully) that of identity as paradox, not identity as onefold-only, as consistency sense.

Games: paradox + faces; coincidence + inconsistent qua distinct – onefold/onefold, consistent/consistent – cases; per analogies, ladder + up/down ways, drabbit + duck/rabbit faces.

256. Now, what about the language which describes my inner experiences and which only I myself can understand? **How** *do I use words to signify my sensations? – As we ordinarily do? Then are my words for sensations tied up with my natural* *expressions of sensation? In that case my language is not a 'private' one. Someone else might understand it as well as I. – But suppose I didn't have any natural expression of sensation, but only had sensations? And now I simply* **associate** *names with sensations, and use these names in descriptions.*

To rehearse. The (PI 201) thesis of the *Investigations* is that identity is paradox, called the rule, as neither of opposite cases + existing as both qua either.

Comment. Per PI 256: the grammar talk qua law talk runs as follows; the private case both is and is not the public case in that it is paradoxically so; it is indirectly so via the paradox case of language; the paradox-face cases are distinct cases as thereby wholly other cases yet – as well – are coincidental cases as the paradox case; compare, from PI 43, meaning/use cases are distinct as well as coincide as the word case; associative connection is paradoxical connection cf. the associated up/down aspects of the ladder.

Games: paradox + faces; word + meaning/use cases; language + private/ public – cf. inner-experience/natural-expression – cases; sensation + sensing/ sensed cases; name + naming/named cases; association + associating/ associated cases; description + describing/described cases; per analogies, ladder + up/down ways, drabbit + duck/rabbit faces.

257. "What would it be like if human beings did not manifest their pains (did not groan, grimace, etc.)? Then it would be impossible to teach a child the use of the word 'toothache'." – Well, let's assume that the child is a genius and invents a name for the sensation by himself! – But then, of course, he couldn't make himself understood when he used the word. – So does he understand the name, without being able to explain its meaning to anyone? – But what does it mean to say that he has 'named his pain'? – How has he managed this naming of pin? And whatever he did, what was its purpose? – When one says "He gave a name to his sensation", one forgets that much must be prepared in the language for mere naming to make sense. And if we speak of someone's giving a name to a pain, the grammar of the word "pain" is what has been prepared here; it indicates the post where the new word is stationed.

To rehearse. The (PI 201) thesis of the *Investigations* is that identity is paradox, called the rule, as neither of opposite cases + existing as both qua either.

Comment. Per PI 257: whether 'pain' is an existing or invented word, it locates – as per PI 43 – in the threefold grammar case (law case) of word + meaning/use cases as the threefold game of paradox + faces, and this as the threefold case of language + private/public aspects; whatever the language game, it is a grammar case as the 'stage-setting' case for a sensation qua a name, as a paradox case, as for its faces its sensing/sensed cases qua its naming/named cases.

Games: paradox + faces; pain as a word + meaning/use cases; sensation + sensing/sensed cases; name + naming/named cases; language + private/public cases; per analogies, ladder + up/down ways, drabbit + duck/rabbit faces.

258. Let's imagine the following case. I want to keep a diary about the recurrence of a certain sensation. To this end I associate it with the sign "S" and write this sign in a calendar for every day on which I have the sensation. – I first want to observe that a definition of the sign cannot be formulated. – But all the same, I can give one to myself as a kind of ostensive definition! – How? Can I point to the sensation? – Not in the ordinary sense. But I speak, or write the sign down, and at the same time I concentrate my attention on the sensation – and so, as it were, point to it inwardly. – But what is this ceremony for? For that is all it seems to be! A definition serves to lay down the meaning of a sign, doesn't it? – Well, that is done precisely by concentrating my attention; for in this way I commit to memory the connection between the sign and the sensation. – But "I commit it to memory" can only mean: this process brings it about that I remember the connection **correctly** *in the future. But in the present case, I have no criterion of correctness. One would like to say: whatever is going to seem correct to me is correct. And that only means that here we can't talk about 'correct'.*

To rehearse. The (PI 201) thesis of the *Investigations* is that identity is paradox, called the rule, as neither of opposite cases + existing as both qua either.

Comment. Per PI 258: grammatically (lawfully) – not logically, not empirically – the text implies as follows; paradox is to faces; as criterion is to qualifying cases; as correctness is to correctly connected – paradoxically connected – cases; as per PI 43, word (here, sensation) is to meaning/use – sensation/ sensation, verb-sense/noun-sense, sensation/"S", feeling/behaviour, ostensive-defining/"S" – cases.

Games: paradox + faces; criterion + qualifying cases; per PI 43, word (here, sensation) + meaning/use aspects (and parallel aspects); word (remembrance, connection) + verb/noun senses; per analogies, ladder + up/down aspects, drabbit + duck/rabbit faces.

*259. Are the rules of the private language **impressions** of rules? – The balance on which impressions are weighed is not the **impression** of a balance.*

To rehearse. The (PI 201) thesis of the *Investigations* is that identity is paradox, called the rule, as neither of opposite cases + existing as both qua either.

Comment. Per PI 259: grammatically (lawfully), rule is to interpretations; as paradox is to faces; as balance is to scales; as language is to private/public cases; as per PI 43, word is to meaning/use – cf. impression/expression – cases.

Games: paradox + faces; rule + interpretations; word + meaning/use cases; language + private/public cases; balance + impression/expression cases; per analogies, ladder + up/down aspects, drabbit + duck/rabbit faces.

*260. "Well, I **believe** that this is the sensation S again." – Perhaps you **believe** that you believe it!*

*Then did the man who made the entry in the calendar make a note of **nothing whatever**? – Don't consider it a matter of course that a person is making a note of something when he makes a mark – say in a calendar. For a note has a function, and this "S" so far has none.*

(One can talk to oneself. – Is everyone who speaks when no one else is present talking to himself?)

To rehearse. The (PI 201) thesis of the *Investigations* is that identity is paradox, called the rule, as neither of opposite cases + existing as both qua either.

Comment. Per PI 260: the grammar sense qua law sense is this; believing is to "S"; as verb-sense believing is to noun-sense believing; as per PI 304, Nothing functional is to Something functional; as sensation is to "S"; as private is to public; paradox faces – say, private-talk/public-talk cases – are cross-referenced cases.

Games: paradox + faces; sensation + feeling/" S" – or belief/" S", or believing/believing (verb-sense/noun-sense) – cases; language + private/public cases; neither nothing nor something + nothing/something – nothing/" S" – cases; per analogies, ladder + up/down ways, drabbit + duck/rabbit faces.

261. What reason have we for calling "S" the sign for a **sensation**? For "sensation" is a word of our common language, which is not a language intelligible only to me. So the use of this word stands in need of a justification which everybody understands. – And it would not help either to say that it need not be a **sensation**; that when he writes "S" he has **Something** – and that is all that can be said. But "has" and "something" also belong to our common language. – So in the end, when one is doing philosophy, one gets to the point where one would like just to emit an inarticulate sound. – But such a sound is an expression only in a particular language-game, which now has to be described.

To rehearse. The (PI 201) thesis of the *Investigations* is that identity is paradox, called the rule, as neither of opposite cases + existing as both qua either.

Comment. Per PI 261: for the grammar qua law case, "S" talk is expression talk (cf. an inarticulate sound) i.e. a public-language case qua a 'something' case; it is cross-referenced with a 'nothing' case i.e. a private-language case, as thereby correctly qua paradoxically that case; here, the paradox case would be language, the private/public cases of which are the paradox faces; in this threefold language game of language + private/public cases (where "S" is the expressed case), all three members of that threefold games talk justify qua warrant one another being the case in that they inhabit one another cf. ladder + up/down aspects, or drabbit + duck/rabbit faces.

Games: paradox + faces; sensation + feeling/" S" – nothing/something – cases; per PI 43, word (language) + meaning/use (private/public) cases; per analogies, ladder + up/down ways, drabbit + duck/rabbit faces.

*262. One might say: someone who has given himself a private explanation of a word must inwardly **resolve** to use the word in such-and-such a way. And how does he resolve that? Should I assume that he invents the technique of applying the word; or that he found it ready-made?*

To rehearse. The (PI 201) thesis of the *Investigations* is that identity is paradox, called the rule, as neither of opposite cases + existing as both qua either.

Comment. Per PI 262: grammatically (lawfully), self-talk as thereby private nevertheless is meaningful only because it is cross-referenced with public language i.e. it is the case of private language as paradoxically public language; per PI 43: the meaning of a word is its us; likewise, the inward resolve re: private explanation aspect of a word is its aspect of use in such-and-such a way in keeping with a ready-made public language.

Games: paradox + faces; rule + aspects; language + private/public aspects; word + meaning/use – resolve/enactment – cases; per analogies, ladder + up/down aspects, drabbit + duck/rabbit faces.

263. "Surely I can (inwardly) resolve to call THIS 'pain' in the future." – "But is it certain that you have resolved this? Are you sure that it was enough for this purpose to concentrate your attention on your feeling?" – An odd question.

To rehearse. The (PI 201) thesis of the *Investigations* is that identity is paradox, called the rule, as neither of opposite cases + existing as both qua either.

Comment. Per PI 263: here, per the grammar qua law, the talk of an inner case of itself alone is a nonsense case in that – to be grammatically sound – the inner case is paradoxically the outer case; per any threefold paradox + faces case, it is that wherein the members indwell one another – cf. ladder + up/down aspects – such that grammatical certainty qua soundness of any of the three being the case is warranted by any one member being the case.

Games: (per PI 216) identity + identical cases cf. per analogy, drabbit + duck/rabbit face; paradox + faces; language + private/public cases; pain qua THIS + feeling/calling – concentrating-on/concentrated-on, resolve/enactment, inner/outer – cases; per PI 43, word + meaning/use cases; per analogies, ladder + up/down aspects, drabbit + duck/rabbit faces.

264. *"Once you know **what** the word signifies, you understand it, you know its whole application."*

To rehearse. The (PI 201) thesis of the *Investigations* is that identity is paradox, called the rule, as neither of opposite cases + existing as both qua either.

Comment. PI 264: the text grammatically (lawfully) translates as that where one knows a word i.e. understands a word i.e. means a word i.e. signifies a word, one thereby paradoxically (per PI 43) makes use of the word i.e. gives the word application i.e. uses the word.

Games: (per PI 216) identity + identical cases cf. per analogy, drabbit + duck/rabbit faces; paradox + faces; word + meaning/use – verb-sense/noun-sense, signifying/use, signifying/application, knowing/known, understanding/understood – cases; per analogies, ladder + up/down aspects, drabbit + duck/rabbit faces.

*265. Let us imagine a table, something like a dictionary, that exists only in our imagination. A dictionary can be used to justify the translation of a word X by a word Y. But are we also to call it a justification if such a table is to be looked up only in the imagination? – "Well, yes; then it is a subjective justification." – But justification consists in appealing to an independent authority – "But surely I can appeal from one memory to another. For example, I don't know if I have remembered the time of departure of a train correctly, and to check it I call to mind how a page of the timetable looked. Isn't this the same sort of case?" No; for this procedure must now actually call forth the **correct** memory. If the mental image of the timetable could not itself be **tested** for correctness, how could it confirm the correctness of the first memory? (As if someone were to buy several copies of today's morning paper to assure himself that what it said was true.)*

Looking up a table in the imagination is no more looking up a table than the image of the result of an imagined experiment is the result of an experiment.

To rehearse. The (PI 201) thesis of the *Investigations* is that identity is paradox, called the rule, as neither of opposite cases + existing as both qua either.

Comment. PI 265: the assorted grammar (law) cases, each as threefold, present as follows; paradox faces are correctly qua paradoxically one another; as are the X/Y word cases, each as its meaning/use cases, each word + meaning/use threefold case as a private/public – subjective/ objective, imaginative/actual – language case; whatever the threefold game, its three members warrant (justify) one another being the case in that they inhabit each other – cf. per analogy, ladder + up/down aspects – such that, given any one of the three as the case, all three thereby are the case; paradox as criterion is a grammatical criterion, not a logical or empirical criterion.

Games: paradox + faces; per PI 43, word (language) + meaning/use (private/public) cases; subjective translation + X/Y cases; objective translation + X/Y cases; translation + subjective/objective cases; remembrance (like imagination, like actuality, like connection) + verb/noun senses; per analogies, ladder + up/down aspects, drabbit + duck/rabbit faces.

*266. I can look at a clock to see what time it is. But I can also look at the dial of a clock in order to **guess** what time it is; or for the same purpose move the hands of a clock till their position strikes me as right. So, the look of a clock may serve to determine the time in more than one way. (Looking at a clock in one's imagination.)*

To rehearse. The (PI 201) thesis of the *Investigations* is that identity is paradox, called the rule, as neither of opposite cases + existing as both qua either.

Comment. Per PI 266: time-telling by the private cases of guessing, intuiting, looking activity, imagining, is not at all – grammatically (lawfully) – time-telling unless any such private action i.e. mental action is bonded paradoxically with the public case of the time actually being shown out by the clock; the mental/extra-mental – private/public – cases are cross-referenced by being paradoxically one another cf. per analogy, the up/down ladder aspects; time is analogously a clock as a grammatical paradox case.

Games: paradox + faces; time + telling/told cases cf. mental/extra-mental cases, private/public cases; clock + clock-meaning/clock-use cases; per PI 43, word + meaning/use cases; per analogies, ladder + up/down aspects, drabbit + dunk/rabbit faces.

267. Suppose I wanted to justify the choice of dimensions for a bridge which I imagine being built, by first imagining making loading tests on the material of the bridge. This would, of course, be to imagine what is called justifying the choice of dimensions for a bridge. But would we also call it justifying an imagined choice of dimensions?

To rehearse. The (PI 201) thesis of the *Investigations* is that identity is paradox, called the rule, as neither of opposite cases + existing as both qua either.

Comment. Per PI 267: grammatically (lawfully), all cases – the bridge, its dimensions, the raw materials, the loading-tests, the choice made – are of an entirety a nonsense, an impossibility, if in the context of a mentality-alone case, the imagination-alone case; to be warranted (justified) as anything grammatical, the entirety requires to be bonded paradoxically with – by being cross-referenced with – the extra-mental case of actual bridge engineering; per any case – imaginative or actual – of threefold grammar, its three members warrant (justify) each other being the case in that they indwell one another such that, given one as the case, thereby the others are the case cf. per analogy, the ladder and its up/down aspects.

Games: paradox + faces; bridge engineering + imagined/actual cases; per PI 43, word + meaning/use cases; language + private/public cases; life + language/deed cases; per analogies, ladder + up/down aspects, drabbit + duck/rabbit faces.

268. Why can't my right hand give my left hand money? – My right hand can put it into my left hand. My right hand can write a deed of gift, and my left hand a receipt. – But the further practical consequences would not be those of a gift. When the left hand has taken the money from the right, and so forth, one will ask, "Well, and now what?" And the same could be asked if a person had given himself a private explanation of a word; I mean, if he has said the word to himself and at the same time has directed his attention to a sensation.

To rehearse. The (PI 201) thesis of the *Investigations* is that identity is paradox, called the rule, as neither of opposite cases + existing as both qua either.

Comment. Per PI 268: money passing between left/right hands is like language passing between privately felt sensation and privately told expression – it is a nonsense, an impossibility (grammatically speaking, lawfully speaking) unless it is bonded paradoxically with a public dimension (a practical-consequences case); the private/public cases cannot exist without one another because being cross-referenced cases, paradoxical cases, coincidental cases cf. per analogy, the ladder case where its way up case is a nonsense except where it is paradoxically a way down case; for it to be a way-up case alone is for it (grammatically speaking) not to be a ladder.

Games: paradox + faces; money, like language + private/public cases; per PI 43, word + meaning/use cases; per analogies, ladder + way-up/way-down aspects, drabbit + duck/rabbit faces.

*269. Let us remember that there are certain criteria in a man's behaviour for his not understanding a word: that it means nothing to him, that he can do nothing with it. And criteria for his 'thinking he understands', attaching some meaning to the word, but not the right one. And lastly, criteria for his understanding the word correctly. In the second case, one might speak of a subjective understanding. And sounds which no one else understands but which I '**appear to understand**' might be called a "private language".*

To rehearse. The (PI 201) thesis of the *Investigations* is that identity is paradox, called the rule, as neither of opposite cases + existing as both qua either.

Comment. Per PI 269: whether the case is that of a word without meaning or of a word involving a subjective mistaken meaning, it is the case of nothing grammatical (lawful) – and this by the criterial threefold grammar of word + meaning/use cases pertaining to the commonly agreed language of human life; grammatically, paradox is to faces; as language is to private/public – subjective/objective – cases; only where bonded correctly qua paradoxically with the objective case is the subjective case grammatical (lawful).

Games: paradox + faces; per PI 43, word (language) + meaning/use (private/public) cases; understanding + verb/noun – cf. mental-process/behaviour, subjective/objective – cases; per analogies, ladder + way-up/way-down aspects, drabbit + duck/rabbit faces.

270. Let us now imagine a use for the entry of the sign "S" in my diary. I find out the following from experience: whenever I have a particular sensation, a manometer shows that my blood pressure is rising. This puts me in a position to report that my blood pressure is rising without using any apparatus. This is a useful result. And now it seems quite indifferent whether I've recognized the *sensation **correctly** or not. Suppose that I regularly make a mistake in identifying it, this does not make any difference at all. And this alone shows that the supposition of this mistake was merely sham. (We, as it were, turned a knob which looked as if it could be used to adjust something in the machine; but it was a mere ornament not connected with the mechanism at all.)*

And what reason do we have here for calling "S" the name of a sensation? Perhaps the kind of way this sign is employed in this language game. – And why a "particular sensation": that is, the same one every time? Well, we're supposing, aren't we, that we write "S" every time.

To rehearse. The (PI 201) thesis of the *Investigations* is that identity is paradox, called the rule, as neither of opposite cases + existing as both qua either.

Comment. Per PI 270: grammatically (lawfully), paradox is to faces; as particular case is to feeling/rising-blood-pressure – feeling/RBP, sensation/RBP, sensation/"S" – cases; whichever the grammatical threefold case, to suppose that a face is not its paradoxical (counterpart) face i.e. to suppose the "S" is not connected with sensation i.e. to suppose that "S" is not correctly qua not paradoxically sensation is a nonsense supposition qua a supposition without any relevance to the paradox case cf. per analogy, the ornamental knob that is a sham qua without any connection to the mechanism.

Games: paradox + faces; mechanism (machine) + parts; particular case cf. PI 216 identity case + identical cases cf. PI 215 sameness case + sensation/" S" – same/same – cases; per analogies, ladder + up/down aspects, drabbit + duck/rabbit faces.

*271. "Imagine a person who could not remember **what** the word 'pain' meant – so that he constantly called different things by that name – but nevertheless used it in accordance with the usual symptoms and presuppositions of pain" – in short, he uses it as we all do. Here I'd like to say: a wheel that can be turned though nothing else moves with it is not part of the mechanism.*

To rehearse. The (PI 201) thesis of the *Investigations* is that identity is paradox, called the rule, as neither of opposite cases + existing as both qua either.

Comment. Per PI 271: the grammar sense qua law sense of the text is this; just as that which betimes is a duck face and betimes a mouse face is not the drabbit case; so, that which betimes is a pain-feeling and betimes a joy-feeling is not the pain case qua a word case; and so, that which betimes is a working-part turning wheel and betimes an idle-part turning wheel is not the mechanism.

Games: paradox + faces; per PI 43, word (language) + meaning/use (private/public) cases; pain + feeling/felt – pain/pain, calling/called, naming/named – cases; mechanism + working-part turning wheel cases; per analogies, ladder + way-up/way-down aspects, drabbit + duck/rabbit faces.

*272. The essential thing about private experience is really not that each person possesses his own specimen, but that nobody knows whether other people also have **this** or something else. The assumption would thus be possible – though unverifiable – that one section of mankind had one visual impression of red, and another section another.*

To rehearse. The (PI 201) thesis of the *Investigations* is that identity is paradox, called the rule, as neither of opposite cases + existing as both qua either.

Comment. Per PI 272: grammatically (lawfully) – not experientially, not empirically, hence whatever the person or section of mankind – every private language case qua paradox face is thereby paradoxically the counterpart public language case; here, paradox is to faces; as per PI 43, word is to meaning/use – cf. essence/expression – cases; as language qua **this** case is to private/public cases; as "red" is to "red"/"red" cases.

Games: paradox (cf. **this**) + faces; word + meaning/use – "red" + "red"/"red" – cases; language + private/public – essential/expressed – cases; per analogies, ladder way-up/way-down aspects, drabbit + duck/rabbit faces.

*273. What about the word "red"? – Am I to say that it signifies something 'confronting us all', and that everyone should really have another word, besides this one, to signify his **own** impression of red? Or is it like this: the word "red" signifies something known to us all; and in addition, for each person, it signifies something known only to him? (Or perhaps, rather: it **refers** to something known only to him.)*

To rehearse. The (PI 201) thesis of the *Investigations* is that identity is paradox, called the rule, as neither of opposite cases + existing as both qua either.

Comment. Per PI 273: the grammar talk qua law talk is this: paradox is to faces; as word is to meaning/use case; as "red" is to "red"/"red" cases; as language is to private/public – own-impression/something-confronting-all, something-known-only-to-self/something-known-to-us all – cases.

Games: paradox + faces; per PI 43, word + meaning/use – signifying/signified, referring-to/referred-to – cases; language + private/public cases; "red" + "red"/"red" cases; per analogies, ladder + way-up/way-down aspects, drabbit + duck/rabbit faces.

*274. Of course, saying that the word "red" **refers** to rather than "signifies" something private does not help us in the least to grasp its function; but it is the more psychologically apt expression for a particular experience in doing philosophy. It is as if, when I uttered the word, I cast a sidelong glance at my own colour impression, as it were, in order to say to myself: I know all right what I mean by the word.*

To rehearse. The (PI 201) thesis of the *Investigations* is that identity is paradox, called the rule, as neither of opposite cases + existing as both qua either.

Comment. Per PI 274: grammatically (lawfully), significance is to signifying/signified cases; as word is to meaning/use cases; as paradox is to faces; as refer-to is to referring-to/referred-to – impression/expression – cases; as language is to private/public cases; as "red" is to "red"/"red" case; as colour knowledge is to own-impression/report – sidelong-glance/utterance – cases.

Games: identity-as-paradox + faces; per PI 43, word + meaning/use cases; language + private/public cases; particular case + impression/expression cases; "red" + "red"/"red" cases; refer-to + referring-to/referred-to cases; per analogies, ladder + way-up/way-down aspects, drabbit + duck/rabbit faces.

*275. Look at the blue of the sky and say to yourself, "How blue the sky is!" – When you do it spontaneously – without philosophical purposes – the idea never crosses your mind that this impression of colour belongs only to **you**. And you have no qualms about exclaiming thus to another. And if you point at anything as you say the words, it is at the sky. I mean: you don't have the pointing-into-yourself feeling that often accompanies 'naming sensations' when one is thinking about the 'private language'. Nor do you think that really you ought to point at the colour not with your hand, but with your attention. (Consider what "to point at something with one's attention" means.)*

To rehearse. The (PI 201) thesis of the *Investigations* is that identity is paradox, called the rule, as neither of opposite cases + existing as both qua either.

Comment. Per PI 275: by this text, grammatically qua lawfully (not empirically), private language is to public language; as self-talk is to social-talk (cf. exclamation-talk); as paradox face is to counterpart face; as colour-impression is to colour-expression; as pointing-into is to pointing-outward; as inner sky-blue sensing is to outer sensed sky-blue; as inner blue is to outer blue; as inner pointing-at/pointed-at cases are to outer pointing-at/pointed-at cases, as inner or outer naming/named cases are to inner or outer naming/named cases; as pointing with the attention is to pointing with the hand; from which assorted language games, each is a threefold grammar as the case of identity-as-paradox + identical faces cf. per analogy, drabbit + duck/rabbit faces, also the comparisons of person + mind/body – mind/behaviour, subjective/objective – cases, also per PI 43, word + meaning/use cases.

Games: paradox + faces (and variants, as per Comment); per analogies, ladder + way-up/way-down aspects, drabbit + duck/rabbit faces.

*276. "But don't we at least **mean** something quite definite when we look at a colour and name our colour impression?" It is virtually as if we detached the colour **impression** from the object, like a membrane. (This ought to arouse our suspicions.)*

To rehearse. The (PI 201) thesis of the *Investigations* is that identity is paradox, called the rule, as neither of opposite cases + existing as both qua either.

Comment. Per PI 276: grammatically qua lawfully, the colour impression is to the colour expression; as word meaning is to word use; as paradox face is to counterpart face; as object face (identity face) is to counterpart face; as colour naming (cf. colour gazing) is to named colour; from which, the threefold impression/object-qua-colour/expression case – cf. impression/object/expression, membrane/object/membrane, face/paradox/ face threefold case – comprises three members as detached-from qua distinct-from one another yet also living in one another cf. the duck/drabbit/rabbit threefold case.

Games: paradox + faces; object + membranes; colour + impression/ expression cases; per PI 43, word + meaning/use cases; coincidence + different (distinct, detached) cases; per analogies, ladder + way-up/way-down aspects, drabbit + duck/rabbit faces.

*277. But how is it even possible for one to be tempted to think that one uses a word to **mean** at one time the colour known to everyone – and at another time the 'visual impression' which **I** am getting **now**? How can there be so much as a temptation here? – I don't turn the same kind of attention on the colour in the two cases. When I mean the colour impression that (as I should like to say) belongs to me alone, I immerse myself in the colour – rather like when I 'can't get my fill of a colour'. That's why it is easier to produce this experience when one is looking at a bright colour, or at a colour scheme which sticks in our memory.*

To rehearse. The (PI 201) thesis of the *Investigations* is that identity is paradox, called the rule, as neither of opposite cases + existing as both qua either.

Comment. Per PI 277: grammatically qua lawfully (not experientially), and whatever the case (bright colour or impressive colour scheme) colour as language is private/public – own-visual-impression/known-to-all, now/all-times, I/others, immersion-in/looking-at, mine-alone/others-owned, insatiably-impacted/normally-impacted – cases; as paradox is to faces; as, per PI 43, word is to meaning/use case; whatever the threefold language game, it bespeaks identity-as-paradox + identical faces cf. ladder + up/down aspects.

Games: paradox + faces; word + meaning/use aspects; language + private/public aspects; colour + impression/expression cases; per analogies, ladder + up/down aspects, drabbit + duck/rabbit faces.

278. *"I know how the colour green looks to **me**" – surely that makes sense! – Certainly; what use of the sentence are you thinking of?*

To rehearse. The (PI 201) thesis of the *Investigations* is that identity is paradox, called the rule, as neither of opposite cases + existing as both qua either.

Comment. Per PI 2787: the text implies grammar cases qua law cases as follows; from PI 43, the meaning aspect of the word green is its use aspect; as a variant language game – the known-to-me aspect of the colour-look (cf. knowledge) case is the known-to-others aspect; the sentence-use aspect as thought of is the sentence-use aspect as paradoxically the sentence-meaning aspect.

Games: paradox + faces; word (sentence) + meaning/use cases; green language + private/public (to-me/to-others) aspects; per analogies, ladder + up/down aspects, drabbit + duck/rabbit faces.

279. *Imagine someone saying, "But I know how tall I am!" and laying his hand on top of his head to indicate it!*

To rehearse. The (PI 201) thesis of the *Investigations* is that identity is paradox, called the rule, as neither of opposite cases + existing as both qua either.

Comment. Per PI 279: the grammar sense qua law sense is this: a private-language only apparently threefold grammar case presents as follows; tallness qua person is to I/myself qua mind/body – cf. hand-on-head/head-under/hand – cases; as paradox is to faces; as indication is to indicating/indicated cases; however, this apparent grammatical case is not grammatical unless bonded paradoxically with a public-language case – for example, a height-measure mechanism as its measuring/measured aspects.

Games: paradox + faces; tallness + subjective/objective cases; per analogies, ladder + up/down aspects, drabbit + duck/rabbit faces.

*280. Someone paints a picture in order to show, for example, how he imagines a stage set. And now I say: "This picture has a double function: it informs others, as pictures or words do – but for the informant it is in addition a representation (or piece of information?) of another kind: for him it is the picture of his image, as it can't be for anyone else. His private impression of the picture tells him what he imagined, in a sense in which the picture can't do this for others." – And what right have I to speak in this second case of a representation or piece of information – if these words were correctly used in the **first** case?*

To rehearse. The (PI 201) thesis of the *Investigations* is that identity is paradox, called the rule, as neither of opposite cases + existing as both qua either.

Comment. Per PI 280: as a threefold grammar (law) sense, paradox is to faces; as per PI 43, word (language) is to meaning/use (private/public) cases; as picture is to inward/outward – impression/expression – aspects; whatever the threefold language game, the flanking aspects are correctly qua paradoxically one another cf. ladder + up/down aspects.

Games: paradox + faces; word + meaning/use cases; language + private/public cases; information + informing/informed cases; picture (painting, representation, image) + verb/noun senses; stage-set + impression/expression cases; per analogies, ladder + up/down aspects, drabbit + duck/rabbit faces.

281. "*But doesn't what you say amount to this: that there is no pain, for example, without **pain-behaviour**?*" – *It amounts to this: that only of a living human being and what resembles (behaves like) a living human being can one say: it has sensations; it sees; is blind; hears; is deaf; is conscious or unconscious.*

To rehearse. The (PI 201) thesis of the *Investigations* is that identity is paradox, called the rule, as neither of opposite cases + existing as both qua either.

Comment. Per PI 281!: grammatically (lawfully), it is not that there is no pain without pain-behaviour; it is that – of pain, referenced to human or humanlike beings – there is no felt-pain without the corresponding paradoxical pain behaviour cf. per analogy, of a ladder, there is no way-up without it paradoxically being a way-down.

Games: paradox + faces; pain + feeling/behaviour cases; per analogies, ladder + up/down aspects, drabbit + duck/rabbit faces.

282. "*But in a fairy tale a pot too can see and hear!*" (*Certainly; but it **can** also talk.*)

"*But a fairy tale only invents what is not the case; it does not talk **nonsense**, does it?*" – *It's not as simple as that. Is it untrue or nonsensical to say that a pot talks? Does one have a clear idea of the circumstances in which we'd say of a pot that it talked? (Even a nonsense poem is not nonsense in the same way as the babble of a baby.)*

*We do indeed say of an inanimate thing that it is in pain: when playing with dolls, for example. But this use of the concept of pain is a secondary one. Imagine a case in which people said **only** of inanimate things that they are in pain; pitied **only** dolls! (When children play trains, their game is connected with their acquaintance with trains. It would nevertheless be possible for the children of a tribe unacquainted with trains to learn this game from others, and to play it without knowing that it was imitating anything. One could say that the game did not make the same kind of **sense** to them as to us.)*

To rehearse. The (PI 201) thesis of the *Investigations* is that identity is paradox, called the rule, as neither of opposite cases + existing as both qua either.

Comment. Per PI 282: whatever case is human or humanised is grammatically (lawfully) a paradox case having to it corresponding paradox faces.

Games: paradox + faces; per PI 43, word + meaning/use cases; per PI 216, identity + identical cases; per PI 201, rule + courses of action; analogy + fiction/fact cases, also inanimate/animate cases, also invented/actual cases, also imitated/real case; per analogies, ladder + up/down aspects, drabbit + duck/rabbit faces.

283. What gives us **so much as the idea** that beings, things, can feel?

Is it that my education has led me to it by drawing my attention to feelings in myself, and now I transfer the idea to objects outside myself? That I recognize that there is something there (in me) which I can call "pain" without getting into conflict with other people's usage? — I do not transfer my idea to stones, plants, and so on.

Couldn't I imagine having frightful pains and, while they were going on, turning to stone. Indeed, how do I know, if I shut my eyes, whether I have not turned into a stone? — And if that has happened, in what sense will **the stone** *have pains? In what sense will they be ascribable to a stone? Why indeed should the pain here have a bearer at all?!*

And can one say of the stone that it has a mind, and **that** *is what has the pain? What has a mind, what have pains, to do with a stone?*

Only of what behaves like a human being can one say that it **has** *pains.*

For one has to say it of a body, or, if you like, of a mind which some body **has**. *And how can a body* **have** *a mind?*

To rehearse. The (PI 201) thesis of the *Investigations* is that identity is paradox, called the rule, as neither of opposite cases + existing as both qua either.

Comment. Per PI 283: the empirical-sense talk in the text translates grammatically (lawfully) as follows; paradox is to faces; as human or any humanised thing is to mind/body cases; as pain is to feeling/felt cases; as pain is to private/public – own/others, own/humanised-things, pain-bearing/borne-pain – cases; as humanised stone is to mind/behaviour – pain-feeling/felt-pain cases; from which, it is the grammar (law) of identity-as-paradox which accounts for the analogy that things feel pain.

Games: paradox + faces; human or humanised + mind/body – cf. pain-feeling/ felt-pain – cases; per analogies, ladder + up/down aspects, drabbit + duck/rabbit.

*284. Look at a stone and imagine it having sensations. – One says to oneself: How could one so much as get the idea of ascribing a **sensation** to a **thing**? One might as well ascribe it to a number! – And now look at a wriggling fly, and at once these difficulties vanish, and pain seems able to get a **foothold** here, where before everything was, so to speak, too **smooth** for it.*

And so, too, a corpse seems to us quite inaccessible to pain. – Our attitude to what is alive and to what is dead is not the same. All our reactions are different. – If someone says, "That cannot simply come from the fact that living beings move in such-and-such ways and dead ones don't", then I want to suggest to him that this is a case of the transition 'from quantity to quality'.

To rehearse. The (PI 201) thesis of the *Investigations* is that identity is paradox, called the rule, as neither of opposite cases + existing as both qua either.

Comment. Per PI 284: the empirical-sense talk translates grammatically (lawfully) as follows; whether of a person or a wriggling fly, or, by analogy and imaginatively, of an inanimate thing, stone, number, corpse, each qua a threefold case of identity-as-paradox + identical cases qua paradox faces, is the threefold case of sensation (say, pain) + feeling/expression – quality/quantity – cases.

Games: paradox + faces; per PI 43, word + meaning/use cases; pain + feeling/behaviour – quality/quantity, aliveness/deadness, animate/inanimate cases; per analogies, ladder + up/down aspects, drabbit + duck/rabbit faces.

*285. Think of the recognition of **facial expressions**. Or of the description of facial expressions – which does not consist in giving the measurements of the face! Think, too, how one can imitate a man's face without seeing one's own in a mirror.*

To rehearse. The (PI 201) thesis of the *Investigations* is that identity is paradox, called the rule, as neither of opposite cases + existing as both qua either.

Comment. Per PI 285: grammatically qua lawfully, paradox is to faces; as per PI 43, word is to meaning/use cases; as a person's face is to expressions; as recognition cf. description cf. imitation is to verb/noun senses; as face is to quality/quantity – cf. meaning/behaviour – cases.

Games: paradox + faces; word (say, face) + meaning/use – quality/quantity, imitating/imitated – cases; per analogies, ladder + up/down aspects, drabbit + duck/rabbit faces.

*286. But isn't it absurd to say of a **body** that it has pain? – And why does one feel an absurdity in that? In what sense does my hand not feel pain, but I in my hand?*

*What sort of issue is this: Is it the **body** that feels pain? – How is it to be decided? How does it become clear that it is **not** the body? – Well, something like this: if someone has a pain in his hand, then the **hand** does not say so (unless it writes it), and one does not comfort the hand, but the sufferer: one looks into his eyes.*

To rehearse. The (PI 201) thesis of the *Investigations* is that identity is paradox, called the rule, as neither of opposite cases + existing as both qua either.

Comment. Per PI 286: in terms of grammatical (lawful) sense, a body, a hand, is a felt case, not a feeling case; person is to mind/body cases; as pain is to feeling/felt cases; as paradox is to (absurdly qua paradoxically connected) faces; grammar is the warrant for deciding – and making clear – that corresponding (mind/body, mind/hand, paining/saying-so, suffering/sufferance, suffering/hand) opposite case are paradox faces.

Games: paradox + faces; paradox + corresponding opposites; person + mind/body – cf. mind/hand, paining/saying-so, suffering/sufferance, suffering/hand – cases; per analogies, ladder + up/down aspects, drabbit + duck/ rabbit faces.

*287. How am I filled with pity **for this human being**? How does it come out what the object of my pity is? (Pity, one may say, is one form of being convinced that someone else is in pain.)*

To rehearse. The (PI 201) thesis of the *Investigations* is that identity is paradox, called the rule, as neither of opposite cases + existing as both qua either.

Comment. Per PI 287: the grammar (law) sense presents as follows: paradoxically is how corresponding opposite cases – this/that persons, subject/object cases, pitying/pitied cases, convincing/convinced cases – are connected.

Games: paradox + faces; person (cf. identity qua ***this human being***) + mind/body aspects; pain + feeling/expression aspects; human pain + subject/object aspects; pity + verb/noun senses; per analogies, ladder + up/down aspects, drabbit + duck/rabbit faces.

*288. I turn to stone, and my pain goes on. – What if I were mistaken, and it was no longer **pain**? – But surely I can't be mistaken here; it means nothing to doubt whether I am in pain! – That is, if someone said "I don't know if what I have is a pain or something else", we would think, perhaps, that he does not know what the English word "pain" means; and we'd explain it to him. – How? Perhaps by means of gestures, or by pricking him with a pin and saying, "See, that's pain!" This explanation of a word, like any other, he might understand rightly, wrongly, or not at all. And he will show which by his use of the word, in this as in other cases.*

*If he now said, for example, "Oh, I know what 'pain' means; what I don't know is whether **this**, that I have now, is pain" – we'd merely shake our heads and have to regard his words as a strange reaction which we can't make anything of. (It would be rather as if we heard someone say seriously, "I distinctly remember that sometime before I was born I believed ...")*

*That expression of doubt has no place in the language-game; but if expressions of sensation – human behaviour – are excluded, it looks as if I might then **legitimately** begin to doubt. My temptation to say that one might take a sensation for something other than what it is arises from this: if I assume the abrogation of the normal language-game with the expression of a sensation, I need a criterion of identity for the sensation; and then the possibility of error also exists.*

To rehearse. The (PI 201) thesis of the *Investigations* is that identity is paradox, called the rule, as neither of opposite cases + existing as both qua either.

Comment. Per PI 288: the grammar sense qua law sense reads as follows; there exist cases of doubt and error-risk in identifying opposite cases other than as paradoxical cases – for example, feeling-pain/pain-felt cases, or per analogy, ladder-ascent/ladder-descent cases; paired opposites are together neither an identity qua onefold sense nor contradictories qua a twofold sense but faces of paradox qua an identity-as-paradox sense; to abrogate this threefold grammar is to use language meaninglessly cf. talk of what one believed prior to one's birth; such abrogation legitimises doubt and error-risk cases; per the threefold grammar, the case of paradox + faces is that of neither-right-nor-wrong + right;-or-wrong/wrong-or-right – eclipsing-or-eclipsed/eclipsed-or-eclipsing – faces; from which, the cases of doubt and error-risk are irrelevant.

Games: paradox + faces; per PI 43, word + meaning/use cases; person, or a humanised stone + mind/body aspects; pain + feeling/behaviour – feeling/expression, feeling/felt – aspects; per analogies, ladder + up/down aspects, drabbit + duck/rabbit faces.

*289. "When I say 'I am in pain', I am at any rate justified **before myself**."* – *What does that mean? Does it mean: "If someone else could know what I am calling 'pain', he would admit that I was using the word correctly"?*

To use a word without a justification does not mean to use it wrongly.

To rehearse. The (PI 201) thesis of the *Investigations* is that identity is paradox, called the rule, as neither of opposite cases + existing as both qua either.

Comment. Per PI 289: in terms of the grammar qua law, what justifies (warrants) any of the paradox + faces – here, the pain + feeling/felt cases or the pain + private/public cases – three cases being the case is any one of them being the case in that all three live in one another cf. ladder + up/down aspects; a justified (warranted) paradox-face case is in function a right-or-wrong/wrong-or-right – eclipsing-or-eclipsed/eclipsed-or-eclipsing – case; from which, a word-use paradox-face case – functioning rightly and wrongly – is not an ungrammatical case, a case without justification.

Games: paradox + faces; pain + feeling/expression cases; language + private/public cases; per PI 43, word + meaning/use aspects; per analogies, ladder + up/down aspects, drabbit + duck/rabbit faces.

290. It is not, of course, that I identify my sensation by means of criteria; it is, rather, that I use the same expression. But it is not as if the language-game **ends** *with this; it begins with it.*

But doesn't it begin with the sensation – which I describe? – Perhaps this word "describe" tricks us here. I say "I describe my state of mind" and "I describe my room". One needs to call to mind the differences between the language-games.

To rehearse. The (PI 201) thesis of the *Investigations* is that identity is paradox, called the rule, as neither of opposite cases + existing as both qua either.

Comment. Per PI 290: from PI 289, identity is nothing definably onefold but is grammatically paradox (sensation, description, mind-state, room) as for its faces identical – verb-sense/noun-sense, sensation/sensation, description/description, same/same – cases; each paradox-face case is its beginning/end – eclipsing/eclipsed – cases; whatever the talk it is to be understood neither logically nor empirically but grammatically qua lawfully.

Games: identity-as-paradox + identical aspects qua paradox faces; identity (sensation, description, mind-sate, room) + verb/noun senses; per PI 43, word + meaning/use cases; per analogies, ladder + up/down aspects, drabbit + duck/rabbit faces.

*291. What we call "**descriptions**" are instruments for particular uses. Think of a machine-drawing, a cross-section, an elevation with measurements, which an engineer has before him. Thinking of a description as a word-picture of the facts has something misleading about it: one tends to think only of such pictures as hang on our walls, which seem simply to depict how a thing looks, what it is like. (These pictures are, as it were, idle.)*

To rehearse. The (PI 201) thesis of the *Investigations* is that identity is paradox, called the rule, as neither of opposite cases + existing as both qua either.

Comment. Per PI 291: an identity (description, instrument, particularity, machine-drawing, word, language, picture) is a paradox case; identity talk as a logical sense talk or as an empirical sense talk is raw material for translation into grammatical talk qua law talk.

Games: paradox + faces; per PI 216, identity + identical cases; description + describing/described cases; instrument + meaning/use cases; particular case + applications; machine-drawing + verb/noun sense; per PI 43, word + meaning/use cases; language + private/public cases; picture + out-pictures; per analogies, ladder + up/down aspects, drabbit + duck/rabbit faces.

292. Don't always think that you read off what you say from the facts; that you depict these in words according to rules! For you would still have to apply the rule in the particular case without guidance.

To rehearse. The (PI 201) thesis of the *Investigations* is that identity is paradox, called the rule, as neither of opposite cases + existing as both qua either.

Comment. Per PI 292: whatever the threefold language game (see Games, below), it looks to nothing other than itself – is its own guide – as a threefold grammar (law) of identity as paradox, exhibiting as its mutually eclipsing faces.

Games: paradox + faces; factuality + reading-off/reading-out aspects; rule + wording/depicted aspects; application case qua particular + applying/ applied aspects; per analogies, ladder + up/down aspects, drabbit + duck/rabbit faces.

*293. If I say of myself that it is only from my own case that I know what the word "pain" means – must I not say **that** of other people too? And how can I generalize the **one** case so irresponsibly?*

*Well, everyone tells me that he knows what pain is only from his own case! – Suppose that everyone had a box with something in it which we call a "beetle". No one can ever look into anyone else's box, and everyone says he knows what a beetle is only by looking at **his** beetle. – Here it would be quite possible for everyone to have something different in his box. One might even imagine such a thing constantly changing. – But what if these people's word "beetle" had a use nonetheless? – If so, it would not be as the name of a thing. The thing in the box doesn't belong to the language-game at all; not even as a **Something**: for the box might even be empty. – No, one can 'divide through' by the thing in the box; it cancels out, whatever it is.*

That is to say, if we construe the grammar of the expression of sensation on the model of 'object and name', the object drops out of consideration as irrelevant.

To rehearse. The (PI 201) thesis of the *Investigations* is that identity is paradox, called the rule, as neither of opposite cases + existing as both qua either.

Comment. PI 293: an identity (a word, a sensation, a pain, a beetle, a description) is a paradox case; it has its paradox faces (meaning/use cases, sensing/sensed cases, pain-feeling/felt-pain cases, boxed-beetle/beetle-talk cases, describing/described cases); a paradox-face case – say, the boxed-beetle case – is of itself nothing where not bonded paradoxically with its counterpart face (the beetle-talk case); of itself, the face is not integral to the threefold grammar (law) of paradox + faces; of itself, the face is thus grammatically irrelevant.

Games: paradox + faces; per PI 43, word + meaning/use cases; beetle + boxed-beetle/described-beetle cases cf. beetle word + beetle-meaning/beetle-use cases; sensation (pain) + private/public – feeling/expressed, own/other's – cases; – cf. pain word + pain-meaning/pain-use cases; per analogies, ladder + up/down aspects, drabbit + duck/ rabbit faces.

*294. If you say that he sees a private picture before him, which he is describing, you have at any rate made an assumption about what he has before him. And this means that you can describe it or do describe it more closely. If you admit that you have no idea what kind of thing it might be that he has before him – then what seduces you into saying, in spite of that, that he has something before him? Isn't it as if I were to say of someone: "He **has** something. But I don't know whether it is money, or debts, or an empty till."*

To rehearse. The (PI 201) thesis of the *Investigations* is that identity is paradox, called the rule, as neither of opposite cases + existing as both qua either.

Comment. Per PI 294: the picturing (the seeing before him) of the picture (as whatever) is a pictured (described) case; as, per PI 43, the meaning of a word is its use; as the face of a paradox is its corresponding other face; as the private aspect of language is its public aspect; as the Nothing (the not knowing) aspect of neither Nothing nor Something is its Something (the known not-knowing) aspect.

Games: paradox + faces (and variants, as per the Comment); per analogies, ladder + up/down aspects, drabbit + duck/rabbit faces.

*295. "I know ... only from my **own** case" – what kind of proposition is this meant to be? An empirical one? No. – A grammatical one?*

*So this is what I imagine: everyone says of himself that he knows what pain is only from his own pain. – Not that people really say that, or are even prepared to say it. But **if** everybody said it – it might be a kind of exclamation. And even if it gives no information, still, it is a picture; and why should we not want to call such a picture before our mind? Imagine an allegorical painting instead of the words.*

Indeed, when we look into ourselves as we do philosophy, we often get to see just such a picture. Virtually a pictorial representation of our grammar. Not facts; but, as it were, illustrated turns of speech.

To rehearse. The (PI 201) thesis of the *Investigations* is that identity is paradox, called the rule, as neither of opposite cases + existing as both qua either.

Comment. Per PI 295: grammatically (from empirical-sense talk as raw material for translation to grammar qua law), the picture (say, pain) is to picturing/pictured (feeling/felt) aspects; as paradox is to faces; as exclamation is to exclaiming/exclaimed cases; as per PI 43, word is to meaning/use – cf. meaning/illustrated turns of speech – case; as imagination is to imagining/imagined, before-the-mind/told-out – case; as allegory is to allegorising/allegorised cases; as representation is to representing/represented cases.

Games: paradox + faces, and variants (as presented in the Comment); per analogies, ladder + up/down aspects, drabbit + duck/rabbit faces.

296. "Right; but there is a Something there all the same, which accompanies my cry of pain! And it is on account of this that I utter it. And this Something is what is important – and frightful." – Only to whom are we telling this? And on what occasion?

To rehearse. The (PI 201) thesis of the *Investigations* is that identity is paradox, called the rule, as neither of opposite cases + existing as both qua either.

Comment. Per PI 296: the text presents where the occasion for it being presented is the grammatical (lawful) investigation of language, as follows: per PI 43, the meaning of a word is its use; per PI 296 the Nothing (as intangible, as frightful feeling) aspect of (say) fright is to its Something (the tangible frightened behaviour) aspect; as the face of a paradox case is to its corresponding other paradox face; as the pain-feeling aspect of pain is to its outcry – telling-out, utterance – aspect.

Games: paradox + faces, and variants (as presented in the Comment); per analogies, ladder + up/down aspects, drabbit + duck/rabbit faces.

297. Of course, if water boils in a pot, steam comes out of the pot, and also a picture of steam comes out of a picture of the pot. But what if one insisted on saying that there must also be something boiling in the picture of the pot?

To rehearse. The (PI 201) thesis of the *Investigations* is that identity is paradox, called the rule, as neither of opposite cases + existing as both qua either.

Comment. Per PI 297: grammatically, the pot – whether real or depicted – is a paradox case, the faces of which are the hidden/visible cases, the private/public cases, the boiling-water/issuing-steam cases; the empirical sense of 'picture' qua empirical identity and its grammatical sense as an identity-as-paradox case are to be distinguished.

Games: paradox + faces; (grammatical) picture + picturing/pictured cases; per PI 43, word + meaning/use cases; language + private/public cases; pot + depicted/real cases; pot (depicted or real) + boiling-water/issuing-steam – hidden/unhidden – cases; per analogies, ladder + up/down aspects, drabbit + duck/rabbit faces.

*298. The very fact that we'd so much like to say "**This** is the important thing" – while we point for ourselves to the sensation – is enough to show how much we are inclined to say something which is not informative.*

To rehearse. The (PI 201) thesis of the *Investigations* is that identity is paradox, called the rule, as neither of opposite cases + existing as both qua either.

Comment. Per PI 298: for its grammar sense (law sense), the text reads as follows: paradox is to faces; as sensation (**this**) is to sensing/sensed – pointing-to/pointed-to, non-informative/informative – cases.

Games: paradox + faces; per PI 43, word + meaning/use cases; sensation (**this**) + sensing/sensed – pointing-to/pointed-to, non-informative/informative – cases; (per PI 304) nothing + Nothing/Something cases; per analogies, ladder + up/down aspects, drabbit + duck/rabbit faces.

*299. Being unable – when we indulge in philosophical thought – to help saying something or other, being irresistibly inclined to say it – does not mean being forced into an **assumption**, or having an immediate insight into, or knowledge of, a state of affairs.*

To rehearse. The (PI 201) thesis of the *Investigations* is that identity is paradox, called the rule, as neither of opposite cases + existing as both qua either.

Comment. Per PI 299: here, per grammar (law), state-of-affairs/verbal-expression cases co-exist neither by force of assumption, nor immediate insight, nor knowledge, but by the warrant of the cases as paradox-faces cases, as thereby inseparably bonded by being coincidental cases cf. per analogy, the ladder's way-up/way-down cases; here, to say Something of a state of affairs is not to bond the sate/Something cases empirically (say, psychologically) but grammatically.

Games: paradox + faces; per PI 43, word + meaning/use – state/expression, state/Something – cases; per analogies, ladder + up/down aspects, drabbit + duck/rabbit faces.

300. It is, one would like to say, not merely the picture of the behaviour that belongs to the language-game with the words "he is in pain", but also the picture of *the pain. Or, not merely the paradigm of the behaviour, but also that of the pain. – It is a misunderstanding to say "The picture of pain enters into the language-game with the word 'pain' ". Pain in the imagination is not a picture, and **it** is not replaceable in the language-game by anything that we'd call a picture. – Imagined pain certainly enters into the language-game in a sense; only not as a picture.*

To rehearse. The (PI 201) thesis of the *Investigations* is that identity is paradox, called the rule, as neither of opposite cases + existing as both qua either.

Comment. Per PI 300: grammatically (lawfully), picture (paradigm, word, imagination) is behaviour (the expression "he is in pain", an imagined case), also – paradoxically – pain-feeling (the imagining case).

Games: paradox + faces; picture + out-pictures (out-pictures qua picturing/pictured cases, verb/noun senses); per PI 43, word + meaning/use cases; pain + feeling/felt – feeling/behaviour, feeling/expression – cases; imagination + imagining/imagined cases; per analogies, ladder + up/down aspects, drabbit + duck/rabbit faces.

301. What is in the imagination is not a picture, but a picture can correspond to it.

To rehearse. The (PI 201) thesis of the *Investigations* is that identity is paradox, called the rule, as neither of opposite cases + existing as both qua either.

Comment. Per PI 301: for its grammar sense (law sense) the text presents thus; a face of paradox is to its corresponding other face; as a picturing aspect of a picture corresponds to a pictured aspect; as an imagining aspect of imagination corresponds to o an imagined aspect.

Games: paradox + faces; picture + picturing/pictured cases; imagination + imagining/imagined cases; per analogies ladder + up/down aspects, drabbit + duck/rabbit faces.

*302. If one has to imagine someone else's pain on the model of one's own, this is none too easy a thing to do: for I have to imagine pain which I **don't feel** on the model of pain which I **do feel**. That is, what I have to do is not simply to make a transition in the imagination from pain in one place to pain in another. As from pain in the hand to pain in the arm. For it is not as if I had to imagine that I feel pain in some part of his body. (Which would also be possible.)*

Pain-behaviour can indicate a painful place – but the person who is suffering is the person who manifests pain.

To rehearse. The (PI 201) thesis of the *Investigations* is that identity is paradox, called the rule, as neither of opposite cases + existing as both qua either.

Comment. Per PI 302: grammatically qua lawfully (not empirically), pain is a paradox case, the faces of which are (say) own-pain/his-pain cases; here, each pain case (own or his) is a paradox case, the faces of which are feeling/behaviour cases.

Games: paradox + faces; pain + feeling/behaviour cases; pain + own/his cases; per analogies, ladder + up/down aspects, drabbit + duck/rabbit faces.

*303. "I can only **believe** that someone else is in pain, but I **know** it if I am." – Yes: one can resolve to say "I believe he is in pain" instead of "He is in pain". But that's all. – What looks like an explanation here, or like a statement about a mental process, in truth just exchanges one way of talking for another which, while we are doing philosophy, seems to us the more apt.*

Just try – in a real case – to doubt someone else's fear or pain!

To rehearse. The (PI 201) thesis of the *Investigations* is that identity is paradox, called the rule, as neither of opposite cases + existing as both qua either.

Comment. Per PI 303: empirically, doubt is either apt or not apt; grammatically, doubt (whether or not empirically apt) is irrelevant; paradox is to faces; as pain is to believing/stating cases or to knowing/stating cases; where paradox and faces – all three – coincide, there is no room for doubting that the case of any of the three warrants the other two equally being the case cf. the threefold case of ladder + way-up/way-down cases.

Games: paradox + faces; pain + mental-process/natural-expression cases; per analogies, ladder + up/down aspects, drabbit + duck/rabbit faces.

304. "But you will surely admit that there is a difference between pain-behaviour with pain and pain-behaviour without pain." – Admit it? What greater difference could there be? – "And yet you again and again reach the conclusion that the sensation itself is a Nothing." – Not at all. It's not a Something, but not a Nothing either! The conclusion was only that a Nothing would render the same service as a Something about which nothing could be said. We've only rejected the grammar which tends to force itself on us here.

The paradox disappears only if we make a radical break with the idea that language always functions in one way, always serves the same purpose: to convey thoughts – which may be about houses, pains, good and evil, or whatever.

To rehearse. The (PI 201) thesis of the *Investigations* is that identity is paradox, called the rule, as neither of opposite cases + existing as both qua either.

Comment. Per PI 304: the ungrammatical (unlawful) paradox to radically break away from is where identity/identity cases are nothing/something cases; the paradox to grammatically (lawfully) turn to is where identical cases qua paradox faces are Nothing/Something cases; it is to be seen that the Nothing case, like the Something case, is per PI 201 an accord/discard case cf. something/nothing case, and these as identical aspects qua paradox faces.

Games: identity-as-paradox + identical paradox faces – where each face functions as its eclipsing/eclipsed, something/nothing, accord/discord, aspects; nothing (qua neither Nothing nor Something) + Nothing/Something cases; per PI 43, word + meaning/use – cf. mentalism/behaviourism – cases; sensation +

verb/noun senses; pain + feeling/expression cases; per analogies, ladder + up/down aspects, drabbit + duck/rabbit faces.

305. "But you surely can't deny that, for example, in remembering, an inner process takes place." – What gives the impression that we want to deny anything? When one says, "Still, an inner process does take place here" – one wants to go on: "After all, you **see** it." And it is this inner process that one means by the word "remembering". – The impression that we wanted to deny something arises from our setting our face against the picture of an 'inner process'. What we deny is that the picture of an inner process gives us the correct idea of the use of the word "remember". Indeed, we're saying that this picture, with its ramifications, stands in the way of our seeing the use of the word as it is.

To rehearse. The (PI 201) thesis of the *Investigations* is that identity is paradox, called the rule, as neither of opposite cases + existing as both qua either.

Comment. Per PI 305: the grammar qua law sense is this; a remembering – seeing, inner process – case is paradoxically a remembered – seen, outer shown – case; as paradox face is its counterpart face; as a picturing case is paradoxically a pictured case; from which, and to be denied, is the ungrammatical view of a picture – cf. a word – as of onefold-only consistency sense.

Games: paradox + faces; per PI 43, word + meaning/use – cf. mental/behavioural – aspects; picture + picturing/pictured cases; remembrance + verb/ noun senses; per analogies, ladder + up/down aspects, drabbit + duck/rabbit faces.

306. Why ever should I deny that there is a mental process? It is only that "There has just taken place in me the mental process of remembering ..." means nothing more than "I have just remembered ..." To deny the mental process would mean to deny the remembering; to deny that anyone ever remembers anything.

To rehearse. The (PI 201) thesis of the *Investigations* is that identity is paradox, called the rule, as neither of opposite cases + existing as both qua either.

Comment. Per PI 306: grammatically (lawfully), the text denies that memory is anything other than a paradox, the faces of which are its remembering/remembered aspects, each aspect as thereby inseparably the other cf. per analogy, ladder + up/down aspects.

Games: paradox + faces; remembrance + verb/noun – remembering/remembered, mental-process/behaviour – senses; per analogies, ladder + up/down aspects, drabbit + duck/rabbit faces.

*307. "Aren't you nevertheless a behaviourist in disguise? Aren't you nevertheless basically saying that everything except human behaviour is a fiction?" – If I speak of a fiction, then it is of a **grammatical** fiction.*

To rehearse. The (PI 201) thesis of the *Investigations* is that identity is paradox, called the rule, as neither of opposite cases + existing as both qua either.

Comment. Per PI 307: the grammar qua law talk of the text says as follows; behaviourism is a grammatical fiction unless behaviour is bonded paradoxically with mental-process.

Games: paradox + faces; per PI 43, word + meaning/use – cf. meaning/behaviour – cases; per analogies, ladder + up/down aspects, drabbit + duck/rabbit faces.

308. How does the philosophical problem about mental processes and states and about behaviourism arise? – The first step is the one that altogether escapes notice. We talk of processes and states, and leave their nature undecided. Sometime perhaps we'll know more about them – we think. But that's just what commits us to a particular way of looking at the matter. For we have a certain conception of what it means to learn to know a process better. (The decisive movement in the conjuring trick has been made, and it was the very one that seemed to us quite innocent.) – And now the analogy which was to make us understand our thoughts falls to pieces. So we have to deny the yet-uncomprehended process in the yet unexplored medium. And now it looks as if we had denied mental processes. And naturally we don't want to deny them.

To rehearse. The (PI 201) thesis of the *Investigations* is that identity is paradox, called the rule, as neither of opposite cases + existing as both qua either.

Comment. Per PI 308: grammatically – lawfully – speaking, the mistaken view is taken that a mental process is a (behaviourally non-understood) identity case whereas it is a (behaviourally understood) identity-aspect case; paradox is to faces; as identity is to identical aspects; as per PI 43, word is to meaning/use – cf. mental-process/behaviour – cases.

Games: paradox + faces; per PI 43, word + meaning/use – cf. mentalistic/behavioural – cases; per analogies, ladder + up/down aspects, drabbit + duck/rabbit faces.

309. What is your aim in philosophy? – To show the fly the way out of the fly-bottle.

To rehearse. The (PI 201) thesis of the *Investigations* is that identity is paradox, called the rule, as neither of opposite cases + existing as both qua either.

Comment. Per PI 309: grammar qua law - talk is this; paradox is to faces; as fly is to bottled/unbottled cases.

Games: paradox + faces; word (language) + meaning/use (private/public) – cf. mental-process/behaviour – cases; fly + bottled/unbottled – within/without, inner/outer – cases; per analogies, ladder + up/down aspects, drabbit + duck/rabbit faces.

310. I tell someone I'm in pain. His attitude to me will then be that of belief, disbelief, suspicion, and so on.

Let's suppose he says, "It's not so bad". – Doesn't that prove that he believes in something behind my utterance of pain? – His attitude is proof of his attitude. Imagine not merely the words "I'm in pain", but also the reply "It's not so bad", replaced by *instinctive noises and gestures.*

74   IDENTITY AS PARADOX

To rehearse. The (PI 201) thesis of the *Investigations* is that identity is paradox, called the rule, as neither of opposite cases + existing as both qua either.

Comment. Per PI 310: grammatically (lawfully), pain is to feeling/told-out cases; as attitude (say, belief, or reply, or instinctive-gesture, and so on) is to verb/noun senses – proving/proven – aspects; as paradox is to faces.

Games: paradox + faces; pain + feeling/behaviour cases; pain + owned/surmised cases; belief + believing/believed cases; attitude-proof + attitude-proving/proven-attitude cases; per analogies, ladder + up/down aspects, drabbit + duck/rabbit faces.

*311. "What greater difference could there be?" – In the case of pain, I believe that I can privately give myself an exhibition of the difference. But the difference between a broken and an unbroken tooth I can exhibit to anyone. – For the private exhibition, however, you don't have to give yourself actual pain; it is enough to **imagine** it – for instance, you screw up your face a bit. And do you know that what you are exhibiting to yourself in this way is pain and not, for example, a facial expression? And how do you know what you are to exhibit to yourself before you do it? This **private** exhibition is an illusion.*

To rehearse. The (PI 201) thesis of the *Investigations* is that identity is paradox, called the rule, as neither of opposite cases + existing as both qua either.

Comment. Per PI 311: paradox is to faces; as coincidence is to difference; as per 43, word (language) is to private/public – cf. self/talk/communicative-talk, private-exhibition/public-exhibition – cases; as pain is to feeling/ expressed cases; as tooth is to now-unbroken/now-broken cases; as imagination (here, as pain) is to imagining/facial-expression cases; whatever the grammatical (lawful case qua threefold language game, the paradox-face cases are indubitably one another cf. ladder + up/down aspects.

Games: paradox + faces; coincidence + difference; per PI 43, word (language) + meaning/use (private/public) cases; per PI 215-PI 216, sameness

+ different same/same cases (cf. the drabbit analogy), identity + identical cases; per analogies, ladder + up/down aspects, drabbit + duck/rabbit faces.

*312. But again, **aren't** the cases of the tooth and the pain similar? For the visual impression in the one corresponds to the sensation of pain in the other. I can exhibit the visual impression to myself as little or as well as the sensation of pain.*

Let's imagine the following. The surfaces of the things around us (stones, plants, etc.) have patches and regions which cause pain in our skin when we touch them. (Perhaps through the chemical composition of these surfaces. But we needn't know that.) In this case, we'd speak of pain-patches on the leaf of a particular plant, just as at present we speak of red patches. I'm supposing that it is useful to us to notice these patches and their shapes; that we can infer important properties of the objects from them.

To rehearse. The (PI 201) thesis of the *Investigations* is that identity is paradox, called the rule, as neither of opposite cases + existing as both qua either.

Comment. PI 312: the grammar talk qua law talk runs as follows; object (a person, a tooth, a stone, a plant leaf) is to inner/outer cases (cf. properties/patches, hidden/observable, private/public); as coincidence is to different qua distinct cases; as paradox is to faces.

Games: paradox + faces; per PI 43, word + meaning/use cases; object + inner/outer – cf. quality/quantity, properties/behaviour – cases; sight (cf. the PI 311 tooth case) seeing/seen cases (be the tooth broken or not); pain + feeling/behaviour cases; per analogies, ladder + up/down aspects, drabbit + duck/rabbit faces.

*313. I can exhibit pain, as I exhibit red, and as I exhibit straight and crooked and trees and stones. – **That** is what we **call** "exhibiting".*

To rehearse. The (PI 201) thesis of the *Investigations* is that identity is paradox, called the rule, as neither of opposite cases + existing as both qua either.

Comment. Per PI 313: grammatically (lawfully), any wordage case (pain, red, straight and crooked, trees, stones) is an exhibition case, a **that** case, a paradox case, the faces of which are the exhibiting/exhibited cases; here, paradox is to faces; as exhibition is to exhibiting/exhibited cases; as picture is to out-pictures (which out-pictures qua paradox faces are picturing/pictured cases).

Games: paradox + faces; pain exhibition + feeling/behaviour – exhibiting/exhibited – cases; per PI 43, word + meaning/use cases. per analogies, ladder + up/down aspects, drabbit + duck/rabbit faces.

314. It indicates a fundamental misunderstanding, if I'm inclined to study my current headache in order to get clear about the philosophical problem of sensation.

To rehearse. The (PI 201) thesis of the *Investigations* is that identity is paradox, called the rule, as neither of opposite cases + existing as both qua either.

Comment. Per PI 314: understanding identity (a sensation, a current headache) is problematic where seen logically as a onefold-only – a consistency – sense, also if seen empirically as a physical experience; grammatically (lawfully), identity is paradox cf. word (say, headache) + meaning/use – cf. logical/empirical – cases.

Games: paradox + faces; sensation (here, a current headache) + sensing/sensed – feeling/felt, feeling/behaviour – cases; per analogies, per PI 43, word + meaning/use cases; ladder + up/down aspects, drabbit + duck/rabbit faces.

*315. Could someone who had **never** felt pain understand the word "pain"? – Is experience to teach me whether this is so or not? – And if we say "A man could not imagine pain without having sometime felt it", how do we know? How can it be decided whether it's true?*

To rehearse. The (PI 201) thesis of the *Investigations* is that identity is paradox, called the rule, as neither of opposite cases + existing as both qua either.

Comment. Per PI 315: grammatically (lawfully), the criterion for understanding the meaning of the pain word is its use in a language – not any empirical pain experience; the pain word is understood in terms of word-use of it as paradoxically its word-meaning talk in terms of pain-feelings talk.

Games: paradox + faces; per PI 43, word + meaning/use cases; pain + feeling/expression cases; per analogies, ladder + up/down aspects, drabbit + duck/rabbit faces.

*316. In order to get clear about the meaning of the word "think", we watch ourselves thinking; what we observe will be what the word means! – But that's just **not** how this concept is used. (It would be as if without knowing how to play chess, I were to try and make out what the word "checkmate" meant by close observation of the last move of a game of chess.)*

To rehearse. The (PI 201) thesis of the *Investigations* is that identity is paradox, called the rule, as neither of opposite cases + existing as both qua either.

Comment. Per PI 316: one learns the grammatical qua lawful meaning of thinking as a word not by empirically watching one's thinking process but by understanding that the word-use determines the word-meaning, likewise, with the checkmate word.

Games: paradox + faces; per PI 43, word (say, thinking, checkmate) + meaning/use cases; per analogies, ladder + up/down aspects, drabbit + duck/rabbit faces.

317. Misleading parallel: a cry, an expression of a pain – a sentence, an expression of a thought.

As if the purpose of a sentence were to convey to one person how it is with another: only, so to speak, in his thinking apparatus, and not in his stomach.

To rehearse. The (PI 201) thesis of the *Investigations* is that identity is paradox, called the rule, as neither of opposite cases + existing as both qua either.

Comment. Per PI 317: grammatically (lawfully), pain is to its feeling/cry-expression aspects; as sentence is its thinking/word-expression aspects; as paradox is its faces; as per PI 43, word is to meaning/use cases; as communication is to its communicating/communicated – conveying/conveyed – aspects.

Games: paradox + faces; word + meaning/use cases; language + private/public cases; communication + communicating/communicated – conveying/conveyed – cases; pain + feeling/behaviour cases; per analogies, ladder + up/down aspects, drabbit + duck/rabbit faces.

*318. When we speak, or write, with thought – I mean, as we normally do – we wouldn't, by and large, say that we think more quickly than we talk; rather, the thought seems **not to be detached** from the expression. On the other hand, however, one does speak of the speed of thought, of how a thought goes through one's head like lightning, of how problems become clear to us at a stroke, and so on. So it is natural to ask whether the same thing happens in lightning-like thought as in speech that is not thoughtless – only extremely accelerated. So that in the first case the clockwork, as it were, runs down all at once, but in the second bit by bit, braked by the words.*

To rehearse. The (PI 201) thesis of the *Investigations* is that identity is paradox, called the rule, as neither of opposite cases + existing as both qua either.

Comment. Per PI 318: grammatically qua lawfully (treating with empirical-sense talk), from PI 43, word is to meaning/use – thinking/speaking, fast/slow – cases; as paradox is to faces.

Games: paradox + faces; language + thinking/speaking – fast/slow – cases; word + meaning/use cases; coincidence + distinct cases; per analogies, ladder + up/down aspects, drabbit + duck/rabbit faces.

319. I can see, or understand, a thought complete before my mind's eye in a flash, in the same sense in which I can make a note of it in a few words or a few pencilled dashes.

What makes this note into an epitome of this thought?

To rehearse. The (PI 201) thesis of the *Investigations* is that identity is paradox, called the rule, as neither of opposite cases + existing as both qua either.

Comment. Per PI 319: the understanding/understanding – verb/noun, thinking/thought, seeing/seen, thinking/note, epitome/expression – cases are paradox faces; here, grammatically qua lawfully, it is thought qua paradox that renders the epitome paradox face as the note paradox face.

Games: paradox + faces; per PI 43, word + meaning/use – cf. understanding/ note, essence/note, epitome/note – cases; rapidity + thinking/note cases; thought + thought/thought – thinking/thinking, verb-sense/noun-sense – cases; per analogies, ladder + up/down aspects, drabbit + duck/ rabbit faces.

320. A lightning-like thought may stand to a spoken thought as an algebraic formula to a sequence of numbers which I develop from it.

When, for example, I am given an algebraic function, I am CERTAIN that I shall be able to work out its values for the arguments 1, 2, 3 ... up to 10. This certainty will be called 'well-grounded', for I have learnt to compute such functions, and so on. In other cases, there will be no grounds – but it will nonetheless be justified by success.

To rehearse. The (PI 201) thesis of the *Investigations* is that identity is paradox, called the rule, as neither of opposite cases + existing as both qua either.

Comment. Per 320: the certainty case is the paradox case, making certain that the paradox faces thereby are certainly qua paradoxically one another cf. per analogy, the up/down ladder-aspects as certainly one another; such faces are the formula/out-work cases; the certainty is there whether or not the out-work is logically well-grounded for it is grammatical qua lawful certainty, not logical certainty.

Games: paradox + faces; per PI 43, word + meaning/use – cf. form/matter, form/content, formula/out-work – cases; per analogies, ladder + up/down aspects, drabbit + duck/rabbit faces.

321. "What happens when a man suddenly understands?" – The question is badly framed. If it is a question about the meaning of the expression "sudden understanding", the answer is not to point to a process to which we give this name. – The question might mean: what are the symptoms of sudden understanding; what are its characteristic mental accompaniments?

(There is no reason to think that a man feels his expressive facial movements, for example, or alterations in his breathing that are characteristic of some emotion. Even if he feels them as soon as he directs his attention towards them.) ((Posture.))

To rehearse. The (PI 201) thesis of the *Investigations* is that identity is paradox, called the rule, as neither of opposite cases + existing as both qua either.

Comment. Per PI 321: the empirical-sense talk is grammatically (lawfully) irrelevant other than as raw material for translation to grammar; grammatically, the verb-sense understanding aspect (cf. mental process) of understanding is its noun-sense aspect (cf. natural accompaniment); as a face of paradox is to its counterpart face; as (from PI 43) the meaning of – a "sudden understanding" wordage is to its use (expression).

Games: paradox + faces; word + meaning/use cases; understanding + verb/noun – cf. thinking/thought, mental-process/natural-accompaniment – cases; per analogies, ladder + up/down aspects, drabbit + duck/rabbit faces.

*322. The question what the expression means is not answered by such a description; and this tempts us to conclude that understanding is a specific, indefinable experience. But one forgets that the question which should be our concern is: how do we **compare** these experiences; what criterion of identity **do we stipulate** for their occurrence?*

To rehearse. The (PI 201) thesis of the *Investigations* is that identity is paradox, called the riper use, as neither of opposite cases + existing as both qua either.

Comment. PI 322: the empirical-sense talk coverts grammatically (lawfully) as follows: understanding is to its expression; as paradox face is to counterpart face; by which, the warrant (criterion) for the understanding/expression cases being the case is each other in that they inhabit one another cf. given the case of either up or down aspect of a ladder, thereby its down or up aspect is the case.

Games: paradox + faces; per PI 216, identity + identical cases; per PI 43, word (understanding) + verb-sense/noun-sense – understanding/expression – cases; per analogies, ladder + up/down aspects, drabbit + duck/rabbit faces.

*323. "Now I know how to go on!" is an exclamation; it corresponds to an instinctive sound, a glad start. Of course, it does not follow from my feeling that I won't find I'm stuck when I do try to go on. – Here there are cases in which I'd say: "When I said I knew how to go on, I **did** know." One will say that if, for example, an unforeseen interruption occurs. But what is unforeseen must not simply be that I get stuck.*

One could also imagine a case in which light was constantly seeming to dawn on someone – he exclaims "Now I have it!", and then can never substantiate this in practice. – It might seem to him as if in the twinkling of an eye he forgot again the meaning of the picture that occurred to him.

To rehearse. The (PI 201) thesis of the *Investigations* is that identity is paradox, called the rule, as neither of opposite cases + existing as both qua either.

Comment. Per PI 323: grammatically (lawfully), knowing how to go on is paradoxically known qua going on; as exclaiming is to exclaimed; as making a glad start is a glad start made; as feeling is to enactment; here, empirical-sense interruptions or cases of forgetfulness do not feature in cases of grammar where opposite cases are one another cf. up/down ladder aspects; picture talk is identity tall, the meaning qua picturing aspect of a picture is its expressed qua pictured aspect.

Games: paradox + faces: per PI 216 identity + identical cases cf. drabbit + duck/rabbit faces; knowledge or understanding + knowing/known – cf. feeling/behaviour, – cases; per PI 43 word + meaning/use cases; per analogies, ladder + up/down aspects, drabbit + duck/rabbit faces.

*324. Would it be correct to say that this is a matter of induction, and that I am as certain that I'll be able to continue the series as I am that this book will drop to the ground when I let it go; and that I'd be no less astonished if I suddenly, and for no obvious reason, got stuck in working out the series than I would be if the book remained hanging in the air instead of falling? – To that I'll reply that we don't need any grounds for **this** certainty either. What could justify the certainty **better** than success?*

To rehearse. The (PI 201) thesis of the *Investigations* is that identity is paradox, called the rule, as neither of opposite cases + existing as both qua either.

Comment. Per PI 324: what warrants the knowing how to go on case being indubitably the actual (successful) going on case is that these are corresponding cases as paradox-face cases which thereby are coincidentally qua paradoxically one another cf. the way-up/way-down rungs of a ladder; per PI 43, word-meaning is word-use; as per ladder analogy, way-up is way-down; as per 324, verb-sense continuation is noun-sense continuation; from which, the certainty talk as paradox talk (see PI 323) is grammatical (lawful) – neither logical nor empirical – talk.

Games: paradox + faces (each face as correct/incorrect qua eclipsing/ eclipsed); word + meaning/use – cf. logical/empirical – cases; continuation

+ continuation/continuation cases i.e. verb-sense/noun-sense cases; per analogies, ladder + up/down aspects, drabbit + duck/rabbit faces.

325. "The certainty that I'll be able to go on after I've had this experience – seen this formula, for example – is simply based on induction." What does this mean? – "The certainty that fire will burn me is based on induction." Does it mean that I reason to myself: "Fire has always burned me, so it will happen now too"? Or is the previous experience the **cause** of my certainty, not its reason? Whether the earlier experience is the cause of the certainty depends on the system of hypotheses, of natural laws, in terms of which we are considering the phenomenon of certainty.

Is such confidence justified? – What people accept as a justification shows how they think and live.

To rehearse. The (PI 201) thesis of the *Investigations* is that identity is paradox, called the rule, as neither of opposite cases + existing as both qua either.

Comment. Per PI 325: the grammar talk qua law talk is this; certainty as paradox (not as either logical or empirical) is to faces; as per PI 43, word is to meaning/use – logical/empirical – cases; from which, humans live and think in paradoxical ways.

Games: paradox + faces; word + meaning/use – cf. logical/empirical – cases; fire + verb/noun senses; causality + causing/caused cases; per analogies, ladder + up/down aspects, drabbit + duck/rabbit faces.

326. We expect **this**, and are surprised at **that**. But the chain of reasons has an end.

To rehearse. The (PI 201) thesis of the *Investigations* is that identity is paradox, called the rule, as neither of opposite cases + existing as both qua either.

Concept. Per PI 326: the gramma (law sense) runs as follows; expecting is to expected; as paradox face is to counterpart face; as **this** is to **that**; as reasoning is to reasoned; as beginning is to end.

Games: paradox + faces; per PI 43, word + meaning/use – cf. expecting/expected, expecting/outcome, expecting/surprise, this/that, reasoning/reasoned, beginning/end – cases; per analogies, ladder + up/down aspects, drabbit + duck/rabbit faces.

327. *"Can one think without speaking?" – And what is **thinking**? Well, don't you ever think? Can't you observe yourself and see what is going on? It should be quite simple. You don't have to wait for it as for an astronomical event, and then perhaps make your observation in a hurry.*

To rehearse. The (PI 201) thesis of the *Investigations* is that identity is paradox, called the rule, as neither of opposite cases + existing as both qua either.

Comment. Per PI 327: the empirical-sense talk translates grammatically qua lawfully as follows; paradox is to faces; as thinking is to thinking/thinking – verb-sense/noun-sense – cases.

Games: paradox + faces; coincidence + distinct cases; per PI 43, word + meaning/use cases; language + thinking/speaking cases; per analogies, ladder + up/down aspects, drabbit + duck/rabbit faces.

328. *Well, what does one call 'thinking'? What has one learnt to use this word for? – If I say I've thought – need I always be right? – What **kind** of mistake is there room for here? Are there circumstances in which one would ask, "Was what I was doing then really thinking; aren't I making a mistake?" Suppose someone takes a measurement in the middle of a train of thought: has he interrupted the thinking if he doesn't say anything to himself while measuring?*

To rehearse. The (PI 201) thesis of the *Investigations* is that identity is paradox, called the rule, as neither of opposite cases + existing as both qua either.

Comment. Per PI 328: grammatically (lawfully), thinking is paradoxically – coincidentally, inseparably, unmistakably, a non-interruptible, – thinking i.e. verb-sense as paradoxically noun-sense i.e. a paradox face as its counterpart paradox face cf. ladder-ascent as paradoxically ladder-descent; of paradox faces, each is as right or correct as it is wrong or incorrect i.e. each is as eclipsing as it is eclipsed.

Games: paradox + faces; thinking + verb/noun senses; per PI 43, word + meaning/use cases; per analogies, ladder + up/down aspects, drabbit + duck/rabbit faces.

329. When I think in words, I don't have 'meanings' in my mind in addition to the verbal expressions; rather, language itself is the vehicle of thought.

To rehearse. The (PI 201) thesis of the *Investigations* is that identity is paradox, called the rule, as neither of opposite cases + existing as both qua either.

Comment. Per PI 329: the analogous case of ladder-ascent/ladder-descent aspects is not that of aspects added to each other; rather, per law talk qua grammar, as paradox faces, they thereby are paradoxically one another (cf. co-vehicular faces); so, it is with the thinking/words – meaning/expression, thought/language-use – cases.

Games: paradox + faces; per PI 43, word + meaning/use – thinking/speaking – meaning/expression, thought/language-use – cases; per analogies, ladder + up/down aspects, drabbit + duck/rabbit faces.

330. Is thinking a kind of speaking? One would like to say that it is what distinguishes speech with thought from talking without thought. – And so it seems to be an accompaniment of speech. A process which may accompany something else or go on by itself.

Say: "Yes, this pen is blunt. Oh well, it'll do." First, with thought; then without thought; then just think the thought without the words. – Well, while writing, I might test the point of my pen, make a face – and then go on writing with a gesture of resignation. – So too I might, while taking various measurements, act in such a way that an onlooker would say that I had wordlessly thought: if two magnitudes are equal to a third, they are equal to one another. – But what constitutes thought here is not some process which has to accompany the words if they are not to be spoken without thought.

To rehearse. The (PI 201) thesis of the *Investigations* is that identity is paradox, called the rule, as neither of opposite cases + existing as both qua either.

Comment. Per PI 330: thinking/speaking cases qua paradox faces coincide (cf. speech with thought as accompaniments of each other) but as distinct cases (cf. thinking/speech cases without each other, each going by itself); from which, whereas the text presents empirical-sense cases of paired opposites, side by side, as it were, each of these cases per pair – grammatically (lawfully) speaking, is paradoxically (coincidentally) the other.

Games: paradox + faces; coincidence + distinct cases; paradox + paired opposites; per PI 43, word + meaning/use – cf. thinking/speaking – cases; third magnitude as equality + two equal magnitudes; per analogies, ladder + up/down aspects, drabbit + duck/rabbit faces.

331. Imagine people who could think only aloud. (As there are people who can read only aloud.)

To rehearse. The (PI 201) thesis of the *Investigations* is that identity is paradox, called the rule, as neither of opposite cases + existing as both qua either.

Comment. Per PI 331: whatever the empirical case or imaginary case, the grammatical qua lawful case is that of paradox + faces as the case of language + thinking/speaking cases; grammatically, silent reading, say, is referenced to reading aloud; public-only thinking as distinct from private-only thinking is also grammatically referenced to its opposite case.

Games: paradox + faces; per PI 43, word (language) + meaning/use – cf. thinking/speaking – cases; per analogies, ladder + up/down aspects, drabbit + duck/rabbit faces.

332. True, we sometimes call accompanying a sentence by a mental process "thinking"; nonetheless, that accompaniment is not what we call a "thought". – Utter a sentence, and think it; utter it with understanding. – And now don't utter it, and just do what you accompanied it with when you uttered it with understanding! – (Sing this song with expression! And now don't sing it, but repeat its expression! – And here too there is something one might repeat: for example, swaying of the body, slower and faster breathing, and so on.)

To rehearse. The (PI 201) thesis of the *Investigations* is that identity is paradox, called the rule, as neither of opposite cases + existing as both qua either.

Comment. Per PI 332: paradox is to companion cases qua faces; as thinking (cf. thought) is to thinking/thinking (thought/thought) – verb-sense/noun-sense – cases; as per PI 43, word (language) is to meaning/use – cf. thinking/ utterance, understanding/utterance – cases; here, of the variant paired paradox-face cases, there cannot be the case of the one without the case of the other (cf. the up/down ladder aspects) other than where the faces are grammatically (lawfully) distinct cases, which nonetheless also coincide as the paradox case.

Games: paradox + faces; accompaniment + accompanying cases; word + meaning/use cases; language + thinking/speaking – private/public – cases; song + singing/expression cases; body + berthing/expression cases; coincidence + distinct cases; per analogies, ladder + up/down aspects, drabbit + duck/rabbit faces.

*333. "Only someone who is **convinced** can say that." – How does the conviction help him when he says it? – Is it present alongside the spoken expression? (Or is it masked by it, as a soft sound by a loud one, so that it can, as it were, no longer be heard when one expresses it out loud?) What if someone were to say, "In order to be able to sing a tune from memory, one has to hear it in one's mind and sing from that"?*

88 IDENTITY AS PARADOX

To rehearse. The (PI 201) thesis of the *Investigations* is that identity is paradox, called the rule, as neither of opposite cases + existing as both qua either.

Comment. Per PI 333: grammatically (lawfully), paradox is to faces; as conviction is to convinced-feeling/spontaneous-expression – cf. soft-sound/loud-noises, nothing-heard/spoken-aloud – cases; as remembrance is to mentally-heard/sung-aloud cases.

Games: paradox + faces; per PI 43, word + meaning/use – cf. mental-process/behaviour – cases; conviction + convincing/convinced cases; per analogies, ladder + up/down aspects, drabbit + duck/rabbit faces.

334. "So you really wanted to say ..." – *We use this phrase in order to lead someone from one form of expression to another. One is tempted to use the following picture: what he really 'wanted to say', what he 'meant', was already present in his mind even before we articulated it. Various kinds of thing may persuade us to give up one expression and to adopt another in its place. To understand this, it's useful to consider the relation in which solutions of mathematical problems stand to their occasion, and the original setting in which they were posed: the concept of trisecting an angle with ruler and compass, when people are trying to do it, and, on the other hand, when it has been proved that there's no such thing.*

To rehearse. The (PI 201) thesis of the *Investigations* is that identity is paradox, called the rule, as neither of opposite cases + existing as both qua either.

Comment. Per PI 334: picture talk is identity-as-paradox talk; per grammar qua law-talk, paradox is to faces; as picture is to picturing/pictured cases; as language is to thinking/expression cases; from which, and where the text's empirical-sense talk or logical-sense talk is converted to grammar, mental/behavioural cases cannot exist other than as paradoxically one another.

Games: paradox + faces; picture + picturing/pictured cases; language + thinking/expression – thinking/saying, thinking/doing – cases; per analogies, ladder + up/down aspects, drabbit + duck/rabbit faces.

*335. What happens when we make an effort – say in writing a letter – to find the right expression for our thoughts? – This way of speaking compares the process to one of translating or describing: the thoughts are already there (perhaps were there in advance), and we merely look for their expression. This picture is more or less appropriate in different cases. – But can't all sorts of things happen here? – I surrender to a mood, and the expression **comes**. Or I have a picture before my mind, and I try to describe it. Or an English expression occurs to me, and I try to recollect the corresponding German one. Or I make a gesture, and ask myself: "What words correspond to this gesture?" And so on.*

Now if it were asked, "Do you have the thought before finding the expression?", what would one have to reply? And what to the question "What did the thought, as it existed before its expression, consist in?"

To rehearse. The (PI 201) thesis of the *Investigations* is that identity is paradox, called the rule, as neither of opposite cases + existing as both qua either.

Comment. Per PI 335: notwithstanding the plentiful ordinary language presented by this text in empirical-sense terms, it rehearses all of the grammar qua law-sense that was said per PI 334; from which, paradox is to faces; as exchange is to different cases.

Games: paradox + faces; mutual eclipse + interchangeable cases; per analogies, ladder + up/down aspects, drabbit + duck/rabbit faces.

336. This case is similar to the one in which someone imagines that one could not think a sentence with the curious word order of German or Latin just as it stands. One first has to think it, and then one arranges the words in that strange order. (A French politician once wrote that it was a peculiarity of the French language that in it words occur in the order in which one thinks them.)

To rehearse. The (PI 201) thesis of the *Investigations* is that identity is paradox, called the rule, as neither of opposite cases + existing as both qua either.

Comment. Per PI 336: notwithstanding the yet further and variant cases of ordinary language presented in empirical-sense terms by this text, it rehearses all that was grammatically (lawfully) said per the PI 334 and PI 335 texts – here, as follows; paradox is to faces; as translation is to (say) German/English cases; what is being rehearsed in a text such as this is that opposite cases cannot grammatically be the case other that as coincidentally so, such that the grammar is threefold as paradox + faces qua coincidence + difference.

Games: paradox + faces; coincidence + difference; mutual eclipse + interchangeable (say) French/German cases; per analogies, ladder + up/down aspects, drabbit + duck/rabbit faces.

337. But didn't I already intend the whole construction of the sentence (for example) at its beginning? So surely it already existed in my mind before I uttered it out loud! – If it was in my mind, still it would not normally be there in some different word order. But here again, we are forming a misleading picture of 'intending': that is, of the use of this word. An intention is embedded in a setting, in human customs and institutions. If the technique of the game of chess did not exist, I could not intend to play a game of chess. To the extent that I do intend the construction of an English sentence in advance, that is made possible by the fact that I can speak English.

To rehearse. The (PI 201) thesis of the *Investigations* is that identity is paradox, called the rule, as neither of opposite cases + existing as both qua either.

Comment. Per PI 337: notwithstanding the yet further and variant cases of ordinary language presented in empirical-sense terms by this text, it rehearses all that was grammatically (lawfully) said per the PI 334-336 texts, here as follows; paradox is to faces; as intention (like chess-play, like translation) is to verb/noun – cf. in-advance/outcome – cases.

Gamesa: paradox + faces; picture + picturing/pictured cases; per PI 43, word + meaning/use cases; language-construction or chess-play or intention + verb/noun senses; per analogies, ladder + up/down aspects, drabbit b+ duck/rabbit faces.

*338. After all, one can only say something if one has learned to talk. Therefore, in order to **want** to say something, one must also have mastered a language; and yet it is clear that one can want to speak without speaking. Just as one can want to dance without dancing.*

*And when one thinks about this, the mind reaches for the **idea** of dancing, speaking, etc.*

To rehearse. The (PI 201) thesis of the *Investigations* is that identity is paradox, called the rule, as neither of opposite cases + existing as both qua either.

Comment. Per PI 338: the grammar qua law-talk of the text is this; paradox faces thereby are and are not one another; as thinking/expression – cf. wanting/wanted, dancing/expression – cases are connected qua referenced to one another and unconnected qua distinct from one another; from which, the faces are referenced also to paradox, just as the thinking/expression cases are referenced also to language; per PI 338, unexpressed private language is nonetheless referenced to public language – otherwise, it would not be the case of language.

Games: paradox + faces; language + private/public cases; per analogies, ladder + up/down aspects, drabbit + duck/rabbit faces.

339. Thinking is not an incorporeal process which lends life and sense to speaking, and which it would be possible to detach from speaking, rather as the Devil took the shadow of Schlemihl from the ground. – But in what way "not an incorporeal process"? Am I acquainted with incorporeal processes, then, only thinking is not one of them? No; in my predicament, I helped myself to the expression "an incorporeal process" as I was trying to explain the meaning of the word "thinking" in a primitive way.

*One could, however, say "Thinking is an incorporeal process" if one were using this to distinguish the grammar of the word "think" from that of, say, the word "eat". Only that makes the difference between the meanings look **too slight**. (It is like saying: numerals are actual, and numbers are non-actual objects.) An inappropriate expression is a sure means of remaining stuck in confusion. It, as it were, bars the way out.*

To rehearse. The (PI 201) thesis of the *Investigations* is that identity is paradox, called the rule, as neither of opposite cases + existing as both qua either.

Comment. Per PI 339: the incorporeal/corporeal terms are not to be taken empirically but are to be taken grammatically (lawfully) as paradox faces, the paradox being the language case; paradox is to faces; as language is to thinking/expression – incorporeal/corporeal – cases.

Games: paradox + faces; language + thinking/expression cases; per analogies, reality + incorporeal/corporal cases, ladder + up/down aspects, drabbit + suck/rabbit faces.

*340. One cannot guess how a word functions. One has to **look** at its application and learn from that.*

*But the difficulty is to remove the prejudice which stands in the way of doing so. It is not a **stupid** prejudice.*

To rehearse. The (PI 201) thesis of the *Investigations* is that identity is paradox, called the rule, as neither of opposite cases + existing as both qua either.

Comment. Per PI 340: as a paradox-face case, a word-use case, like its corresponding word-meaning case qua counterpart paradox-face case, functions as a focal case, also as a non-focal face; the word-meaning is not fixed as per the traditional perspective of identity-gamma whereby meaning is consistency; this onefold-only perspective is prejudicial – not stupidly so but simply traditionally so – to seeing the grammar qua law to be threefold as that of paradox + faces, and variants.

Games: paradox + faces; per PI 43, word + meaning/use cases; per analogies, ladder + up/down aspects, drabbit + duck/rabbit faces

341. Speech with and without thought is to be compared to playing a piece of music with and without thought.

To rehearse. The (PI 201) thesis of the *Investigations* is that identity is paradox, called the rule, as neither of opposite cases + existing as both qua either.

Comment. Per PI 341: the grammar sense qua law sense of the text presents as follows; of the thinking/speaking cases, each without the other is a distinct paradox face; each with the other is the paradox case of language; paradox is to faces; as language is to thinking/spoken cases; as music is to thinking/played cases.

Games: paradox + faces; language + thinking/expression cases; music + thinking/expression cases; per analogies, ladder + up/down aspects, drabbit + duck/rabbit faces

*342. William James, in order to show that thought is possible without speech, quotes the reminiscences of a deaf-mute, Mr Ballard, who wrote that in his early youth, even before he could speak, he had had thoughts about God and the world. – What could that mean!? – Ballard writes: "It was during those delightful rides, some two or three years before my initiation into the rudiments of written language, that I began to ask myself the question: how came the world into being?" – Are you sure – one would like to ask – that this is the correct translation of your wordless thoughts into words? And why does this question – which otherwise seems not to exist – arise here? Do I want to say that the writer's memory deceives him? – I don't even know if I'd say **that**. These recollections are a strange memory phenomenon – and I don't know what conclusions one can draw from them about the narrator's past!*

To rehearse. The (PI 201) thesis of the *Investigations* is that identity is paradox, called the rule, as neither of opposite cases + existing as both qua either.

Comment. Per PI 342: the text recounts – and questions – the case of thoughts existing which are not referenced to speech; the implication is that thou/speech cases are cross-referenced cases, with both referenced to language as a third party; whilst the thought/speech cases cf. paradox faces are without each other in that they are distinct cases as thereby each not the other, as well as are without one another in that they eclipse and are eclipsed by one another, they nonetheless are inseparable cases in that they coincide as the case of language cf. the case of paradox; such is the grammar qua law sense of PI 342.

Games: paradox + faces; per PI 43, word (say, memory) + meaning/use (memorising/memorised) cases; language + thinking/speaking – private/public – cases; per analogies, ladder + up/down ways, drabbit + duck/rabbit faces.

343. The words with which I express my memory are my memory reaction.

To rehearse. The (PI 201) thesis of the *Investigations* is that identity is paradox, called the rule, as neither of opposite cases + existing as both qua either.

Comment. Per PI 343: grammatically (lawfully), action stands to reaction; as a remembering case stands to a remembered case qua expression case or report case; as a paradox-face case stands to its corresponding other paradox-face case.

Gamesa: paradox + faces; per PI 43, word + meaning/use cases; memory + remembering/repot – cf. action/reaction – cases; per analogies, ladder + up/down aspects, drabbit + d

344. Is it conceivable that people should never speak an audible language, but should nevertheless talk to themselves inwardly, in the imagination?

"If people talked only inwardly, to themselves, then they would merely be doing **always** what, as it is, they do **sometimes**." – So it is quite easy to imagine this;

one need only make the easy transition from some to all. (Similarly, "An infinitely long row of trees is simply one that does **not** come to an end.") Our criterion for someone's saying something to himself is what he tells us, as well as the rest of his behaviour; and we say that someone talks to himself only if, in the ordinary sense of the words, he **can talk**. And we do not say it of a parrot; or of a gramophone.

To rehearse. The (PI 201) thesis of the *Investigations* is that identity is paradox, called the rule, as neither of opposite cases + existing as both qua either.

Comment. Per PI 344: grammatically (as lawful sense), per PI 43, word (language) is to meaning/use (private/public) cases; as paradox qua always is to this/that – sometimes/sometimes – faces; from which, there is neither a private case without its public counterpart case (the people in the text) nor vice versa (parrot, gramophone).

Games: paradox + faces; always + sometimes/sometimes cases; infinite + finite/finite cases; word (language) + meaning/use (private/public) cases; per analogies, ladder + up/down aspects, drabbit + /rabbit faces.

345. "What sometimes happens might always happen." – What kind of proposition is that? It is similar to this one: If "F(a)" makes sense, "(x).F(x)" makes sense.

"If it is possible for someone to make a false move in some game, then it could be that everybody made nothing but false moves in every game." – So we're tempted to misunderstand the logic of our expressions here, to give an incorrect account of the use of our words.

Orders are sometimes not obeyed. But what would it be like if no orders were **ever** obeyed? The concept of an order would have lost its purpose.

To rehearse. The (PI 201) thesis of the *Investigations* is that identity is paradox, called the rule, as neither of opposite cases + existing as both qua either.

96 IDENTITY AS PARADOX

Comment. Per PI 345: grammatically (as lawful sense), paradox is to faces; as always is to this/that – sometimes/sometimes – faces; from which, it is the game, or the order, that is the always case; the false-move aspect or the non-obeyed aspect is a sometimes aspect.

Games: paradox + face; always + sometimes/sometimes cases cf. PI 215, sameness + same/same cases; per analogies, ladder + ascent/descent aspects, drabbit + duck/rabbit faces.

346. But couldn't we imagine God's suddenly giving a parrot reason, and its now saying things to itself? – But here it is important that, in order to arrive at this idea, I had recourse to the notion of a deity.

To rehearse. The (PI 201) thesis of the *Investigations* is that identity is paradox, called the rule, as neither of opposite cases + existing as both qua either.

Comment. Per PI 346: the grammar qua law-talk sense is this; paradox is to faces; as per PI 43, word (language) is to meaning/use (private/public) cases; from which, it is the case of something out of this world (cf. divine causality) qua the ungrammatical case that what is not a human form of life (the parrot) should be a paradox case (cf. word qua language case), the faces of which are reason/expression (cf. meaning/use qua private/public) cases.

Games: paradox + faces; language + private/public cases; word + meaning/use cases; per analogies, ladder + up/down aspects, drabbit + duck/rabbit faces.

347. "But at least I know from my own case what it means 'to say things to oneself'. And if I were deprived of the organs of speech, I could still conduct internal monologues."

*If I know it only from my own case, then **I** know only what I call that, not what anyone else does.*

To rehearse. The (PI 201) thesis of the *Investigations* is that identity is paradox, called the rule, as neither of opposite cases + existing as both qua either.

Comment. PI 347: one can only know – see to be grammatical qua lawful – one's own case to be a private language case where it is referenced to a shared human language case with public expression; compare – the case of *I* is just such a case only as a person case as well as a myself case; whatever the language game, opposite cases are cross-referenced as paradox faces inhabiting one another cf. the up/down aspects of a ladder, as well as where the opposite cases are referenced to a their-party case, viz., their-coincidence case as a paradox case.

Games: paradox + faces; language + private/public cases; per PI 43, word + meaning/use cases; person + I/myself – mind/body, thinking/speaking, mental/behavioural – cases; per analogies, ladder + up/down aspects, drabbit + duck/rabbit faces.

*348. "All these deaf-mutes have learned only a sign-language, but each of them talks to himself inwardly in a vocal language." – Well, don't you understand that? – How should I know whether I understand it?! – What can I do with this information (if that's what it is)? The whole idea of understanding smells fishy here. I don't know whether I am to say I understand it, or I don't understand it. I'm inclined to answer "It's an English sentence; **apparently** quite in order – that is, until one wants to do something with it; it has a connection with other sentences, which makes it difficult for us to say that one doesn't really know what it tells us. Anyone who has not become insensitive by doing philosophy notices that there is something wrong here."*

To rehearse. The (PI 201) thesis of the *Investigations* is that identity is paradox, called the rule, as neither of opposite cases + existing as both qua either.

Comment. Per PI 348: the grammar qua law-sense of the text is this; language exhibits not as vocal/gestured cases but as meaning/gestured cases, or meaning/vocal cases; per PI 43, word is to meaning/use – meaning/vocal, meaning/written, meaning-gestured – cases; as language is to private/public cases; as paradox is to faces.

Gamesa: paradox + faces; language (the shared language of humankind) + private/public – thinking/speaking, thinking/gesturing – cases; word + meaning/use cases; per analogies, ladder + up/down aspects, drabbit + duck/rabbit faces.

349. "But this assumption surely makes good sense!" – Yes; in ordinary circumstances these words and this picture have an application with which we are familiar. – But if we suppose a case in which this application does not exist, we become aware for the first time of the nakedness, as it were, of the words and the picture.

To rehearse. The (PI 201) thesis of the *Investigations* is that identity is paradox, called the rule, as neither of opposite cases + existing as both qua either.

Comment. Per PI 349: grammatically (lawfully) paradox i.e. picture is to faces; as per PI 43, word is to meaning/use cases; where it is assumed that opposite cases are the case but not seen as paradoxically one another, the assumed case is stripped of grammatical sense cf. per analogy, a ladder seen as up/down aspects but not paradoxically so.

Games: paradox + faces; picture + picturing/pictured cases; per PI 43, word (language) + meaning/use – meaning/application, private/public – cases; per analogies, ladder + up/down aspects, drabbit + duck/rabbit faces.

350. "But if I suppose that someone has a pain, then I am simply supposing that he has just the same as I have so often had." – That gets us no further. It is as if I were to say, "You surely know what 'It's 5 o'clock here' means; so you also know what 'It's 5 o'clock on the sun' means. It means simply that it is just the same time there as it is here when it is 5 o'clock." – The explanation by means of **sameness** *does not work here. For I know well enough that one can call 5 o'clock* here and 5 o'clock there "the same time", but do not know in what cases one is to speak of its being the same time here and there.

In exactly the same way, it is no explanation to say: the supposition that he has a pain is simply the supposition that he has the same as I. For what's surely clear to me is **this** part of grammar: that one will say that the stove has the same experience as I if one says: it's in pain and I'm in pain.

To rehearse. The (PI 201) thesis of the *Investigations* is that identity is paradox, called the rule, as neither of opposite cases + existing as both qua either.

Comment. Per PI 350: by supposition, opposites are the case – self and another have the same pain, 5 o'clock on Earth and on the sun, same time here and same time there; such supposition as to there being opposite case same/same cases is ungrammatical (unlawful) unless the opposite cases qua same/same cases are faces of a paradox case called sameness; per PI 215, sameness is to opposite same/same cases cf. per analogy, drabbit + duck/rabbit faces; as paradox is to faces; as pain is to pain/pain – own/his, own/stove – cases.

Games: paradox + faces; sameness + same/same cases; pain + pain/pain – his/mine, own/stove's – cases; same time + 5 pm/5 pm cases – Earth/sun, here/there – case; per analogies, ladder + up/down aspects, drabbit + duck/rabbit faces.

*351. Yet we keep wanting to say: "A sensation of pain is a sensation of pain – whether **he** has it, or **I** have it, no matter how I come to know whether he has a pain or not." – I might go along with that. – And when you ask me, "Don't you know, then, what I mean when I say that the stove is in pain?", I can reply: "These words may lead me to imagine all sorts of things; but their usefulness goes no further." And I can also imagine something in connection with the words: "Just now it was 5 o'clock in the afternoon on the sun" – such as a grandfather clock which shows 5. – But a still better example would be that of the application of "above" and "beneath" to the globe. Here we all have a quite clear idea of what* *"above" and "beneath" mean. I see well enough that I am on top; the earth is surely beneath me! (And don't smile at this example. We are indeed all taught at elementary school that it is stupid to talk like that. But it is much easier to bury a problem than to solve it.) And it is only reflection that shows us that in this case "above" and "beneath" cannot be used in the customary way. (That we might, for instance, say that the people at the antipodes are 'beneath' our part of the earth, but must then also recognize it as right for them to use the same expression about us.)*

To rehearse. The (PI 201) thesis of the *Investigations* is that identity is paradox, called the rule, as neither of opposite cases + existing as both qua either.

Comment. Per PI 351: grammatically (lawfully), to say that pain is a sameness, whether his or mine, whether the stove's or mine, or that time is a sameness, whether here or on the sun, or that the Earth is a sameness, whether at one pole or the other pole, is to say that identity-as-paradox is a sameness, whether as one paradox face or as the corresponding other paradox face cf. a ladder is a sameness as same/same cases qua up/down aspects; whatever the opposite cases, they are indeed distinct cases yet which coincide as the case of opposition: opposition is a sameness, whether as same/same cases qua this-opposite/that-opposite cases cf. drabbit is a sameness, whether same/same cases qua duck/rabbit faces.

Games: paradox + faces; per PI 215, sameness + same/same cases; pain + pain/pain – his/mine, the-stove's/mine – cases; time + time/time – on-Earth/on-sun – cases; Earth + Earth/Earth – this-pole/that-pol, say above/below – cases; per analogies, ladder + up/down aspects, drabbit + duck/rabbit faces.

352. At this point, our thinking plays us a strange trick. That is, we want to quote the law of excluded middle and say: "Either such an image floats before his mind, or it does not; there is no third possibility!" – We encounter this curious argument also in other regions of philosophy. "In the infinite expansion of π either the group '7777' occurs, or it does not–a there is no third possibility." That is to say: God sees – but we don't know. But what does that mean? – We use a picture: the picture of a visible series, the whole of which one person can survey and another can't. Here the law of excluded middle says: it must look either like **this** or like **that**. So really – and this is surely obvious – it says nothing at all, but gives us a picture. And the problem is now supposed to be: does reality accord with the picture or not? And this picture **seems** to determine what we have to do, what to look for, and how – but it does not, precisely because we do not know how it is to be applied. Here, saying "There is no third possibility" or "There really isn't a third possibility!" expresses our inability to turn our eyes away from this picture – a picture which looks as if it must already contain both the problem and its solution, while all the time we **feel** that it is not so.

Similarly, when it is said "Either he has this sensation, or he doesn't", what primarily occurs to us is a picture which already seems to determine the sense of the statements **unequivocally**: "Now you know what is in question", one would like to say. And that's just what it does not tell you.

To rehearse. The (PI 201) thesis of the *Investigations* is that identity is paradox, called the rule, as neither of opposite cases + existing as both qua either.

Comment. Per PI 352: for its grammar (law sense), the text reads as follows; picture talk is identity-as-paradox talk; the focus of the text is the excluded-middle law of thought by which an identity is an either/or-but-not-contradictorily-both case; but the *Investigations* has shown that identity is paradox as neither of its faces in its being distinct from them (cf. excluded middle), also either of its faces in that it exists by turns as each of them (cf. opposites), also both of its faces in that it is their coincidence (cf. included middle); from which, identity as a fixed, unequivocal, onefold-only picture of consistency is to be replaced by the picture that is an identity as paradox, a third party to the paradox-face cases – cases which function grammatically as complementary and mutually eclipsing faces.

Games: identity-as-paradox + identical faces (cf. drabbit + duck/rabbit faces); picture + picturing/pictured cases; third party + opposite – either/or, this/that, this-to-me/that-top-thee, 7777/no-7777, mental-image/no-image – cases; nothing at all (excluded middle) + either/or cases; reality + accord/no-accord – cf. pro-real/anti-real – cases; picture + determination/ no-determination cases; coincidence (included middle) + problem/solution extremes; per analogies, ladder + up/down aspects, drabbit + duck/rabbit faces.

353. Asking whether and how a proposition can be verified is only a special form of the question "How do you mean?" The answer is a contribution to the grammar of the proposition.

To rehearse. The (PI 201) thesis of the *Investigations* is that identity is paradox, called the rule, as neither of opposite cases + existing as both qua either.

Comment. Per PI 353: grammatically (lawfully), from PI 43, the meaning of a sentence is its use (its verification); as face of paradox is to its counterpart face.

Games: paradox + faces; word + meaning/use cases; sentence + meaning/verification cases; per analogies, ladder + up/down aspects, drabbit + duck/rabbit faces.

*354. The fluctuation in grammar between criteria and symptoms makes it look as if there were nothing at all but symptoms. We say, for example, "Experience teaches that there is rain when the barometer falls, but it also teaches that there is rain when we have certain feelings of wet and cold, or such-and-such visual impressions." As an argument in support of this, one says that these sense impressions can deceive us. But here one overlooks the fact that their deceiving us precisely **about rain** rests on a definition.*

To rehearse. The (PI 201) thesis of the *Investigations* is that identity is paradox, called the rule, as neither of opposite cases + existing as both qua either.

Comment. Per PI 354: by its grammar quo law sense, against the definition of rain as evidenced by the falling barometer reading, and where rain-sensation is discounted as subject to deception, there is the threefold grammar as follows; paradox is to faces; as rain is to sensation/barometer-reading cases; as per PI 43, word is to meaning/use cases.

Gamers: paradox + faces; criterion + symptoms; word + meaning/use cases; rain + subjective/objective – sensation/barometer-reading – cases; per analogies, ladder + up/down aspects, drabbit + duck/rabbit faces.

355. The point here is not that our sense impressions can lie to us, but that we understand their language. (And this language, like any other, rests on convention.)

To rehearse. The (PI 201) thesis of the *Investigations* is that identity is paradox, called the rule, as neither of opposite cases + existing as both qua either.

Comment. Per PI 355: the grammar qua law sense is this; conventionally, sensation language is language of sensation as defined identity – it is either this or that identity and not contradictorily both; against this ungrammatical conventional perspective, there is the threefold grammatical (language-game) understanding whereby sensation is to sensing/sensed – this/that – cases; as paradox is to faces.

Games: paradox + faces; per PI 43, word (language) + meaning/use (private/public) cases; sensation + sensing/sensed – this/that, subjective/ objective – cases; per analogies, ladder + up/down aspects, drabbit + duck/ rabbit faces.

356. One is inclined to say: "Either it is raining, or it isn't – how I know, how the message has reached me, is another matter." But then let's put the question like this: What do I call "a message that it is raining"? (Or have I only word of this message too?) And what gives this 'message' the character of a message about something? Doesn't the form of our expression mislead us here? For isn't it a misleading metaphor to say, "My eyes send me the message that there is a chair over there"?

To rehearse. The (PI 201) thesis of the *Investigations* is that identity is paradox, called the rule, as neither of opposite cases + existing as both qua either.

Comment. Per PI 356: the text reads grammatically (lawfully) as follows; a messaging aspect of a message is its messaged aspect; as, per PI 43, the meaning of a word is its use; as the mental-process aspect of a person is his behavioural aspect; as a face of paradox is its corresponding other face; as the chair-seeing aspect of a chair sight is its chair-seen aspect; as the informing aspect of information is its informed aspect; as the either-it-is aspect of a raining case is its or-it-isn't aspect; as the knowing aspect of a knowledge is its known aspect; as, per analogy, the ascent aspect of a ladder is its descent aspect; this assorted threefold game talk is not grammatically misleading; misleading cases are the either/or cases (and variants), seen as contradictory identities rather than as complementary identical cases qua paradox faces.

Games: paradox + faces (and variants, as per the PI 356 Comment); per analogies, ladder + up/down aspects, drabbit + duck/rabbit faces.

*357. We do not say that **possibly** a dog talks to itself. Is that because we are so minutely acquainted with its mind? Well, one might say this: if one sees the behaviour of a living being, one sees its mind. — But do I also say in my own case that I am talking to myself, because I am behaving in such-and-such a way? — I do **not** say it from observation of my behaviour. But it makes sense only because I do behave in this way. — So isn't it because I **mean** it that it makes sense?*

To rehearse. The (PI 201) thesis of the *Investigations* is that identity is paradox, called the rule, as neither of opposite cases + existing as both qua either.

Comment. Per PI 357: that word-behaviour determines word-meaning is a grammatical (lawful) case, not a logical possibility case and not an empirical case to be verified by observation alone.

Games: paradox + faces; per PI 43, word + meaning/use cases; living being + brain-process/enactment – believing/believed, mental/behavioural, non-observable/observable, possible/practical – cases; language + private/public cases; per analogies, ladder + up/down aspects, drabbit + duck/rabbit faces.

*358. But isn't it our **meaning** it that gives sense to the sentence? (And here, of course, belongs the fact that one cannot mean a senseless sequence of words.) And* *meaning something lies within the domain of the mind. But it is also something private! It is the intangible Something; comparable only to consciousness itself.*

*How **could** one find this ludicrous? After all, it is, as it were, a dream of our language.*

To rehearse. The (PI 201) thesis of the *Investigations* is that identity is paradox, called the rule, as neither of opposite cases + existing as both qua either.

Comment. Per PI 358: the grammar qua law sense is this; a paradox face is to its counterpart face; as per PI 43, word-meaning is to word-use cf. as person-mind is to person-body, or as private language is to public language; as per PI 304, Nothing (cf. intangible) is to Something (cf. tangible) cf. as person-consciousness is to person-enactment; from which, to say that paired opposites are one another as ludicrously qua contradictorily so is to say grammatically that they are paradoxically (not consistently, not contradictorily) one another.

Games: paradox + faces; word + meaning/use cases; language + private/public – self-talk/behaviour, consciousness/enactment, intangible/ tangible, in-dream/in-actuality – cases; person + mind/body cases; per PI 304, nothing qua neither Nothing nor Something + Nothing/Something cases; per analogies, ladder + up/down aspects, drabbit + duck/rabbit faces.

359. Could a machine think? – Could it be in pain? – Well, is the human body to be called such a machine? It surely comes as close as possible to being such a machine.

To rehearse. The (PI 201) thesis of the *Investigations* is that identity is paradox, called the rule, as neither of opposite cases + existing as both qua either.

Comment. Per PI 359: a machine is paradoxically a consciousness where it is a body as paradoxically a mind i.e. as the grammar (law sense) of a face of paradox as thereby paradoxically its corresponding other face; for the case of shared human language, it is not said, other than analogously (as, say, in an animation cartoon), that a mindless machine thinks; rather, it is said non-analogously that the inner mechanisms of a machine are paradoxically its outer working.

Games: paradox + faces; person + mind/body cases cf. machine + inner-workings/outer-enactment cases; thinking, like pain + verb/noun senses; per analogies, ladder + up/down aspects, drabbit + duck/rabbit faces.

360. But surely a machine cannot think! – Is that an empirical statement? No. We say only of a human being and what is like one that it thinks. We also say it of dolls; and perhaps even of ghosts. Regard the word "to think" as an instrument!

To rehearse. The (PI 201) thesis of the *Investigations* is that identity is paradox, called the rule, as neither of opposite cases + existing as both qua either.

Comment. Per PI 360: by the thesis of identity as paradox + faces, to say that machines think is to say nothing relevant; but to say that the body as a machine is paradoxically a mind is grammatical (lawful); here, cases such as dolls and spirits go proxy for humans such that these cases thereby have consciousness as paradoxically behaviours; 'thinking' as a word, is meaningful as paradoxically a tool qua a use; of course – as in a cartoon strip, say – a machine which goes proxy for a human or humanlike being may be said to think, to be alive, have a mind, and so on.

Games: paradox + faces; human or humanlike or humanised + thinking/behaving cases i.e. consciousness/enactment caseate i.e. mind/body cases; per PI 43, word + meaning/use cases; per analogies, ladder + up/down aspects, drabbit + duck/rabbit faces.

361. The chair is thinking to itself...

WHERE? In one of its parts? Or outside its body; in the air around it? Or not **anywhere** *at all? But then what is the difference between this chair's talking silently to itself and another one's doing so, next to it? – But then how is it with man: where* *does he talk to himself? How come that this question seems senseless; and that no specification of a place is necessary, except just that this man is talking silently to himself? Whereas the question of **where** the chair talks silently to itself seems to demand an answer. – The reason is: we want to know **how** the chair is supposed to be like a human being; whether, for instance, its head is at the top of the back, and so on.*

*What is it like to talk silently to oneself; what goes on there? – How am I to explain it? Well, only in the way in which you can teach someone the meaning of the expression "to talk silently to oneself". And we **do** learn the meaning of that as children. – Only no one is going to say that the person who teaches it to us tells us 'what goes on here'.*

To rehearse. The (PI 201) thesis of the *Investigations* is that identity is paradox, called the rule, as neither of opposite cases + existing as both qua either.

Comment. Per PI 361: the empirical-sense talk of the text grammatically (lawfully) translates as follows; by PI 43, a word as language (be the word "human" or "chair") is to its meaning/use – private/public, thinking/expression, mind/body – cases; as paradox is to faces; per each case of threefold grammar, the three members locate in one another cf. per analogy, ladder + up/down aspects; per grammar, thinking, like silent self-talk, as a word-meaning case, locates not in a place but in a word-use case.

Games: paradox + faces; word + meaning/use cases; language + private/public – thinking/expression – cases; per analogies, ladder + up/down aspects, drabbit + duck/rabbit faces.

*362. Rather, it seems to us as though, in this case, the instructor **conveyed** the meaning to the pupil – without telling him directly; but in the end, the pupil is brought to the point of giving himself the correct ostensive definition. And this is where our illusion lies.*

To rehearse. The (PI 201) thesis of the *Investigations* is that identity is paradox, called the rule, as neither of opposite cases + existing as both qua either.

Comment. PI 362: though a child might take the self as a thing to be defined or located in his head, the grammar (law sense) to displace this illusion (this non-grammatical case) is this: per PI 43, the meaning of a word (here, "self") is its use; as communication is to conveying/conveyed cases; as the face of a paradox is its counterpart face.

Games: paradox + faces; word + meaning/use cases; language + private/public – thinking/expression, self-tall/behaviour – cases; per analogies, ladder + up/down aspects, drabbit + duck/rabbit faces.

363. "But when I imagine something, something **goes on**, doesn't it?" Well, something goes on a and then I make a noise. What for? Presumably in order to communicate what went on. – But how, in general, does one communicate something? When does one say that something is being communicated? – What is the language-game of communicating something?

I'd like to say: you regard it much too much as a matter of course that one can communicate anything to anyone. That is to say, we are so much accustomed to communicating in speech, in conversation, that it looks to us as if the whole point of communicating lay in this: that someone else grasps the sense of my words – which is something mental – that he, as it were, takes it into his own mind. If he then does something further with it as well, that is no part of the immediate purpose of language.

One would like to say "It is through my communicating it that he comes to **know** that I am in pain; it produces this mental phenomenon; everything else is immaterial to the communicating". As for what this remarkable phenomenon of knowledge is – that can be taken care of later. Mental processes just are strange. (It is as if one said, "The clock shows us the time. **What** time is, is not yet settled. And as regards the point of telling the time a that doesn't come in here.")

To rehearse. The (PI 201) thesis of the *Investigations* is that identity is paradox, called the rule, as neither of opposite cases + existing as both qua either.

Comment. PI 363: grammatically (lawfully), the word "tell" is examined; just as the face of a paradox is its counterpart face; so per PI 43, the meaning of a word is its use; so the telling-out (communicating) aspect of the telling (communication) is its told-out (communicated) aspect; so per implication, the mental qua immaterial aspect of (say) pain is its behavioural qua material aspect; so per implication, the knowing aspect of knowledge is its known qua what's-told (time told) aspect.

Games: paradox + faces; word (tell, purpose, time) + meaning/use – telling/told, purposing/purposed, verb-sense-time/noun-sense-time – cases; communication + verb-sense/noun-sense – sender/receiver – cases; per analogies, ladder + up/down aspects, drabbit + duck/rabbit faces.

*364. Someone does a calculation in his head. He uses the result, let's say, for building a bridge or a machine. – Do you want to say that it wasn't **really** by a calculation that he arrived at this number? That it has, say, just dropped into his lap, after some sort of reverie? There surely must have been calculation going on, and there was. For he **knows** that, and how, he calculated; and the correct result he got would be inexplicable without calculation. – But what if I said: "It **seems to him** just as if he had calculated. And why should the correct result be explicable? Is it not incomprehensible enough, that without saying a word, without making a note, he was able to CALCULATE?" -*

*Is calculating in the imagination in some sense less real than calculating on paper? It is **real** – calculating-in-the-head. – Is it similar to calculating on paper? – I don't know whether to call it similar. Is a bit of white paper with black lines on it similar to a human body?*

To rehearse. The (PI 201) thesis of the *Investigations* is that identity is paradox, called the rule, as neither of opposite cases + existing as both qua either.

Comment. Per PI 364: the grammar qua law sense of the text is this; calculation is to calculating/calculated – going-on/going-on, knowing-that/ that-known, knowing-how/how-known, in-head/real, in-reverie/real, seemingly/ actually, imaginatively/on-paper – cases; as paradox is to faces, as per PI 43, word is to meaning/use cases; as bridge or machine is to building/ building (verb-sense/noun-sense) cases; here, per each of these language games, each paradox-face case is as explicably correct as it is incorrect, as functionally eclipsing as it is functionally eclipsed; more, the calculating case is incomprehensibly qua paradoxically – not consistently, not contradictorily – the calculated case; paradox is to faces; as similarity is to similar/similar cases cf. PI 215 whereby sameness is to same/same cases cf. per analogy, as drabbit is to duck/rabbit faces; as calculation is to mental/behavioural – mind/body, meaning/matter, in-mind/on-paper – cases.

Games: paradox + faces; word + meaning/use cases; language + private/public cases; calculation + mental/physical – mental/actual – cases; person + mind/body cases; knowledge + knowing/performing cases; per analogies, ladder + up/down aspects, drabbit + duck/rabbit faces.

365. Do Adelheid and the Bishop play a **real** *game of chess? – Of course. They are not merely pretending to do so – which would also be possible as part of a play. – But the game, for example, has no beginning! – Of course it has; otherwise it would not be a game of chess. –*

To rehearse. The (PI 201) thesis of the *Investigations* is that identity is paradox, called the rule, as neither of opposite cases + existing as both qua either.

Comment. Per PI 365: grammatically (lawfully, not empirically, not logically), for chess as an identity-as-paradox case, if it is real and has an ending (a not-beginning) it thereby paradoxically is unreal and has a beginning (a not-ending).

Games: paradox + faces; chess + unreal/real – also beginning/ending – cases; per analogies, ladder + up/down aspects, drabbit + duck/rabbit faces.

366. Is calculating in the head less real than calculating on paper? – One is, perhaps, inclined to say some such thing; but one can get oneself to think the opposite as well by telling oneself: paper, ink, and so on are only logical constructions out of our sense-data.

*"I have done the multiplication ... in my head" – don't I **believe** such a statement? – But was it really a multiplication? It was not merely 'a' multiplication, but **this** one – in the head. This is the point at which I go wrong. For I now want to say: it was some mental process **corresponding** to the multiplication on paper. So it would make sense to say: "This process in the mind corresponds to **this** process on paper." And it would then make sense to talk of a method of projection according to which the image of the sign was a representation of the sign itself.*

To rehearse. The (PI 201) thesis of the *Investigations* is that identity is paradox, called the rule, as neither of opposite cases + existing as both qua either.

Comment. Per PI 366: grammatically (lawfully), an identity-as-paradox case – a **this** case – here, as a mathematical case, is for its paradox faces its mental/physical cases; these correspond with one another not by being alongside each other but precisely in being paradoxically one another cf. ladder + up/down aspects; the faces involve in mutual eclipse.

Games: paradox + faces; **this** + this/this cases; per PI 43, word (say, calculation) meaning/use – calculating/calculated, in-head/on-paper, mental/physical – cases; correspondence + corresponding cases; projection + projecting/projected cases; sign + image/representation cases; multiplication + logical-construction/sense-data case; per analogies, ladder + up/down aspects, drabbit + duck/rabbit faces.

367. A mental image is the image which is described when someone describes what he imagines.

To rehearse. The (PI 201) thesis of the *Investigations* is that identity is paradox, called the rule, as neither of opposite cases + existing as both qua either.

112   IDENTITY AS PARADOX

Comment. Per PI 367: the grammar qua lawful sense of the text is this; the mental image-describing aspect of an image-description is its extra-mental described-image aspect; as per PI 43, the meaning of a word is its use; as a face of paradox is its counterpart face.

Games: paradox + faces; word + meaning/use cases; imagination + imagining/imagined cases; description + describing/described cases i.e. mental-process/expressed cases; per analogies, ladder + up/down aspects, drabbit + duck/rabbit faces.

*368. I describe a room to someone, and then get him to paint an **impressionistic** picture from this description to show that he has understood it. – Now he paints the chairs which I described as green, dark red; where I said "yellow", he paints blue. – That is the impression which he got of that room. And now I say: "Quite right! That's what it looks like."*

To rehearse. The (PI 201) thesis of the *Investigations* is that identity is paradox, called the rule, as neither of opposite cases + existing as both qua either.

Comment. Per PI 368: the grammar (law) reads as follows; picture talk is identity-as-paradox talk; the painting is of reality as paradoxically non-reality (impressionistic).

Games: paradox (picture) + faces; painting + non-reality/reality cases i.e. impression/actual cases i.e. green/red cases, yellow/blue cases; per analogies, ladder + up/down aspects, drabbit + duck/rabbit faces.

*369. One is inclined to ask: "What is it like – what goes on – when one calculates in one's head?" – And in a particular case, the answer may be "First I add 17 and 18, then I subtract 39 ..." But that is not the answer to our question. What is called calculating in one's head is not explained in **this** way.*

To rehearse. The (PI 201) thesis of the *Investigations* is that identity is paradox, called the rule, as neither of opposite cases + existing as both qua either.

Comment. Per PI 369: grammatically (lawfully), per a particular case as an identity-as-paradox case, the answer given was an empirical one, not a grammatical one; grammatically, just as there is the threefold case as the paradox + faces, so there is the threefold case as the sum + mental-process/actual-result cases.

Games: paradox + faces; per a particular word, and by PI 43, word + meaning/use cases; per a particular sum, sum + mental-process/actual-result – mental/behavioural – cases; calculation qua a **this** case + calculating/calculated – in-head/expressed – cases; per analogies, ladder + up/down aspects, drabbit + duck/rabbit faces.

370. One ought to ask, not what images are or what goes on when one imagines something, but how the word "imagination" is used. But that does not mean that I want to talk only about words. For the question of what imagination essentially is, is as much about the word "imagination" as my question. And I am only saying that this question is not to be clarified – neither for the person who does the imagining, nor for anyone else – by pointing; nor yet by a description of some process. The first question also asks for clarification of a word; but it makes us expect a wrong kind of answer.

To rehearse. The (PI 201) thesis of the *Investigations* is that identity is paradox, called the rule, as neither of opposite cases + existing as both qua either.

Comment. PI 370: concerning grammar qua law, a word (here, "imagination") is questioned not only as a word-meaning (word-essence) but also as a word-use (word-practice); here, the imagination word case is being questioned neither logically nor empirically but grammatically; grammatically, paradox is to faces; as per PI 43, word is to meaning/use cases; as imagination is to imagining/imagined – mental/behavioural – case.

Games: paradox + faces; word (imagination) + meaning/use – imagining/imagined, mental/behavioural – cases; per analogies, ladder + up/down aspects, drabbit + duck/rabbit faces.

*371. **Essence** is expressed in grammar.*

To rehearse. The (PI 201) thesis of the *Investigations* is that identity is paradox, called the rule, as neither of opposite cases + existing as both qua either.

Comment. Per PI 371: grammatically (lawfully), essence is expressed; as meaning is use; as paradox face is its corresponding other face.

Games: paradox + faces; per PI 43, word + meaning/use – essence/expression – cases; per analogies, ladder + up/down aspects, drabbit + duck/rabbit faces.

372. Consider: "The only correlate in language to an objective necessity is an arbitrary rule. It is the only thing which one can milk out of this objective necessity into a proposition."

To rehearse. The (PI 201) thesis of the *Investigations* is that identity is paradox, called the rule, as neither of opposite cases + existing as both qua either.

Comment. Per PI 372: the grammar qua law sense of the text is this; objectivity qua rule is to necessary/arbitrary cases; as per PI 43, word is to meaning/use – cf. logical/empirical – cases; as paradox is to faces.

Games: paradox + faces; word (sentence) + meaning/use – necessary/arbitrary, logical/empirical, mental/behavioural, essential/expressed – cases; correlation + correlating/correlated cases; per analogies, ladder + up/down aspects, drabbit + duck/rabbit faces.

373. Grammar tells what kind of object anything is. (Theology as grammar.)

To rehearse. The (PI 201) thesis of the *Investigations* is that identity is paradox, called the rule, as neither of opposite cases + existing as both qua either.

Comment. Per PI 373: grammatically (lawfully), from PI 43, a word qua object (here, theology) is for its kind qua meaning its use; as a paradox face is its counterpart face.

Games: paradox + faces; word + meaning/use cases; object (objectivity qua neither subjective nor objective, neither subject nor object) + subjective/objective cases; per analogies, ladder + up/down aspects, drabbit + duck/rabbit faces.

*374. The great difficulty here is not to present the matter as if there were something one **couldn't** do. As if there really were an object, from which I extract a description, which I am not in a position to show anyone. – And the best that I can propose is that we yield to the temptation to use this picture, but then investigate what the **application** of the picture looks like.*

To rehearse. The (PI 201) thesis of the *Investigations* is that identity is paradox, called the rule, as neither of opposite cases + existing as both qua either.

Comment. Per PI 374: in terms of grammar (law), picture talk is identity-as-paradox talk; a private language cases as a paradox-face case is grammatically not a case that cannot be exhibited for it exhibits as paradoxically a corresponding public case qua counterpart paradox-face case.

Games: paradox + faces; picture + picturing/pictured cases; per PI 43, word (language) + meaning/use – meaning/application, private/public – cases; per analogies, ladder + up/down aspects, drabbit + duck/rabbit faces.

375. How does one teach someone to read silently to himself? How does one know when he can do so? How does he himself know that he is doing what is required of him?

To rehearse. The (PI 201) thesis of the *Investigations* is that identity is paradox, called the rule, as neither of opposite cases + existing as both qua either.

Comment. Per PI 375: for its grammar qua law sense (not logical sense, not empirical sense) the text reads thus; the silent-reading/reading-aloud cases – grammatically – are paradoxically one another; to learn or teach the one is thereby to learn or teach the other; to know how to carry out the one is to know how the other is thereby carried out.

Games: paradox + faces; reading + silent/aloud cases; per analogies, ladder + up/down aspects, drabbit + duck/rabbit faces.

*376. When I say the ABC silently to myself, what is the criterion that shows that I am doing the same as someone else who silently repeats it to himself? It might be found that the same thing goes on in my larynx and in his. (And similarly when we both think of the same thing, wish the same, and so on.) But then did we learn the use of the words "to say such-and-such to oneself" by someone's pointing to a process in the larynx or the brain? Is it not also perfectly possible that my auditory image of the sound **a** and his correspond to different physiological processes? The question is: How does one **compare** images?*

To rehearse. The (PI 201) thesis of the *Investigations* is that identity is paradox, called the rule, as neither of opposite cases + existing as both qua either.

Comment. Per PI 376: the empirical-sense talk in the text translates grammatically (lawfully) as follows; private language is referenced to public language; by which, paradox is to faces; as language is to private/public cases; as per PI 215 sereneness (similarity) is to same/same (similar/similar) cases cf. as drabbit is to duck/rabbit faces; as coincidence (correspondence, comparison) is to distinct (corresponding – cf. compared – different) cases.

Games: paradox + faces; per PI 43, word (language) + meaning/use (private/public) cases; coincidence (correspondence, comparison) + distinct (corresponding – cf. compared – different) cases; sereneness (similarity) + same/same (similar/similar) case; per analogies, ladder + up/down aspects, drabbit + duck/rabbit faces.

*377. A logician will perhaps think: The same is the same – how a person satisfies himself of sameness is a psychological question. (High is high – it is a matter of psychology that one sometimes **sees**, and sometimes **hears** it.)*

What is the criterion for the sameness of two images? – What is the criterion for the redness of an image? For me, when it's someone else's image: what he says and does. – For myself, when it's my image: nothing. And what goes for "red" also goes for "same".

To rehearse. The (PI 201) thesis of the *Investigations* is that identity is paradox, called the rule, as neither of opposite cases + existing as both qua either.

Comment. Per PI 377: grammatically qua lawfully – neither logically nor empirically, including psychologically – sameness is to same/same cases (as per PI 215); as redness is to "red"/"red" cases; as per PI 43, word is to meaning/use cases ; as imagery qua coincidence is to imaging/imaged – meaning/saying, meaning/doing – cases; as imagery qua nothing (as distinct from – hence neither – meaning nor use) is to meaning/use cases; throughout these grammar cases, the criterion for each threefold paradox + faces case is each of its three members in that all three live in one mother – cf. ladder + up/down cases – hence, given any of the three as the case, it warrants the other two equally being the case.

Games: paradox + faces; sameness + same/same cases; per analogies, ladder + up/down aspects, drabbit + duck/rabbit faces.

378. "Before I judge that two images which I have are the same, surely I must recognize them as the same." And when that has happened, how am I to know that the word "same" describes what I recognize? Only if I can express my recognition in some other way, and if it is possible for someone else to teach me that "same" is the correct word here.

For if I need a warrant for using a word, it must also be a warrant for someone else.

To rehearse. The (PI 201) thesis of the *Investigations* is that identity is paradox, called the rule, as neither of opposite cases + existing as both qua either.

Comment. Per PI 378: the grammatical qua lawful warrant for each of the three members of each threefold language game of paradox + faces is one another;

this is because all three inhabit one another cf. per analogy ladder + up/down ways; hence, per language game, given any of its three as the case, it warrants the other two being the case; per PI 215, the threefold game is sameness + same/same cases; variants are judgement or recognition + verb/noun senses.

Games: paradox + faces; sameness + same/same cases; per PI 43, word (say, image) + meaning/use – imaging/imaged – cases; per analogies, ladder + up/down aspects, + duck/rabbit faces.

*379. First I recognize it as **this**; and then I remember what it is called. – Consider: in what case can one rightly say this?*

To rehearse. The (PI 201) thesis of the *Investigations* is that identity is paradox, called the rule, as neither of opposite cases + existing as both qua either.

Comment. Per PI 379: it is properly grammatical (lawful) to say as follows: paradox is to faces; as **this** case is to identical cases; as recognition or remembrance is to verb/noun sense; as per PI 43, word is to meaning/use cases.

Games: paradox qua **this** + faces; word + meaning/use – meaning/calling – cases; recognition or remembrance+ verb/noun senses; per analogies, ladder + up/down aspects, drabbit + duck/rabbit faces.

*380. How do I recognize that this is red? – "I see that it is **this**; and then I know that that is what this is called." This? – What?! What kind of answer to this question makes sense?*

(You keep on steering towards an inner ostensive explanation.)

*I could not apply any rules to a **private** transition from what is seen to words. Here the rules really would hang in the air; for the institution of their application is lacking.*

To rehearse. The (PI 201) thesis of the *Investigations* is that identity is paradox, called the rule, as neither of opposite cases + existing as both qua either.

Comment. Per PI 380: concerning identity qua *thisness*: its private aspect (thinking, recognising, seeing, knowing, calling) hangs in the air as unruly qua non-grammatical unless paradoxically a public aspect (spoken, recognised, seen, known, called); identity is paradox, not ostensive definition qua consistency sense; the PI 380 questions make paradoxical sense; opposite case transition into one another as grammatically (lawfully) the case in that the opposites live in one another cf. ladder's up/down aspects or, per PI 43, word-meaning/word-use aspects.

Games: paradox + faces; language + private/public cases; word + meaning/ use cases; per PI 215, sameness + same/same cases cf. per analogy, drabbit + duck/rabbit faces; redness + "red"/"red" cases; recognition + recognising/ recognised cases; sight + seeing/seen cases; knowledge + knowing/known cases; call + calling/called cases; *this* + mental/physical – say, thinking/ spoken – cases; per analogies, ladder + up/down aspects, drabbit + duck/ rabbit faces.

381. How do I recognize that this colour is red? – One answer would be: "I have learnt English."

To rehearse. The (PI 201) thesis of the *Investigations* is that identity is paradox, called the rule, as neither of opposite cases + existing as both qua either.

Comment. Per PI 381: the text reads for its grammar qua law sense as follows; to speak a language is to speak its words; to speak a word is to mean the word; from which, per PI 43, word (say, "red") is to meaning/use cases; as paradox is to faces; as recognition it to verb/noun senses.

Games: paradox + faces; word ("red") + meaning/use cases; recognition + verb/noun senses; per analogies, ladder + up/down aspects, drabbit + duck/rabbit faces.

*382. How can I **justify** forming this image in response to this word?*

*Has anyone shown me the image of the colour blue and told me that **it** is the image of blue?*

*What is the meaning of the words "**this** image"? How does one point at an image? How does one point twice at the same image?*

To rehearse. The (PI 201) thesis of the *Investigations* is that identity is paradox, called the rule, as neither of opposite cases + existing as both qua either.

Comment. Per PI 382: **it** talk, like **this** talk, is identity-as-paradox talk; by PI 43, word (it, this, blue, image) is to meaning/use – cf. imaging/imaged – cases; as paradox is to faces; as point-at is to pointing-at/pointed-at cases; as per PI 215, sameness is to same/same cases; the talk of pointing twice at the same image is a talk of face/face cases qua pointing-at/pointed-at (imaging/imaged, same/same) cases referenced to the point-at case (image case, sameness case); image-forming/imaged-response cases, referenced to image qua word, is a threefold grammar (law sense) case – cf. word + meaning/use – wherein the three members inhabit one another cf. ladder + up/down aspects such that any one of the three members as the case is the warrant (justification) for the other two being the case.

Games: paradox (it, this) + faces; word (blue) + meaning/use cases; image + imaging/imaged cases; point-at + pointing-at/pointed-at cases; sameness + same/same cases; per analogies, drabbit + duck/rabbit faces ladder + up/down aspects.

*383. We do not analyse a phenomenon (for example, thinking) but a concept (for example, that of thinking), and hence the application of a word. So it may look as if what we were doing were nominalism. Nominalists make the mistake of interpreting all words as **names**, and so of not really describing their use, but only, so to speak, giving a paper draft on such a description.*

To rehearse. The (PI 201) thesis of the *Investigations* is that identity is paradox, called the rule, as neither of opposite cases + existing as both qua either.

Comment. Per PI 383: the grammar qua law sense is this; against Nominalism, a concept (say, thinking) as a naming case is paradoxically a practice as a named case; paradox is to faces; as per PI 43, word is to meaning/use – meaning/practice, concept/application, (say) thinking/thought – cases; as name is to naming/named – cf. paper-draft/use – cases

Games: paradox + faces; word + meaning/use cases; language + thinking/ expression cases; per analogies, ladder + up/down aspects, drabbit + duck/ rabbit faces.

*384. You learned the **concept** 'pain' in learning language.*

To rehearse. The (PI 201) thesis of the *Investigations* is that identity is paradox, called the rule, as neither of opposite cases + existing as both qua either.

Comment. Per PI 384: for its grammar (law sense) the text reads as this; pain is to feeling/behaviour cases; as paradox is to faces; as per PI 43, word (language) is to meaning/use (private/public) – concept/application – cases.

Games: paradox + faces; word (say, pain) + meaning/use cases i.e. concept/ application cases; pain + pain-feeling/pain-behaviour cases; per analogies, ladder + up/down aspects, drabbit + duck/rabbit faces.

385. Ask yourself: Is it conceivable that someone learn to calculate in his head without ever calculating aloud or on paper? – "Learning it" presumably means: being brought to the point of being able to do it. Only the question arises, what will count as a criterion for being able to do it? – But is it also possible for some tribe to be acquainted only with calculation in the head, and with no other kind? Here one has to ask oneself: "What will that look like?" – And so one will have to depict it as a limiting case. And the question will then arise whether we still want to apply the concept of calculating in the head here – or whether in such circumstances it has lost its purpose, because the phenomena now gravitate towards another paradigm.

To rehearse. The (PI 201) thesis of the *Investigations* is that identity is paradox, called the rule, as neither of opposite cases + existing as both qua either.

Comment. Per PI 385: the ungrammatical case is the onefold-only private-language case alone; grammatically (lawfully), paradox is to faces; as language is to private/public cases; in that all three members of a threefold grammar inhabit one another cf. ladder + up/down aspects, each member as the case is the criterion or warrant for the other two members being the case.

Games: paradox + faces; calculation as a language + calculating/calculated cases as private/public cases; per PI 43, word + meaning/use cases; per analogies, ladder + up/down aspects, drabbit + duck/rabbit faces.

*386. "But why have you so little confidence in yourself? Ordinarily you know perfectly well what is called 'calculating'. So if you say that you have calculated in the imagination, then you will have done so. If you had **not** calculated, you would not have said you had. Equally, if you say that you see something red in the imagination, then it will **be** red. You know what 'red' is elsewhere. – And further: you don't always rely on agreement with other people; for you often report that you have seen something no one else has." – But I do have confidence in myself – I say without hesitation that I have done this calculation in my head, have imagined this colour. The difficulty is not that I doubt whether I really imagined anything red. But it is **this**: that we should be able, just like that, to point out or describe the colour we have imagined, that mapping the image into reality presents no difficulty at all. Do they then look so alike that one might mix them up? – But I can also recognize a man from a drawing straight off. – Well, but can I ask: "What does an actual mental image of this colour look like?" or "What sort of thing is it?"; can I **learn** this?*

*(I cannot accept his testimony, because it is not **testimony**. It tells me only what he is **inclined** to say.)*

To rehearse. The (PI 201) thesis of the *Investigations* is that identity is paradox, called the rule, as neither of opposite cases + existing as both qua either.

Comment. Per PI 386 grammar qua law sense: **this** talk is identity-as-paradox talk; a private – calculating, imagining, seeing-red, internal, own, mentalistic, pointing-out, describing, mapping, recognising, inclination – case is paradoxically (cf. confidently, unhesitatingly, indubitably) a public – calculated, imagined, seen-red, external, another's, behavioural qua real qua actual, pointed-out, described, mapped, recognised, testimony – case ; from which, paradox-faces case are different qua distinct cases yet cases which are alike (cf. per PI 215 same/same cases cf. ladder's up/down aspects); the cases are nixed qua coincidental cases with paradox as their coincidence; to learn that there is a private case qua case of word-meaning is to learn it to be paradoxically a public case qua a case of word-behaviour cf. per PI 43, word-meaning is word-use.

Games: paradox + faces; word + meaning/use cases; language + private/public cases (and variants, as per Comment); per analogies, ladder + up/down aspects, drabbit + duck/rabbit faces.

*387. The **deep** aspect readily eludes us.*

To rehearse. The (PI 201) thesis of the *Investigations* is that identity is paradox, called the rule, as neither of opposite cases + existing as both qua either.

Comment. Per PI 387: grammatically (lawfully), a paradox-face case is to its corresponding other paradox-face case, as an elusive deep case is to its readily seen surface case; here, the deep case readily seen as elusive is the elusive-deep/readily-seen cases as paradoxically one another.

Games: paradox + faces; per PI 43, word + meaning/use cases i.e. elusive/seen cases i.e. deep/surface cases; per analogies, ladder + up/down aspects, drabbit + duck/rabbit faces.

*388. "I don't see anything violet here, but I can show it you if you give me a paint box." How can one **know** that one can show it if ..., in other words, that one can recognize it if one sees it?*

*How do I know from my **mental image**, what the colour really looks like?*

How do I know that I'll be able to do something? That is, that the state I am in now is that of being able to do that thing?

To rehearse. The (PI 201) thesis of the *Investigations* is that identity is paradox, called the rule, as neither of opposite cases + existing as both qua either.

Comment. Per PI 388: the grammar qua lawful sense is this; colour-seeing is seen-colour; as paradox face is its counterpart face; as knowing is known; as showing is shown; as recognising is recognised; as mentalistic is behavioural; as imaging is imaged; as thinking is doing; as per PI 43, word-meaning is word-use; as enabling is enabled; as mind-state is enactment.

Games: paradox + faces (and variants, as per Comment): per analogies, ladder + up/down aspects, drabbit + duck/rabbit faces.

*389. "A mental image must be more like its object than any picture. For however similar I make the picture to what it is supposed to represent, it may still be the picture of something else. But it is an intrinsic feature of a mental image that it is the image of **this** and of nothing else." That is how one might come to regard a mental image as a super-likeness.*

To rehearse. The (PI 201) thesis of the *Investigations* is that identity is paradox, called the rule, as neither of opposite cases + existing as both qua either.

Comment. Per PI 389: grammatically (lawfully), the text distinguishes between the onefold-sense of an empirical-sense picture and the grammatical picture case qua case of identity-as-paradox; paradox is to faces; as a **this** case is to super-likeness (similar/similar) cases cf. PI 215 as sameness is to same/same cases cf. per analogy, as ladder is to up/down aspects; as per PI 43, ward is to meaning/use – mentalistic/behavioural, imaging/imaged, subject/object – cases; as picture is to picturing/pictured cases; as representation is to representing/represented cases; as **this** is to intrinsic/extrinsic cases; from which, paradox-face cases are distinct case such that each to the other is a something-else case.

Games: paradox qua **this** + faces; word (language) + meaning/use (private/public) cases (and variants as per Comment); per analogies, ladder + up/down aspects, drabbit + duck/rabbit faces.

390. Could one imagine a stone's having consciousness? And if someone can – why should that not prove merely that such image-mongery is of no interest to us?

To rehearse. The (PI 201) thesis of the *Investigations* is that identity is paradox, called the rule, as neither of opposite cases + existing as both qua either.

Comment. Per PI 390: the text presents its grammar qua lawful sense thus: to say of a stone qua matter that is has consciousness qua meaning, is to say of paradox qua one face that it has a corresponding other face; this talk (cf. image-mongery talk) is of interest as grammatical talk.

Games: paradox + faces; per PI 43, word + meaning/use cases; stone + consciousness/matter cases; per analogies, ladder + up/down aspects, drabbit + duck/rabbit faces.

391. I can perhaps even imagine (though it is not easy) that each of the people whom I see in the street is in frightful pain, but is adroitly concealing it. And it is important that I have to imagine adroit concealment here. That I do not simply say to myself: "Well, his mind is in pain: but what has that to do with his body?" or "After all, it need not show in his body". – And if I imagine this – what do I do? What do I say to myself? How do I look at the people? Perhaps I look at one and think, "It must be difficult to laugh when one is in such pain", and much else of the same kind. I, as it were, play a part, **act** as if the others were in pain. When I do this, one might say that I am imagining ...

To rehearse. The (PI 201) thesis of the *Investigations* is that identity is paradox, called the rule, as neither of opposite cases + existing as both qua either.

Comment. Per PI 391: the grammar qua lawful sense is this; the case is that of imagination qua play-activity as its imagining/imagined cases; it is the case of a concealment with its concealing/concealed cases i.e. the case of pain with its mental/behavioural cases; personalised, it is the case of a person with his mind/body natures; it may be the case of a person with inner-pain/outward-laughter cases; grammatically, it is the case of identity-as-paradox with its identical casers qua paradox faces cf. drabbit with its duck/rabbit faces.

Gamesa: paradox + faces; imagination, also, concealment + verb/noun senses; pain + mental/behavioural cases; per PI 43, word + meaning/use cases; per analogies, ladder + up/down aspects, drabbit + duck/rabbit faces.

392. "When I imagine he's in pain, all that really goes on in me is ..." Then someone else says: "I believe I can also imagine it **without** thinking ..." ("I believe I can think without words.") That comes to nothing. The analysis oscillates between natural science and grammar.

To rehearse. The (PI 201) thesis of the *Investigations* is that identity is paradox, called the rule, as neither of opposite cases + existing as both qua either.

Comment. Per PI 392: grammatically (lawfully), to say that the analysis oscillates between natural science and grammar is to say that the text travels to-and-fro between the raw material off explicit empirical-sense talk and its translation into implied grammatic threefold cases (assorted language games); by which, imagining (cf. thinking, believing) is to imagined (thought, believed) cases; as nothing going on is to something gone on; as paradox face is to counterpart face; from which, a paradox case (word, belief, imagination, thinking) existing as a face (word-meaning, believing imagining, thinking) which is without being paradoxically a counterpart face (word-use, believed, imagined, thought) is nothing qua non-grammatical cf. ladder as a way-up aspect which aspect is not paradoxically a way-down aspect.

Games: paradox + faces; per PI 43, word (language, pain, imagination, belief, thinking) + meaning/use – private/public, imagining/imagined, feeling/expression, believing/believed, thinking qua verb-sense/noun-sense – cases; per analogies, ladder + up/down aspects, drabbit + duck/rabbit faces.

393. "When I imagine that someone who is laughing is really in pain, I don't imagine any pain-behaviour, for I see just the opposite. So **_what_** do I imagine?" – I have already said what. And for that, I do not necessarily have to imagine that _**I**_ feel pain. – "But then what is the process of imagining it?" – Well, where (outside philosophy) do we use the words "I can imagine that he is in pain", or "I imagine that ...", or "Imagine that ..."?

One says, for example, to someone who has to play a part on-stage: "Here you must imagine that this man is in pain and is concealing this" – and now we give him no directions, don't tell him what he is **_actually_** to do. For this reason too, the suggested analysis is not to the point. – We now watch the actor, who is imagining this situation.

To rehearse. The (PI 201) thesis of the *Investigations* is that identity is paradox, called the rule, as neither of opposite cases + existing as both qua either.

Comment. Per PI 393: for the text, its grammar qua lawful sense, psychological material converts to grammar, as follows; person is to pain/laughter – feeling/behaviour – cases; as paradox is to faces; as coincidence is to opposites (distinct cases); as imagination is to verb/noun – imagining-what/what-imagined, mental/behavioural, thinking/saying – cases; as pain-concealment-actor is to pain-concealing-acting/concealed-pain-enactment cases; as actuality is to actualising/actualised cases.

Games: paradox + faces; imagination + imagining/imagined – imagining/enactment – cases; play-actor + pain/laughter cases; per analogies, ladder + up/down aspects, drabbit + duck/rabbit faces.

394. In what sort of circumstances would we ask someone: "What actually went on in you as you imagined this?" – And what sort of answer do we expect?

To rehearse. The (PI 201) thesis of the *Investigations* is that identity is paradox, called the rule, as neither of opposite cases + existing as both qua either.

Comment. Per PI 394: the grammar qua lawful sense is this; under the circumstances of philosophical investigation targeting grammar the question may arise as to the identity of an imagining case, the grammatical answer being the imagined case, and where imagination is the identity case as a paradox case, the faces of which are the imagining/imagined aspects.

Games: paradox + faces; per PI 216, identity + identical cases cf. drabbit + duck/rabbit faces; imagination + imagining/imagined cases; per PI 43, word (language) + meaning/use (private/public) cases; per analogies, ladder + up/down aspects, drabbit + duck/rabbit faces.

395. There is a lack of clarity about the role of imaginability in our investigation. Namely, about the extent to which it ensures that a sentence makes sense.

To rehearse. The (PI 201) thesis of the *Investigations* is that identity is paradox, called the rule, as neither of opposite cases + existing as both qua either.

Comment. Per PI 395: grammatically (lawfully), for philosophical investigation, it is to be made clear that the imaginability role is an identity-as-paradox role, the identical aspects qua paradox faces of which are the verb/noun senses cf. imagination qua paradox and imagining/imagined paradox faces.

Games: paradox + faces; per PI 216, identity + identical cases cf. ladder + up/down ways; imaginability + verb/noun senses; imagination + imagining/imagined aspects; per PI 43, word + meaning/use cases; per analogies, ladder + ascent/descent aspects, drabbit + duck/rabbit faces.

396. It is no more essential to the understanding of a sentence that one should imagine something in connection with it than that one should make a sketch from it.

To rehearse. The (PI 201) thesis of the *Investigations* is that identity is paradox, called the rule, as neither of opposite cases + existing as both qua either.

Comment. Per PI 396: grammatically (lawfully), the essence qua meaning qua verb-sense understanding of a sentence is as much its use in terms of an imagined (imaged, spoken, understood, written, gestured) case as it is in terms of a sketched case; from which, paradox is to faces; as understanding, like sketch, is to verb/noun senses; as per PI 43, word is to meaning/use cases.

Games: identity-as-paradox + identical faces; word (language) + meaning/use (private/public) cases; sentence + essence/expression – understanding/understood – cases; sketch + sketching/sketched cases; imagination + imagining/ imagined – mental/enactment – cases; per analogies, ladder + up/down aspects, drabbit + duck/rabbit faces.

397. Instead of "imaginability", one can also say here: representability in a particular medium of representation. And such a representation may indeed safely point a way to a further use of a sentence. On the other hand, a picture may obtrude itself upon us and be of no use at all.

To rehearse. The (PI 201) thesis of the *Investigations* is that identity is paradox, called the rule, as neither of opposite cases + existing as both qua either.

Comment. PI 397: assorted grammatical (lawful) cases are these: the verb-sense aspect of a particular case (imaginability, representability, imagination, representation) is its noun-sense aspect; as per PI 43, the meaning of a sentence is its use; as the face of a paradox case is its corresponding other face; as the picturing aspect of a picture is its pictured aspect; here, the case of picture, if taken as a onefold-only sense – rather than as third-party identity-as-paradox sense in a threefold grammar case – would be ungrammatical (obtrusive, unlawful); identity (say, the picture case) is an identity-as-paradox sense, not a consistency sense.

Games: paradox + faces; per PI 216 identity + identical aspects cf. drabbit + duck/rabbit faces; particular case (imaginability, imagination, representability, representation) + verb/noun senses; word + meaning/use case; per analogies, ladder + up/down aspects, drabbit + duck/rabbit faces.

398. "But when I imagine something, or even actually **see** objects, surely I have **got** something which my neighbour has not." – I understand you. You want to look about you and say: "At any rate only **I** have got THIS." – What are these words for? They serve no purpose. – Indeed, can't one add: "There is here no question of a 'seeing' – and therefore none of a 'having' – nor of a subject, nor therefore of the I either"? Couldn't I ask: In what sense have you **got** what you are talking about and saying that only you have got it? Do you possess it? You do not even **see** it. Don't you really have to say that no one has got it? And indeed, it's clear: if you logically exclude other people's having something, it loses its sense to say that you have it.

But what are you then talking about? It's true I said that I knew deep down what you meant. But that meant that I knew how one thinks to conceive this object, to see it, to gesture at it, as it were, by looking and pointing. I know how one stares ahead and looks about one in this case – and the rest. I think one can say: you are talking (if, for example, you are sitting in a room) of the 'visual room'. That which has no owner is the 'visual room'. I can as little own it as I can walk about it, or look at it, or point at it. In so far as it cannot belong to anyone else, it doesn't belong to me either. Or again, in so far as I want to apply the same form *of expression to it as to the material room in which I sit, it doesn't belong to me. Its description need not mention an owner. Indeed, it need not have an owner. But then the visual room **cannot** have an owner. "For" – one might say – "it has no master outside it, and none inside it either."*

Think of a picture of a landscape, an imaginary landscape with a house in it. – Someone asks "Whose house is that?" – The answer, by the way, might be "It belongs to the farmer who is sitting on the bench in front of it". But then he cannot, for example, step into his house.

To rehearse. The (PI 201) thesis of the *Investigations* is that identity is paradox, called the rule, as neither of opposite cases + existing as both qua either.

Comment. PI 398: grammatically (lawfully), paradox is to faces; as picture qua THIS cf. ownership is to verb/noun senses; as per PI 43, word (language) is to meaning/use (private/public) – cf. visual-room/landscape-house, inside/outside, subjective/objective, seeing/seen, imagining/imagined, owning/owned – cases; by which, the private aspect as a distinct case cannot in this respect be other than paradoxically connected with its counterpart public aspect nor can it be other than coincidentally connected with the language case, which language case as a paradox case is the coincidence of the private/public aspects.

Games: paradox + faces (and variants, as per the Comment); per analogies, ladder + up/down aspects, drabbit + duck/rabbit faces.

399. One could also say: surely the owner of the visual room has to be of the same nature as it; but he isn't inside it, and there is no outside.

To rehearse. The (PI 201) thesis of the *Investigations* is that identity is paradox, called the rule, as neither of opposite cases + existing as both qua either.

Comment. Per PI 399: the grammar qua lawful sense is this; paradox is to faces; as (per PI 398) THIS is to visual-room/landscape-house cases; as ownership is to owner/owned cases; from which, the room aspect of the THIS case and the owner aspect of the ownership cases share the same grammatical nature in that each is a paradox-face case.

Games: paradox + faces; ownership + verb/noun senses; word (language) + meaning/use (private/public) cases; THIS + inside/outside – visual-room/landscape-house – cases; per analogies, ladder + up/down aspects, drabbit + duck/rabbit faces.

400. The visual room seemed like a discovery, as it were; but what its discoverer really found was a new way of speaking, a new comparison, and, one could even say, a new experience.

To rehearse. The (PI 201) thesis of the *Investigations* is that identity is paradox, called the rule, as neither of opposite cases + existing as both qua either.

Comment. Per PI 400: for its grammar (lawful sense), the text reads as follows; the earlier PI 398 visual-room talk is not a discovery talk of an identity but is a variant talk of the room as a private-language aspect of identity-as-paradox case, where that case is called a language case.

Games: paradox + faces; per PI 43, word qua language + meaning/use – private/public – cases cf. per PI 398, THIS + visual-room/landscape-house – inside/outside – cases; per analogies, ladder + up/down aspects, drabbit + duck/rabbit faces.

401. You interpret the new conception as the seeing of a new object. You interpret a grammatical movement that you have made as a quasi-physical phenomenon which you are observing. (Remember, for example, the question "Are sense-data the stuff of which the universe is made?")

But my expression "You have made a 'grammatical' movement" is not unobjectionable. Above all, you have found a new conception. As if you had invented a new way of painting; or, again, a new metre, or a new kind of song.

To rehearse. The (PI 201) thesis of the *Investigations* is that identity is paradox, called the rule, as neither of opposite cases + existing as both qua either.

Comment. Per PI 401: the grammar (law sense) is this; new-conception talk is variant grammatical (lawful) talk; paradox + faces talk is variantly the PI 398 THIS + visual-room/landscape-house – inside/outside – talk; here, the visual room is not an observable new object qua identity but is a variant grammatical identity-as-paradox face (interpretation).

Games: paradox + faces; per PI 398, THIS (whether as object, painting, metre, song) + interpretations; per PI 43, word (language) + meaning/use (private/public – cf. inside/outside, visual-room/landscape – cases; per analogies, ladder + up/down aspects, drabbit + duck/rabbit faces.

402. "It's true that I say 'I now have such-and-such a visual image', but the words 'I have' are merely a sign for **others**; the visual world is described **completely** by the description of the visual image." – You mean: the words "I have" are like "Attention please!" You're inclined to say that it should really have been expressed differently. Perhaps simply by making a sign with one's hand and then giving a description. – When, as in this case, one disapproves of the expressions of ordinary language (which, after all, do their duty), we have got a picture in our heads which conflicts with the picture of our ordinary way of speaking. At the same time, we're tempted to say that our way of speaking does not describe the facts as they really are. As if, for example, the proposition "he has pains" could be false in some other way than by that man's **not** having pains. As if the form of expression were saying something false, even when the proposition faute de mieux asserted something true.

For **this** is what disputes between idealists, solipsists and realists look like. The one party attacks the normal form of expression as if they were attacking an assertion; the others defend it, as if they were stating facts recognized by every reasonable human being.

To rehearse. The (PI 201) thesis of the *Investigations* is that identity is paradox, called the rule, as neither of opposite cases + existing as both qua either.

Comment. Per PI 402: the grammar (law sense) is this; to say that one has got such-and-such a visual image is to say that there is (as an image case) an imaged imaging; this talk converts ordinary language to grammar (law sense); by which, paradox is to faces; as image is to verb/noun senses; rather than targeting language in this way to convert it to grammar, received-philosophy scholars (idealists, solipsists, realists) target logical form, disputing its interpretation, each in his own way from own received-sense premises; in terms of grammar, however, seemingly conflicting cases are corresponding complimentary paradox-faces cases which thereby completely determine one another cf. par analogy, the up/down aspects of a ladder.

Games: paradox + faces; per PI 43, word (language) + meaning/use (private/public) cases; image + imaging/imaged cases cf. PI 398 THIS + visual-room/landscape-house cases, also Solipsism + Idealism/Realism cases; has (say, pain) + verb/noun senses; per analogies, ladder + up/down aspects, drabbit + duck/rabbit faces.

*403. If I were to reserve the word "pain" solely for what I had previously called "my pain", and others "L.W.'s pain", I'd do other people no injustice, so long as a notation were provided in which the loss of the word "pain" in other contexts were somehow made good. Other people would still be pitied, treated by doctors, and so on. It would, of course, be **no** objection to this way of talking to say "But look here, other people have just the same as you!"*

*But what would I gain from this new mode of representation? Nothing. But then the solipsist does not **want** any practical advantage when he advances his view either!*

To rehearse. The (PI 201) thesis of the *Investigations* is that identity is paradox, called the rule, as neither of opposite cases + existing as both qua either.

Comment. Per PI 403: the grammar (law) says this: paradox is to faces; as representation (pain, some other notion, the solipsistic mind) is to interpretations; here, whatever the representation case, as a paradox case, exhibiting its faces, it wants for nothing as a grammatical qua law-of-identity case; this talk converts the identity-as-consistency thesis (cf. the solipsist case) to the grammar of the identity-as-paradox thesis.

Games: paradox + faces; representation + interpretations; per analogies, ladder + up/down aspects, drabbit + duck/rabbit faces.

404. "When I say 'I am in pain', I don't point to a person who is in pain, since in a certain sense I don't know **who** is." And this can be given a justification. For the main point is: I didn't say that such-and-such a person was in pain, but "I am ...". Now, in saying this, I don't name any person. Just as I don't name anyone when I **groan** with pain. Though someone else sees who is in pain from the groaning.

What does it mean to know **who** is in pain? It means, for example, to know which man in this room is in pain: for instance, that it's the one who is sitting over there, or the one who is standing in that corner, the tall one over there with the fair hair, and so on. – What am I getting at? At the fact that there is a great variety of criteria for the 'identity' of a person.

Now, which of them leads me to say that **I** am in pain? None

To rehearse. The (PI 201) thesis of the *Investigations* is that identity is paradox, called the rule, as neither of opposite cases + existing as both qua either.

Comment. Per PI 404: grammatically (lawfully), the PI 403 representation-talk is the PI 404 am-talk; am-talk is being-talk, identity-talk, paradox-talk; from which, identity-as-paradox is to identical faces cf. per analogy, as drabbit is to duck/rabbit faces; as am-talk is to I/pain – feeling/expression – cases; in this games talk, person talk does not feature; in a variant game, paradox is to faces as person is to mind/bod cases, or as person is to (say) this-man/that-man cases.

Games: paradox + faces; am + feeling/report – cf. feeling/groaning-out – cases; representation + interpretations; per analogies, ladder + up/down aspects, drabbit + duck/rabbit faces.

*405. "But at any rate when you say 'I'm in pain', you want to draw the attention of others to a particular person." — The answer could be: No, I just want to draw their attention to **myself**.*

To rehearse. The (PI 201) thesis of the *Investigations* is that identity is paradox, called the rule, as neither of opposite cases + existing as both qua either.

Comment. Per PI 405: in terms of grammar qua law sense; am -talk is identity-as-paradox talk; paradox is to faces; as am-talk is to I/myself cases; for this game, person-talk is irrelevant.

Games: paradox + faces; representation + interpretations; am + I/myself — cf. feeling/behaviour, feeling/report, feeling/pain, feeling/groaning-out — cases; per analogies, ladder + up/down aspects, drabbit + duck/rabbit faces.

*406. "But surely what you want to do with the words 'I am ...' is to distinguish between **yourself** and **other** people." — Can this be said in every case? Even when I merely groan? And even when I 'want to distinguish' between myself and other people — do I want to distinguish between the person L.W. and the person N.N.?*

To rehearse. The (PI 201) thesis of the *Investigations* is that identity is paradox, called the rule, as neither of opposite cases + existing as both qua either.

Comment. Per PI 406: for identity-grammar (identity-law), am-talk is identity-as-paradox talk; paradox is to faces; as am-talk is to interpretations (I/myself, feeling/report, pain/behaviour, feeling/groaning-out, private/public, person/person, L.W./N.N.).

Games: paradox + faces; representation + interpretations (and variants, as per the Comment); per analogies, ladder + up/down aspects, drabbit + duck/rabbit faces.

407. It would be possible to imagine someone groaning out: "Someone is in pain — I don't know who!" — whereupon people would hurry to help him, the one who groaned.

To rehearse. The (PI 201) thesis of the *Investigations* is that identity is paradox, called the rule, as neither of opposite cases + existing as both qua either.

Comment. Per PI 407: grammatically qua lawfully – neither empirically nor logically – paradox is to faces; as someone is to feeling/expression – here, as pain/groaning-out – cases.

Games: paradox + faces; per PI 43, word (language) + meaning/use (private/public) cases; representation + interpretations; someone (I don't know who) + feeling/expression – pain/groan – cases; per analogies, ladder + up/down aspects, drabbit + duck/rabbit faces.

408. *"But you aren't in doubt whether it is you or someone else who is in pain!" – The proposition "I don't know whether I or someone else is in pain" would be a logical product, and one of its factors would be: "I don't know whether I am in pain or not" – and that is not a significant sentence.*

To rehearse. The (PI 201) thesis of the *Investigations* is that identity is paradox, called the rule, as neither of opposite cases + existing as both qua either.

Comment. Per PI 408: logic is insignificant other than as raw material for grammatical conversion; grammatically (lawfully), the case of someone cf. I-don't-know-who is a paradox case, the faces of which are the feeling/expression (pain/report) cases; here, it is the three feeling/someone/report cases which are indubitably qua inseparably connected in that each lives in the other two so that given any of the three as the case the others thereby are the case cf. ladder + up/down aspects.

Games: paradox + faces; representation + interpretations; someone (I don't know who) + felling/report – pain-told-out – cases; per analogies, ladder + up/down aspects, drabbit + duck/rabbit faces.

409. *Imagine several people standing in a circle, myself among them. One of us, sometimes this one, sometimes that, is connected to the poles of an electrostatic*

generator without our being able to see this. I observe the faces of the others and try to see which of us has just been given an electric shock. — At one point I say: "Now I know who it is — it's me." In this sense I could also say: "Now I know who is feeling the shocks — it's me." This would be a rather odd way of speaking. — But if I suppose that I can feel an electric shock even when someone else is being given one, then the form of expression "Now I know who ..." becomes quite inappropriate. It does not belong to this game.

To rehearse. The (PI 201) thesis of the *Investigations* is that identity is paradox, called the rule, as neither of opposite cases + existing as both qua either.

Comment. Per PI 409: for its grammar (law sense), the text reads as follows; is-talk (as in It's-me talk) is identity-as-paradox talk; paradox is to faces; as is-talk is to I/me cases; as electrification is to this-person/that-person cases (including the L.W. person) cf. the am-talk of previous texts.

Games: paradox + faces; representation + interpretations; is-talk + I/me cases cf. persons, also electrification + persons – cases; per analogies, ladder + up/down aspects, drabbit + duck/rabbit faces.

410. "I" doesn't name a person, nor "here" a place, and "this" is not a name. But they are connected with names. Names are explained by means of them. It is also true that it is characteristic of physics not to use these words.

To rehearse. The (PI 201) thesis of the *Investigations* is that identity is paradox, called the rule, as neither of opposite cases + existing as both qua either.

Comment. Per PI 410: grammatically (lawfully), paradox is to faces; as play life is to games; as I, or here, or this, is to names; as physics is to descriptions.

Games: paradox + faces; representation + interpretations (and variants, as per Comment); per analogies, ladder + up/down aspects, drabbit + duck/rabbit faces.

411. Consider how the following questions can be applied, and how decided:

*(1) "Are these books **my** books?"*
*(2) "Is this foot **my** foot?"*
*(3) "Is this body **my** body?"*
*(4) "Is this sensation **my** sensation?"*

Each of these questions has practical (non-philosophical) applications.

For (2): Think of cases in which my foot is anaesthetized or paralysed. Under certain circumstances, the question could be settled by finding out whether I can feel pain in this foot.

*For (3): Here one might be pointing to a reflection in a mirror. But in certain circumstances, one might touch a body and ask the question. In others, it means the same as "Does my body look like **that**?"*

*For (4): But which sensation is **this** one? That is, how is one using the demonstrative pronoun here? Certainly otherwise than in, say, the first example. Here, again, one goes astray, because one imagines that by directing one's attention to a sensation, one is pointing at it.*

To rehearse. The (PI 201) thesis of the *Investigations* is that identity is paradox, called the rule, as neither of opposite cases + existing as both qua either.

Comment. Per PI 411: is-talk, like are-talk, is identity-as-paradox talk, like the am-talk of the previous texts; each of these talk cases is a representation-talk; the empirical-sense talk of PI 411 translates to the grammatical (lawful) talk as follows; paradox is to faces; as are-talk is to these-books/my-books cases; as is-talk is to this-foot/my-foot, or this-body/my-body, or this-sensation/my-sensation, cases.

Games: paradox + face; representation + interpretations (and variants, as per Comment); per analogies, ladder + up/down aspects, drabbit + duck/rabbit faces.

*412. The feeling of an unbridgeable gulf between consciousness and brain process: how come that this plays no role in reflections of ordinary life? This idea of a difference in kind is accompanied by slight giddiness – which occurs when we are doing logical tricks. (The same giddiness attacks us when dealing with certain theorems in set theory.) When does this feeling occur in the present case? It is when I, for example, turn my attention in a particular way on to my own consciousness and, astonished, say to myself: "this is supposed to be produced by a process in the brain!" – as it were clutching my forehead. – But what can it mean to speak of "turning my attention on to my own consciousness"? There is surely nothing more extraordinary than that there should be any such thing! What I described with these words (which are not used in this way in ordinary life) was an act of gazing. I gazed fixedly in front of me – but **not** at any particular point or object. My eyes were wide open, brows not contracted (as they mostly are when I am interested in a particular object). No such interest preceded this gazing. My glance was vacant; or again, **like** that of someone admiring the illumination of the sky and drinking in the light.*

Note that the sentence which I uttered as a paradox ("THIS is produced by a brain process!") has nothing paradoxical about it. I could have said it in the course of an experiment whose purpose was to show that an effect of light which I see is produced by stimulation of a particular part of the brain. – But I did not utter the sentence in the surroundings in which it would have had an everyday and unparadoxical sense. And my attention was not such as would have been in keeping with that experiment. (If it had been, my gaze would have been intent, not vacant.)

To rehearse. The (PI 201) thesis of the *Investigations* is that identity is paradox, called the rule, as neither of opposite cases + existing as both qua either.

Comment. Per PI 212: the text puts out in terms of grammar qua law and not referenced to unparadoxical logical-sense surroundings or empirical-sense surroundings other than these as raw material for grammatical (paradoxical) surroundings; the surroundings convert grammatically as follows; paradox is to faces; as coincidence is to different qua distinct cases; as gulf or vacancy is to unbridgeable cases; as THIS is to min/brain – consciousness/behaviour – cases; as per PI 216, identity is to identical cases cf. per analogy as drabbit is to duck/rabbit faces;

Games: paradox + faces; THIS qua attending-to with vacant look + consciousness/brain case; per analogies, ladder + up/down aspects, drabbit + duck/rabbit faces.

413. Here we have a case of introspection, not unlike that which gave William James the idea that the 'self' consisted mainly of 'peculiar motions in the head and between the head and throat'. And James's introspection showed, not the meaning of the word "self" (so far as it means something like "person", "human being", "he himself", "I myself"), or any analysis of such a being, but the state of a philosopher's attention when he says the word "self" to himself and tries to analyse its meaning. (And much could be learned from this.)

To rehearse. The (PI 201) thesis of the *Investigations* is that identity is paradox, called the rule, as neither of opposite cases + existing as both qua either.

Comment. Per PI 413: grammatically (lawfully), the case of the self is to introspection/report aspects (so Wittgenstein, on James); as paradox is too its faces.

Games: paradox + faces; self + mind-state/verbal-report aspects cf. person + mind/body aspects cf. self + I/me aspects cf. PI 412 attending-to + consciousness/brain aspects; per analogies, ladder + up/down aspects, drabbit + duck/rabbit faces.

414. You think that after all you must be weaving a piece of cloth: because you are sitting at a loom – even if it is empty – and going through the motions of weaving.

To rehearse. The (PI 201) thesis of the *Investigations* is that identity is paradox, called the rule, as neither of opposite cases + existing as both qua either.

Comment. Per PI 414: the grammar (law sense) reads as follows; language is to thinking/enactment cases; as loom is to weaving/motions cases; as per PI 304, emptiness is to Nothing/Something cases; as a paradox face is to faces.

Games: paradox qua neither of – distinct from – its faces + faces; emptiness + weaving/motions aspects; per PI 43, word + meaning/practice aspects; per analogies, ladder + up/down aspects; aspects, drabbit + duck/rabbit faces.

415. What we are supplying are really remarks on the natural history of human beings; not curiosities, however, but facts that no one has doubted, which have escaped notice only because they are always before our eyes.

To rehearse. The (PI 201) thesis of the *Investigations* is that identity is paradox, called the rule, as neither of opposite cases + existing as both qua either.

Comment. Per PI 415: the grammar qua law sense is this: the text reminds one that the *Investigations* philosophy has to do with the grammatical treatment of the empirical and everyday discourse which is the raw material for grammatical analysis, a raw material in plain sight; this has to do with what is hidden in plain sight i.e. the threefold grammar of identity-as-paradox + identical faces cf. per analogy, drabbit + duck/rabbit faces.

Games: paradox + faces.; per analogies, ladder + up/down aspects, drabbit + duck/rabbit faces.

*416. "Human beings agree in saying that they see, hear, feel, and so on (even though some are blind and some are deaf). So they are their own witnesses that they have **consciousness**." – But how strange this is! Whom do I really inform if I say "I have consciousness"? What is the purpose of saying this to myself, and how can another person understand me? – Now, sentences like "I see", "I hear", "I am conscious" really have their uses. I tell a doctor "Now I can hear with this ear again", or I tell someone who believes I am in a faint "I am conscious again", and so on.*

To rehearse. The (PI 201) thesis of the *Investigations* is that identity is paradox, called the rule, as neither of opposite cases + existing as both qua either.

Comment. Per PI 416: grammatically (lawfully), human beings agree in using words to report what they mean, such as that, in one way or another, they are conscious, hear, and so on; here, each being, as a self, is an identity as paradox, the faces of which are the consciousness/report aspects; the purpose of all such paradox talk is to render ordinary language grammatical.

Games: paradox faces; per PI 216, identity + identical cases cf. drabbit + duck/rabbit faces; per PI 43, word + meaning/use aspects; self + consciousness/report aspects; per analogies, ladder + up/down aspects, drabbit + duck/rabbit faces.

417. Do I observe myself, then, and perceive that I am seeing or conscious? And why talk about observation at all? Why not simply say "I perceive I am conscious"? – But what are the words "I perceive" for here – why not say "I am conscious"? But don't the words "I perceive" here show that I am attending to my consciousness? – which is ordinarily not the case. – If so, then the sentence "I perceive I am conscious" does not say that I am conscious, but that my attention is focused in such-and-such a way.

But isn't it a particular experience that occasions my saying "I am conscious again"? – **What** *experience? In what situations do we say it?*

To rehearse. The (PI 201) thesis of the *Investigations* is that identity is paradox, called the rule, as neither of opposite cases + existing as both qua either.

Comment. Per PI 417: the grammar qua law sense is this: consciousness (perception) is to verb/noun senses; as paradox is to faces; the point of such talk is to translate ordinary language into grammatical terms to show that grammar as the threefold case of identity-as-paradox and identical faces cf. drabbit + duck/rabbit faces.

Gamesa: paradox + faces; as per PI 43, word + meaning/use cases; consciousness qua perception + verb/noun cases; per analogies, ladder + up/down aspects, drabbit + duck/rabbit faces.

418. Is my having consciousness a fact of experience?

But doesn't one say that human beings have consciousness, and that trees or stones do not? – What would it be like if it were otherwise? – Would human beings all be unconscious? – No; not in the ordinary sense of the word. But I, for instance, would not have consciousness – as I now in fact have it.

To rehearse. The (PI 201) thesis of the *Investigations* is that identity is paradox, called the rule, as neither of opposite cases + existing as both qua either.

Comment. Per PI 418: grammatically (lawfully), empirical talk – experiential talk – is the raw material analysed grammatically by the *Investigations* philosophy; by it, paradox is to faces; as person is to conscious/physical cases; as stone (say) is to meaning/material cases; from which, PI 418 looks to the grammar of consciousness, not its experiential status; persons are conscious, otherwise unconscious i.e. a person is an identity as paradox, the faces of which are conscious/unconscious – mental/physical cf. meaning/matter – aspects.

Games: paradox + faces; per PI 43, word + meaning/use cases; stone + meaning/material cases; person + conscious/body cases; per analogies, ladder + up/down aspects, drabbit + duck/rabbit faces.

419. *In what circumstances shall I say that a tribe has a* **chief**? *And the chief must surely have* **consciousness**. *Surely he mustn't be without consciousness!*

To rehearse. The (PI 201) thesis of the *Investigations* is that identity is paradox, called the rule, as neither of opposite cases + existing as both qua either.

Comment. Per PI 419: the grammar qua law sense is this: paradox is to faces; as tribe (community, writ small as person) is to chief/others (head/body) cases; as consciousness (self) is to conscious/conscious (mental/behavioural) cases; consciousness role-plays as self, or as mental process or as (living) behaviour; likewise, language role-plays as word, or as meaning, or as use.

Games: paradox + faces; tribe + chief/others cases; person + head/body aspects; self + conscious/behavioural aspects; per PI 43, word + meaning/

use – meaning/material – aspects; per analogies, ladder + up/down aspects, drabbit + duck/rabbit faces.

420. But can't I imagine that people around me are automata, lack consciousness, even though they behave in the same way as usual? – If I imagine it now – alone in my room – I see people with fixed looks (as in a trance) going about their business – the idea is perhaps a little uncanny. But just try to hang on to this idea in the midst of your ordinary intercourse with others – in the street, say! Say to yourself, for example: "The children over there are mere automata; all their liveliness is mere automatism." And you will either find these words becoming quite empty; or you will produce in yourself some kind of uncanny feeling, or something of the sort.

Seeing a living human being as an automaton is analogous to seeing one figure as a limiting case or variant of another; the cross-pieces of a window as a swastika, for example.

To rehearse. The (PI 201) thesis of the *Investigations* is that identity is paradox, called the rule, as neither of opposite cases + existing as both qua either.

Comment. Per PI 420: grammatically (lawfully), person is to mind/behaviour cases; as robot is to program/behaviour cases; as uncanniness is to conscious/unconscious cases; as vacancy (trance, fixed stare) qua neither of opposite cases is to opposite cases; as automation is to child-liveliness/child-lifelessness cases; as mutual eclipse is to interchanging swastika/window-cross-pieces limiting cases; as paradox is to faces; talk of life in connection with automation is talk of meaning in connection with matter, the ethereal in connection with the gross, the mind in connection with the body, mentality in connection with physicality, and so on. It is talk of distinct paradox faces coinciding as the paradox case.

Games: paradox + faces; per PI 43, word + meaning/use cases; person + consciousness/behaviour cases; robot + unconscious/behaviour – program/behaviour cases; child-automation + lively/robotic cases; vacancy qua neutralism + opposite cases; word + meaning/use cases cf. swastika/

window-cross-pieces cases; per analogies, ladder + up/down aspects, drabbit + duck/rabbit faces.

421. It seems paradoxical to us that in a single report we should make such a medley, mixing physical states and states of consciousness up together: "He suffered great torments and tossed about restlessly." It is quite usual; so why does it seem paradoxical to us? Because we want to say that the sentence is about both tangibles and intangibles. – But does it worry you if I say: "These three struts give the building stability?" Are three and stability tangible? – Regard the sentence as an instrument, and its sense as its employment.

To rehearse. The (PI 201) thesis of the *Investigations* is that identity is paradox, called the rule, as neither of opposite cases + existing as both qua either.

Comment. Per PI 421: the grammar qua law sense is this: by PI 43, the meaning of a word is its use; the sense of a sentence is its employment; per PI 421, the torment aspect of the sufferer case is the restless-movement aspect; the stability aspect of a construction case is its struts aspect; the face of a paradox is its counterpart face.

Games: paradox + faces; wordage + meaning/use case: sentence qua tool + sense/employment cases; person + consciousness/behaviour cases i.e. mental/physical cases i.e. intangible/tangible cases cf. torment/restlessness cases; construction + stability/struts cases i.e. intangible/tangible cases; per analogies, ladder + up/down aspects, drabbit + duck/rabbit faces.

422. What do I believe in when I believe that man has a soul? What do I believe in when I believe that this substance contains two carbon rings? In both cases, there is a picture in the foreground, but the sense lies far in the background; that is, the application of the picture is not easy to survey.

To rehearse. The (PI 201) thesis of the *Investigations* is that identity is paradox, called the rule, as neither of opposite cases + existing as both qua either.

Comment. Per PI 422: the grammar (law sense) is this: paradox is to faces; as picture is to out-pictures; as representation (say, belief, religious or scientific) is to background/foreground (say, grammar/language, word-meaning/word-use, eclipsed-face/eclipsing-face) interpretations; as per PI 43, word (language) is to meaning/use (private/public) – cf. sense/application, hardly-surveyed/easily-surveyed – cases.

Games: paradox + faces; (and variants, as per the Comment); per analogies, ladder + up/down aspects, drabbit + duck/rabbit faces.

*423. **Certainly** all these things happen in you. – And now just let me understand the expression we use. – The picture is there. And I am not disputing its validity in particular cases. – Only let me now understand its application.*

To rehearse. The (PI 201) thesis of the *Investigations* is that identity is paradox, called the rule, as neither of opposite cases + existing as both qua either.

Comment. Per PI 423: grammatically (lawfully), certainty is to uncertainty qua changeability (cf. happenings); as paradox is to faces; as per PI 43, word (language) is to meaning/use (private/public) – understanding/expression, sense/application – cases; as picture qua particular case is to interpretations.

Games: paradox + faces (and variants, as per the Comment); per analogies, ladder + up/down aspects, drabbit + duck/rabbit faces.

*424. The picture is there; and I do not dispute its **correctness**. But **what** is its application? Think of the picture of blindness as a darkness in the mind or in the head of a blind person.*

To rehearse. The (PI 201) thesis of the *Investigations* is that identity is paradox, called the rule, as neither of opposite cases + existing as both qua either.

Comment. Per PI 424: the grammar qua law talk presents as follows; paradox is to faces; as picture is to out-pictures; as correctness is to interpretations;

as per PI 43, word (language) is to meaning/use (private/public) – sense/application, darkness/light, blindness/sighted – cases.

Games: paradox + faces (and variants, as per the Comment); per analogies, ladder + up/down aspects, drabbit + duck/rabbit faces.

425. While in innumerable cases we exert ourselves to find a picture, and once it is found, the application, as it were, comes about automatically, here we already have a picture which obtrudes itself on us at every turn — but does not help us out of the difficulty, which begins only now.

*If I ask, for example, "How am I to imagine **this** mechanism fitting into **this** casing?" — perhaps a drawing reduced in scale may serve to answer me. Then I can be told: "You see, it fits like **this**." Or perhaps even: "Why are you surprised? See how it works **here**; well, it is the same there." — Of course, the latter no longer explains anything: it merely invites me to apply the picture I was given.*

To rehearse. The (PI 201) thesis of the *Investigations* is that identity is paradox, called the rule, as neither of opposite cases + existing as both qua either.

Comment. Per PI 425: the grammar (law) is this: talk of an obtruding picture and its applications is talk of an ungrammatical case of identity-as-consistency and its applications; the grammatical case is the picture as a paradox, the faces of which are its meaning/use – meaning/application – cases; from which, paradox is to faces; as representation (imagination, fit, wordage, sameness, thisness, location) is to interpretations (imagining/imagined cases, fitting-into/fitted-into cases, meaning/application cases, same/same cases, here/there cases).

Games: paradox + face; picture + meaning/application cases; per PI 43, word + meaning/use cases; per PI 215, sameness + same/same cases cf. drabbit analogy; per analogies, ladder + up/down aspects, drabbit + duck/rabbit faces.

426. A picture is conjured up which seems to fix the sense unambiguously. The actual use, compared with that traced out by the picture, seems like something muddied. Here again, what is going on is the same as in set theory: the form of expression seems to have been tailored for a god, who knows what we cannot know; he sees all of those infinite series, and he sees into the consciousness of human beings. For us, however, these forms of expression are like vestments, which we may put on, but cannot do much with, since we lack the effective power that would give them point and purpose.

In the actual use of these expressions we, as it were, make detours, go by side roads. We see the straight highway before us, but of course cannot use it, because it is permanently closed.

To rehearse. The (PI 201) thesis of the *Investigations* is that identity is paradox, called the rule, as neither of opposite cases + existing as both qua either.

Comment. Per PI 426: grammar talk (law talk) is this; the identity-as-consistency (as unambiguity) case is ungrammatical (a conjuring act); it makes for meaning qua form (point or purpose) as unclear expression qua application (muddied, perplexing, mysterious, divinely-robed, pontifically-dressed), making for the absence of straight talk (cf. the permanently closed highway) and instead for circumlocution (cf. detour); the grammatical case is that of identity-as-paradox, with paradox as the straight or certain highway and its interchanging faces as the cases of detour.; here mystery does not feature other than as raw material to be analysed such that it is paradoxically non-mysterious cf. word-meaning is paradoxically word-use.

Games: paradox + faces (and variants, as per the Comment); per analogies, ladder + up/down aspects; drabbit + duck/rabbit faces.

427. "While I was speaking to him, I did not know what was going on in his head." In saying this, one is not thinking of brain processes, but of thought processes. This picture should be taken seriously. We really would like to see into his head. And yet we only mean what we ordinarily mean by saying that we would like to know what he is thinking. I want to say: we have this vivid picture – and that use, apparently contradicting the picture, which expresses something mental.

To rehearse. The (PI 201) thesis of the *Investigations* is that identity is paradox, called the rule, as neither of opposite cases + existing as both qua either.

Comment. Per PI 427: grammatically (lawfully), the case of a picture qua an identity-as-consistency is ungrammatical; grammatically, there is the picture qua identity-as-paradox; by which, paradox is to faces; as per PI 43, word (language) is to meaning/use (private/public) – cf. mind/brain, thinking/head, mental/behavioural – cases; whatever the language game, the paradox-face cases are not contradictories but complementary or counterpart cases cf. per analogy, the ladder's way-up as oppositely its way-down.

Games: paradox + fasces; per PI 43, word + meaning/use cases; person + thought/head cases i.e. mental-process/brain-activity cases.; (in mixed-talk terms) word + psychical/use cases; per analogies, ladder + up/down aspects, drabbit + duck/rabbit faces.

428. *"A thought – what a strange thing!" – but it does not strike us as strange when we are thinking. A thought does not strike us as mysterious while we are thinking, but only when we say, as it were retrospectively, "How was that possible?" How was it possible for a thought to deal with this **very** object? It seems to us as if we had captured reality with the thought.*

To rehearse. The (PI 201) thesis of the *Investigations* is that identity is paradox, called the rule, as neither of opposite cases + existing as both qua either.

Comment. Per PI 428: grammatically (lawfully) – as distinct from empirically – the threefold case is paradox + faces as the threefold case of object + thought/reality cases; a variant would be this – reality + thought/object cases cf. reality + subject/object cases; in this variant the **very** object is the real object; the reality case thus can play different roles in the different language games, each threefold grammar qua game bespeaking identity as paradox.

Games: paradox + faces; per PI 43, word + meaning/use cases; reality + thought/object – mysterious/plain – cases; per analogies, ladder + up/down aspects, drabbit + duck/rabbit faces.

*429. The agreement, the harmony, between thought and reality consists in this: that if I say falsely that something is **red**, then all the same, it is **red** that it isn't. And in this: that if I want to explain the word "red" to someone, in the sentence "That is not red", I do so by pointing to something that **is** red.*

To rehearse. The (PI 201) thesis of the *Investigations* is that identity is paradox, called the rule, as neither of opposite cases + existing as both qua either.

Comment. Per PI 429: the grammar qua law sense presents as follows; from PI 216, identity-as-paradox (cf. harmony, agreement) is to identical faces cf. per analogy, drabbit + duck/rabbit faces; as red is to "red"/"red" – cf. meaning/pointing – cases; as per PI 215, sameness is to same/same cases.

Games: paradox + faces; per PI 43, word (language) + meaning/use (private/public) cases; sameness + same/same cases; something qua redness + "red"/"red" cases; object + thought/reality cases; agreement + agreed cases; harmony + harmonised cases; per analogies, ladder + up/down aspects, drabbit + duck/rabbit faces.

430. "Put a ruler against this object; it does not say that the object is so-and-so long. Rather, it is in itself – I am tempted to say – dead, and achieves nothing of what a thought can achieve." – It is as if we had imagined that the essential thing about a living human being was the outward form. Then we made a lump of wood into that form and were abashed to see the lifeless block, lacking any similarity to a living creature.

To rehearse. The (PI 201) thesis of the *Investigations* is that identity is paradox, called the rule, as neither of opposite cases + existing as both qua either.

Comment. Per P 430: grammatically (lawfully), paradox is to paradox-face cases; as person is to mind/body natures; as rule is to informative/lifeless cases.

Games: paradox + faces; per PI 43, word + meaning/use cases; person + thinking/speaking cases; object + length/rule cases cf. thought/speech cases, form/matter cases, essence/expression cases, living/dead case; block + form/lifeless cases; per analogies, ladder + up/down aspects, drabbit + duck/rabbit faces.

431. "There is a gap between an order and its execution. It has to be closed by the process of understanding."

*"Only in the process of understanding does the order mean that we are to do THIS. The **order** – why, that is nothing but sounds, ink-marks."*

To rehearse. The (PI 201) thesis of the *Investigations* is that identity is paradox, called the rule, as neither of opposite cases + existing as both qua either.

Comment. Per P 431: the grammar (law) is this: for an identity-as-paradox case i.e. a THIS case, paradox is to faces, as gap qua neither of the paradox faces is to both of the paradox faces cf. as gap is to order/execution cases; as closure qua coincidence of paradox faces is to paradox faces cf. as (from PI 43) understanding qua word is to meaning/use – meaning/sound, meaning/marks – cases; as object is to thought/reality cases.

Games: paradox + faces; word + meaning/use cases; understanding as a word + meaning/sounds-or-ink-marks cases, understanding as a human activity + order/execution cases; per analogies, ladder + up/down aspects, drabbit + duck/rabbit faces.

*432. Every sign **by itself** seems dead. **What** gives it life? – In use it **lives**. Is it there that it has living breath within it? – Or is the **use** its breath?*

To rehearse. The (PI 201) thesis of the *Investigations* is that identity is paradox, called the rule, as neither of opposite cases + existing as both qua either.

Comment. Per P 432: the grammar qua law sense presents as follows: in terms of identity law stating of identity that *it is itself,* the it aspect of the is case is the itself aspect; as the identical face of an identity-as-paradox case is the counterpart identical face cf. per analogy, as the duck face of drabbit is the rabbit face; as per PI 43, the meaning of a word is its use; as the signing aspect of a sign is its signed aspect; as the living aspect of life is its lived aspect; as the mind aspect of the breath (spirit, person) is the body aspect; as the living of a life (cf. sign) is its behavioural usefulness.

Games: paradox + faces; word (and variants, as per the Comment); per analogies, ladder + up/down aspects, drabbit + duck/rabbit faces.

433. When we give an order, it may look as if the ultimate thing sought by the order had to remain unexpressed, as there is still a gap between an order and its execution. Say I want someone to make a particular movement: for example, to raise his arm. To make my order quite clear, I demonstrate the movement to him. This picture seems unambiguous until the question is raised: how does he know that **he is to make that movement**? *– How does he know at all what he is to do with the signs I give him, whatever they are? – Perhaps I shall now try to supplement the order with further signs, by pointing from myself to him, by making encouraging gestures, and so forth. Here it looks as if the order were beginning to stammer.*

As if the sign were precariously trying to induce understanding in us. – But if we now understand it, in what signs do we do so?

To rehearse. The (PI 201) thesis of the *Investigations* is that identity is paradox, called the rule, as neither of opposite cases + existing as both qua either.

Comment. Per P 433: grammatically (lawfully), picture talk, here as a particular-movement talk, is identity-as-paradox talk, gulf talk, an understanding talk; the paradox faces are the cases of order/execution, demonstrating/witness, meaning/enactment, signing/signed; the faces are connected precariously or as stutteringly qua not consistently qua paradoxically; it is paradox which brings together opposite cases in coincidence, from which they out-picture in interchange, each as ever the other cf. drabbit + duck/rabbit faces.

Games: paradox + faces; per PI 43, word + meaning/use cases; understanding + order/execution cases; sign + signing/ signed cases; gap qua neither of opposites + both opposites; coincidence + distinct cases; per analogies, ladder + up/down aspects, drabbit + duck/rabbit faces.

434. The gesture – one would like to say – tries to prefigure, but can't do so.

To rehearse. The (PI 201) thesis of the *Investigations* is that identity is paradox, called the rule, as neither of opposite cases + existing as both qua either.

Comment. Per PI 434: the grammar (law talk) is this; a gesturing case cannot be prefiguring other than as paradoxically a gestured qua prefigured case.

Games: paradox + faces; per PI 43, word (here, gesture) + meaning/use – gestating/gestured, prefiguring/prefigured – cases; per analogies, ladder + up/down aspects, drabbit + duck/rabbit faces, coin + head/tail faces.

435. If it is asked, "How does a sentence manage to represent?" – the answer might be: "Don't you know? Surely you see it, when you use one." After all, nothing is concealed.

How does a sentence do it? – Don't you know? After all, nothing is hidden.

But when given the answer "But you know how a sentence does it, after all, nothing is concealed", one would like to retort, "Yes, but it all goes by so quickly, and I should like to see it, as it were, more fully laid out."

To rehearse. The (PI 201) thesis of the *Investigations* is that identity is paradox, called the rule, as neither of opposite cases + existing as both qua either.

Comment. Per PI 435: in terms of grammar qua law sense, by PI 43, a sentience qua representation is to its meaning/use – representing/represented – cases; as paradox is to its faces; no face is permanently hidden in the sense that, by turns, the faces out-picture the paradox case; equally, they do not lie alongside one another but inhabit one another such that each out-pictures instantaneously cf. ladder + up/down aspects.

Games: paradox + faces; sentence (word) + meaning/use cases; representation + verb/noun senses; per analogies, ladder + up/down aspects, drabbit + duck/rabbit faces.

436. Here it is easy to get into that dead end in philosophizing where one believes that the difficulty of the problem consists in our having to describe phenomena that evade our grasp, the present experience that slips quickly by, or something akin – where we find ordinary language too crude, and it looks as if we were dealing not with the phenomena of everyday conversation, but with ones that "are evanescent, and, in their coming to be and passing away, tend to produce those others".

(Augustine: Manifestissima et usitatissima sunt, et Eidem rursus nimis latent, et nova est inventio eorum.)

To rehearse. The (PI 201) thesis of the *Investigations* is that identity is paradox, called the rule, as neither of opposite cases + existing as both qua either.

Comment. Per PI 436: grammatically (lawfully), the quote from Augustine translates as follows: "*They are the most obvious and the most common, and the same again are too hidden, and their discovery is new.*"; the threefold grammar is that of a rapidity qua mutually eclipsing (of its faces) activity, but where the faces are nonetheless hidden from sight as paradoxically readily seen; ordinary language translates grammatically such that the paradox case evades discovery other than as a plain discovery in terms of its ever-changing faces (see PI 201 re: grasping the rule in terms of its accordant/discordant courses of action).

Games: paradox qua mutual-eclipse activity + rapidly mutually eclipsing faces; per analogies, ladder + up/down aspects, drabbit + duck/rabbit faces.

437. A wish seems already to know what will or would satisfy it; a proposition, a thought, to know what makes it true – even when there is nothing there! Whence this determining of what is not yet there? This despotic demand? ("The hardness of the logical must".)

To rehearse. The (PI 201) thesis of the *Investigations* is that identity is paradox, called the rule, as neither of opposite cases + existing as both qua either.

Comment. Per PI 437: the grammar qua law sense is this; paradox is to its faces; as wish is to its wishing/wished cases; as thought is to its thinking/thoughts cases; as per PI 43, word is to its meaning/use cases; as per PI 304 cf. PI 201, neither anything nor nothing – neither accord nor conflict – is to its Nothing/Something cases; talk of a despotic demand, the hardness of the logical must, is talk of the onefold-only identity-grammar of consistency – by which paradox is either accounted nonsense or is shorn of one of its faces to render it as consistency-only, as a must; rather it is, grammatically, that per every threefold game talk of paradox + faces, each of the three members being the case warrant the others being the case in that all three inhabit one another cf. drabbit + duck/rabbit faces.

Games: paradox + faces; per PI 43, word + meaning/use cases; per PI 304, neither + Nothing/Something cases; wish (thought) + wishing/wished cases (thinking/thoughts cases); per analogies, ladder + up/down aspects, drabbit + duck/rabbit faces.

438. "A plan, as such, is something unsatisfied." (Like a wish, an expectation, a conjecture, and so on.)

Here I mean: expectation is unsatisfied, because it is an expectation of something; a belief, an opinion, is unsatisfied, because it is an opinion that something is the case, something real, something outside the process of believing.

To rehearse. The (PI 201) thesis of the *Investigations* is that identity is paradox, called the rule, as neither of opposite cases + existing as both qua either.

Comment. Per PI 438: the text reads for its grammar (law sense) as follows; verb-sense plan (cf. verb-sense cases of wish, expectation, belief, conjecture, opinion, and so on) is to an outside (differing) case; as paradox face is to its corresponding other paradox face as a distinctly other face; a plan without its corresponding outcome is unsatisfied, as is the ascent aspect of a ladder without a descent aspect; logically or empirically opposites exist in parallel whereas grammatically they exist as paradoxically one another.

Games: paradox + faces; plan (cf. wish, expectation, belief, conjecture, opinion, and so on) + verb/noun senses; per analogies, ladder + up/down aspects, drabbit + duck/rabbit faces.

439. In what sense can one call wishes, expectations, beliefs, etc. "unsatisfied"? What is our prototype of non-satisfaction? Is it a hollow space? And would one call that "unsatisfied"? Wouldn't this be a metaphor too? — Isn't what we call non-satisfaction — say, hunger — a feeling?

In a particular system of expressions we can describe an object by means of the words "satisfied" and "unsatisfied". For example, if we stipulate that a hollow cylinder is to be called "an unsatisfied cylinder", and the solid cylinder that fills it "its satisfaction".

To rehearse. The (PI 201) thesis of the *Investigations* is that identity is paradox, called the rule, as neither of opposite cases + existing as both qua either.

Comment. Per PI 439: the text treats with satisfaction grammatically (lawfully), not in either its logical or empirical sense other than these as raw material cases for grammatical analysis; paradox (say, as wish, belief, expectation, etc.) is to faces; as coincidence is to distinct cases; as satisfaction is to non-satisfaction cases; as per analogy, cylinder fitted into cylinder casing is to solid/hollow aspects; as filled stomach is to food/hungry cases.

Games: paradox + faces; coincidence + distinct cases; mutual-satisfaction + mutually satisfying/satisfied cases; per analogies ladder + mutually eclipsing up/down aspects, drabbit + mutually eclipsing duck/rabbit faces.

*440. Saying "I'd like an apple" does not mean: I believe an apple will quell my feeling of non-satisfaction. **This** utterance is an expression not of a wish but of non-satisfaction.*

To rehearse. The (PI 201) thesis of the *Investigations* is that identity is paradox, called the rule, as neither of opposite cases + existing as both qua either.

Comment. Per PI 440: grammatically (lawfully), paradox faces are non-satisfaction cases qua distinct faces (cf. up/down aspects of a ladder) as well as are the satisfaction case qua paradox as their coincidence (cf. the ladder), and as well as are mutually satisfying/satisfied faces.

Games: paradox + faces; coincidence + distinct cases; satisfaction + mutually satisfying/satisfied cases; utterance (cf. like, want, wish) qua **this** + mutually eclipsing feeling/expression cases; per analogies, ladder + up/down aspects, drabbit + duck/rabbit faces.

441. By nature and by a particular training, a particular education, we are predisposed to express wishes in certain circumstances. (A wish is, of course, not such a 'circumstance'.) In this game, the question as to whether I know what I wish before my wish is fulfilled cannot arise at all. And the fact that some event stops my wishing does not mean that it fulfils it. Perhaps I wouldn't have been satisfied if my wish had been satisfied.

On the other hand, the word "wish" is also used in this way: "I don't know myself what I wish for." ("For wishes themselves are a veil between us and the thing wished for.")

Suppose someone asked, "Do I know what I long for before I get it?" If I have learned to talk, then I do.

To rehearse. The (PI 201) thesis of the *Investigations* is that identity is paradox, called the rule, as neither of opposite cases + existing as both qua either.

Comment. Per PI 441: whatever the logical-sense or the empirical sense of the text, it converts to grammatical qua lawful sense; the text questions if a wishing or longing-for case can stand alone; grammatically, the wishing-for aspect of a wish is to its wished-for aspect (cf. its enacted aspect, its fulfilled aspect); as a face of paradox is to its counterpart face.

Games: paradox + faces; wish + wishing-for/wished-for cases; longing + thinking/talking aspects; per analogies, ladder + up/down aspects, drabbit + duck/rabbit faces.

442. I see someone aiming a gun and say "I expect a bang". The shot is fired. – What! – was that what you expected? So did that bang somehow already exist in your expectation? Or is it just that your expectation agrees in some other respect with what occurred; that that noise was not contained in your expectation, and merely supervened as an accidental property when the expectation was being fulfilled? – But no, if the noise had not occurred, my expectation would not have been fulfilled; the noise fulfilled it; it was not an accompaniment of the fulfilment like a second guest accompanying the one I expected. Was the feature of the event that was not also in the expectation something accidental, an extra provided by fate? – But then, what was **not** an extra? Did something of the shot already occur in my expectation? – Then what *was* extra? for wasn't I expecting the whole shot.

"The bang was not as loud as I had expected." – "Then was there a louder bang in your expectation?"

To rehearse. The (PI 201) thesis of the *Investigations* is that identity is paradox, called the rule, as neither of opposite cases + existing as both qua either.

Comment. Per PI 442: logical and empirical talk converts to grammar (law sense) as follows: paradox is to faces; as expectation (cf. occurrence) is to verb/noun senses; as gunfire is to firing/report cases; as coincidence (cf. faces agreeing-with or contained-in or existing-in one another) is to distinct cases (cf. cases not contained in one another, together by fate, in accidental accompaniment, involving supervening fulfilment); by which, distinct faces as also coincidental faces cannot exist as entirely without one another.

Games: paradox faces; coincidence + distinct cases; gunfire + firing/fired cases; per analogies, ladder + up/down aspects, drabbit + duck/rabbit faces.

443. *"The red which you imagine is surely not the same (not the same thing) as the red which you see in front of you; so how can you say that it is what you imagined?" – But haven't we an analogous case with the sentences "Here is a red patch" and "Here there isn't a red patch". The word "red" occurs in both; so this word can't indicate the presence of something red.*

To rehearse. The (PI 201) thesis of the *Investigations* is that identity is paradox, called the rule, as neither of opposite cases + existing as both qua either.

Comment. Per PI 443: the grammar qua law sense is this; the imaginary/actual – isn't/is – cases of red are not one another in being distinct paradox-faces cases as well as are one another in being the coincidence case of red as a paradox case.

Games: paradox + faces; red patch + imaginary/real cases; (per PI 215) sameness + same/same cases cf. per analogies, ladder + up/down aspects, drabbit + duck/rabbit faces.

444. One may have the feeling that in the sentence "I expect he is coming" one is using the words "he is coming" in a different sense from the one they have in the assertion "He is coming". But if that were so, how could I say that my expectation had been fulfilled? If I wanted to explain the words "he" and "is coming", say by means of ostensive explanations, the same explanations of these words would go for both sentences.

But now one might ask: what does his coming look like? – The door opens, someone walks in, and so on. – What does my expecting him to come look like? – I walk up and down the room, look at the clock now and then, and so on. – But the one sequence of events has not the slightest similarity to the other! So how can one use the same words in describing them? – But then perhaps I say, as I walk up and down: "I expect he'll come in." – Now there is a similarity here. But of what kind?!

To rehearse. The (PI 201) thesis of the *Investigations* is that identity is paradox, called the rule, as neither of opposite cases + existing as both qua either.

Comment. Per PI 444: the grammar (law talk) presents in the following manner; paradox is to faces; as the he-is-coming expectation is to the expecting-he-is-coming/he-is-coming-as-expected cases; as per PI 215 sameness (similarity) is to same/same (similar/similar) cases cf. per analogy, drabbit is to duck/rabbit faces.

Games: paradox + faces; coincidence + distinct cases; he-is-coming + expectancy-talk/fulfilment-talk cases; per analogies, ladder + up/down aspects, drabbit + duck/rabbit faces.

445. It is in language that an expectation and its fulfilment make contact.

To rehearse. The (PI 201) thesis of the *Investigations* is that identity is paradox, called the rule, as neither of opposite cases + existing as both qua either.

Comment. Per PI 445: grammatically (lawfully), PI 43 states that the meaning of a word is its use; as per PI 445, the expecting aspect of a language of expectation is its expected (fulfilled) aspect; contact talk is paradox-case talk, coincidence talk.

Games: paradox + faces; coincidence + distinct cases; word + meaning/use cases; language + private/public cases; expectation + expecting/fulfilment cases; per analogies, ladder + up/down aspects, drabbit + duck/rabbit faces.

446. It would be odd to say: "A process looks different when it happens from when it doesn't happen." Or: "A red patch looks different when it is there from when it isn't there – but language abstracts from this difference, for it speaks of a red patch whether it is there or not."

To rehearse. The (PI 201) thesis of the *Investigations* is that identity is paradox, called the rule, as neither of opposite cases + existing as both qua either.

Comment. Per PI 446: the grammar qua law sense presents as follows; a paradox (cf. process, red patch) is as much an eclipsing (happening, present) case as it is an eclipsed (non-happening, absent) case.

Games: paradox + face; coincidence (process, red patch) + difference qua is/isn't happening-cases; per analogies, ladder + up/down aspects, drabbit + duck/rabbit faces.

447. The feeling is as if the negation of a proposition had first, in a certain sense, to make it true, in order to be able to negate it.

(The assertion of the negating proposition contains the proposition which is negated, but not the assertion of it.)

To rehearse. The (PI 201) thesis of the *Investigations* is that identity is paradox, called the rule, as neither of opposite cases + existing as both qua either.

Comment. Per PI 447: grammatically (lawfully), a paradox (cf. proposition) is as much an eclipsing (affirmation) case as it is an eclipsed (negation) case;

truth and falsehood alike are referenced to the proposition case; the assertion of a paradox (cf. proposition), as thereby also the assertion of its faces (cf. affirmation/negation cases), is the threefold grammar case.

Games: paradox + face; proposition + mutually eclipsing affirmation/negation cases; per analogies, ladder + up/down aspects, drabbit + duck/rabbit faces.

*448. "If I say I did **not** dream last night, still I must know where to look for a dream; that is, 'I dreamt', applied to this actual situation, may be false, but mustn't be nonsense." – Does that mean, then, that you did, after all, feel something, as it were the hint of a dream, which made you aware of the place which a dream would have occupied?*

Again, if I say "I have no pain in my arm", does that mean that I have a shadow of a sensation of pain, which, as it were, indicates the place where a pain could have been?

In what sense does my present painless state contain the possibility of pain?

If someone says, "For the word 'pain' to have a meaning, it is necessary that pain should be recognized as such when it occurs" – one can reply: "It is not more necessary than that the absence of pain should be recognized."

To rehearse. The (PI 201) thesis of the *Investigations* is that identity is paradox, called the rule, as neither of opposite cases + existing as both qua either.

Comment. Per PI 448: the grammar (law talk) is this; a paradox (cf. sleeps, pain) is as much an eclipsing (dreaming, present i.e. painful) case as it is an eclipsed (dreamless, absent i.e. pain-free) case.

Games: paradox (dream, pain) mutually eclipsing verb/noun senses; per analogies, ladder + up/down aspects, drabbit + duck/rabbit faces.

449. "But mustn't I know what it would be like if I were in pain?" – One can't shake oneself free of the idea that using a sentence consists in imagining something for every word.

*One fails to bear in mind the fact that one **calculates**, operates, with words, and in due course transforms them into this or that picture. – It is as if one believed that a written order for a cow, which someone is to hand over to me, always had to be accompanied by a mental image of a cow if the order was not to lose its sense.*

To rehearse. The (PI 201) thesis of the *Investigations* is that identity is paradox, called the rule, as neither of opposite cases + existing as both qua either.

Comment. Per PI 449: in terms of grammar qua law sense, picture talk is identity-as-paradox talk; empirical talk and experience are cases of raw material for grammatical treatment; grammatically, pain talk is to painful/pain-free talk; as paradox is to faces; as per PI 43, picture qua word, sentence, in terms, say of cow talk, is to meaning/use – mental image/ written-order – aspects.

Games: paradox + faces; word + meaning/use cases; picture + picturing/ pictured out-pictures; pain + presence/absence – what-is/what-could-be, affirmation/negation – aspects; cow + mental-process/written-order – imaging/imaged – aspects; per analogies, ladder + up/down aspects, drabbit + duck/rabbit faces.

*450. Knowing what someone looks like: being able to imagine it – but also: being able to **mimic** it. Need one imagine it in order to mimic it? And isn't mimicking it just as good as imagining it?*

To rehearse. The (PI 201) thesis of the *Investigations* is that identity is paradox, called the rule, as neither of opposite cases + existing as both qua either.

Comment. Per PI 450: grammatically (lawfully), a paradox-face case of a paradox case is its corresponding other paradox-face case; as a knowing aspect of a knowledge case is a known aspect; as an imagining aspect of imagination is its imagined aspect; as a mimicking aspect of mimicry is its mimicked aspect.

Games: paradox + faces; knowledge + knowing/known cases; imagination + imagining/imagined cases; mimicry + mimicking/mimicked cases i.e. copying/copied cases; per analogies, ladder + up/down aspects, drabbit + duck/rabbit faces.

451. What if I give someone the order "Imagine a red circle here" – and now I say: understanding the order means knowing what it is like for it to have been carried out – or even: being able to imagine what it is like ...?

To rehearse. The (PI 201) thesis of the *Investigations* is that identity is paradox, called the rule, as neither of opposite cases + existing as both qua either.

Comment. Per PI 451: for the grammar qua law sense, by PI 43, to mean a word is to uses the word, not to use a meaning; to understand an order X (= to imagine a red circle here) is to execute an order, not to execute an understanding; a paradox face counterparts a paradox face, not the paradox case.

Games: paradox + faces; word + meaning/use cases; order qua carry-out case + carrying-out/carried-out cases; understanding + verb/noun senses; knowledge + knowing/known cases; per analogies, ladder + up/down aspects, drabbit + duck/rabbit faces.

*452. I want to say: "If someone could see an expectation, the mental process, then he'd surely see **what** was being expected." – But that's just how it is: anyone who sees the expression of an expectation will see what is being expected. And in what other way, in what other sense, could one see it?*

To rehearse. The (PI 201) thesis of the *Investigations* is that identity is paradox, called the rule, as neither of opposite cases + existing as both qua either.

Comment. Per PI 452: the grammar (law talk) is this; per PI 43, the meaning of a word is its use; per PI 452, the expressing aspect of an expression case is its expressed aspect; the expecting aspect of an expectation case is its expected aspect.

Games: paradox + faces; word + meaning/use cases; expectation + expecting/expected − expecting/expression, mental-process/what's-expected − cases; per analogies, ladder + up/down aspects, drabbit + duck/rabbit faces.

*453. Anyone who perceived my expecting should perceive directly **what** was expected – that is, not **infer** it from the process he perceived! – But to say that someone perceives an expectation **makes no sense**. Unless it means something like: he perceives the manifestations of expectation. To say of an expectant person that he perceives his expectation, instead of saying "he expects" would be an idiotic distortion of the words.*

To rehearse. The (PI 201) thesis of the *Investigations* is that identity is paradox, called the rule, as neither of opposite cases + existing as both qua either.

Comment. Per PI 453: the grammar (law) presents as follows; the face of a paradox is its counterpart face; as per PI 43, the meaning of a word is its use; as the verb sense (cf. mental-process aspect) of a perception or expectation or manifestation is a noun sense (cf. behavioural aspect).

Games: paradox + faces; expectation and parallels + verb/noun senses; per analogies, ladder + up/down aspects, drabbit + duck/rabbit faces.

*454. "Everything is already there in ..." How does it come about that this arrow → à **points**? Doesn't it seem to carry within it something extraneous to itself? – "No, not the dead line on paper; only a mental thing, the meaning, can do that." – That is both true and false. The arrow points only in the application that a living creature makes of it.*

*This pointing is **not** a hocus-pocus that can be performed only by the mind.*

To rehearse. The (PI 201) thesis of the *Investigations* is that identity is paradox, called the rule, as neither of opposite cases + existing as both qua either.

Comment. Per PI 454: grammatically (lawfully), the pointing case is to its verb/noun senses; as paradox is to faces; as per PI 43, word is to meaning/use (meaning/application) – contained-within/extraneous, it/itself, mental/behavioural, mind/enactment, living/dead, meaning/matter – cases; from which, each paradox-face case is as true as it is false, as eclipsing in function as eclipsed; the pointing case qua paradox case is not merely exhibited by the pointing qua verb-sense aspect (cf. mind) but by the pointing/pointing qua verb-sense/noun-sense paradox-face cases in tandem; such is the grammar as thus not hocus pocus qua ungrammatical.

Games: paradox + faces; arrow qua pointing case + meaning/behaviour aspects where each aspect is as presenting (eclipsing) as it is non-presenting (eclipsed) i.e. as truly pointing as it is falsely punting; per analogies, ladder + up/down aspects, drabbit + duck/rabbit faces.

455. We are inclined to say: "When we mean something, there is no dead picture here (no matter of what kind), but, rather, it's like going towards someone." We go towards the thing we mean.

To rehearse. The (PI 201) thesis of the *Investigations* is that identity is paradox, called the rule, as neither of opposite cases + existing as both qua either.

Comment. Per PI 455: the grammar qua law sense reads as follows; by PI 43, word meaning goes up to – is referenced to – word use; as face of paradox is paradoxically its counterpart face; as picture is to picturing/pictured cases.

Games: paradox + faces; word + meaning/use – cf. meaning/matter, living/dead – cases; picture + out-pictures; per analogies, ladder + up/down aspects, drabbit + duck/rabbit faces.

456. "When one means something, it is oneself that means"; so one sets oneself in motion. One rushes ahead, and so cannot also observe one's rushing ahead. Indeed not.

To rehearse. The (PI 201) thesis of the *Investigations* is that identity is paradox, called the rule, as neither of opposite cases + existing as both qua either.

Comment. Per PI 456: the grammar (law sense) is this; oneself is means use cases; as paradox is face as counterpart face; as observation, like motion, like a rushing-ahead case, is verb/noun senses.

Games: paradox + faces; per PI 43, word + meaning/use cases; movement + verb/noun – rushing/observed – aspects; per analogies, ladder + up/down aspects, drabbit + duck/rabbit faces.

457. Yes, meaning something is like going towards someone.

To rehearse. The (PI 201) thesis of the *Investigations* is that identity is paradox, called the rule, as neither of opposite cases + existing as both qua either.

Comment. Per PI 457: grammatically (lawfully), from PI 43, word meaning goes towards – is referenced to – word use; as face of paradox is referenced to its counterpart face.

Games: paradox + faces; word + meaning/use cases; per analogies, ladder + up/down aspects, drabbit + duck/rabbit faces.

*458. "An order orders its own execution." So it knows its execution before it is even there? – But that was a grammatical proposition, and it says: if an order runs "Do such-and-such", then **doing such-and-such** is called "executing the order".*

To rehearse. The (PI 201) thesis of the *Investigations* is that identity is paradox, called the rule, as neither of opposite cases + existing as both qua either.

Comment. Per 458: in terms of grammar qua law sense; the face of a paradox case is its corresponding other face; as, per PI 43, the meaning of a word is its use; as, per PI 458, the ordering ('Do X') aspect of an order is its ('Doing X') executed aspect; as the coincidental aspect of a coincidence case is its other coincidental aspect.

Games: paradox + faces; order + ordering/ordered cases i.e. ordering/executed cases; per analogies, ladder + up/down aspects, drabbit + duck/rabbit faces.

*459. We say "The order orders **this**", and do it; but also: "The order orders this: I am to ..." We translate it at one time into a sentence, at another into a demonstration, and at another into action.*

To rehearse. The (PI 201) thesis of the *Investigations* is that identity is paradox, called the rule, as neither of opposite cases + existing as both qua either.

Comment. Per PI 459: the text presents its grammar (law sense) as follows; the this-case is an identity-as-paradox case; its threefold grammar of identity-as-paradox + identical faces is the threefold case of order + ordering/ordered cases.

Games: paradox + faces; **this** + ordering/ordered – ordering/action, order/demonstration – cases; per analogies, ladder + up/down aspects, drabbit + duck/rabbit faces.

460. Could a justification of an action as the execution of an order run like this: "You said 'Bring me a yellow flower', whereupon this flower gave me a feeling of satisfaction; that's why I've brought it"? Wouldn't one have to reply: "But I didn't tell you to bring me a flower that would give you that sort of feeling in response to my words!"?

To rehearse. The (PI 201) thesis of the *Investigations* is that identity is paradox, called the rule, as neither of opposite cases + existing as both qua either.

Comment. Per PI 460: by PI 43, the meaning of a wordage is its use; grammatically (lawfully) – neither logically nor empirically – the meaning of the "Bring me a flower" wordage is not the usage "Bring me a yellow flower" nor "Bring me a satisfying flower"; from which, the alien usage cases do not justify qua warrant either the "Bring me a flower" wordage nor its meaning; paradox is to faces; as word is to meaning/use cases; as "Bring me a flower" qua order is to bringing/brought (bringing/enactment) cases qua ordering/ordered (ordering/enactment) cases.

Games: paradox + faces; word + meaning/use cases; order + ordering/ordered cases; bringing (a flower) + verb/noun senses; per analogies, ladder + up/down aspects, drabbit + duck/rabbit faces.

461. *In what sense does an order anticipate its fulfilment? – By now ordering **just that** which later on is carried out? – But this would surely have to run: "which later on is carried out, or again is not carried out". And that says nothing.*

"But even if my wish does not determine what is going to be the case, still it does, so to speak, determine the theme of a fact, no matter whether such a fact fulfils the wish or not." We are, as it were, surprised, not at someone's knowing the future, but at his being able to prophesy at all (right or wrong).

As if the mere prophecy, no matter whether true or false, foreshadowed the future; whereas it knows nothing of the future and cannot know less than nothing.

To rehearse. The (PI 201) thesis of the *Investigations* is that identity is paradox, called the rule, as neither of opposite cases + existing as both qua either.

Comment. Per PI 461: the grammar qua law sense is this; whatever the paradox case (prophecy, foreshadowing, anticipation, wish, order, fulfilment, satisfaction) its faces as verb/sense cases – cf. present/future cases, foretelling/foretold cases – are unconnected qua distinct cases as well as are connected qua coincidental cases cf. per paradox, drabbit +

duck/rabbit faces; each face (each sense) is an eclipsing/eclipsed – is/is-not, right/wrong, true/false – face.

Games: paradox + faces; prophecy + verb/noun senses (and variants, as per the Comment); per analogies, ladder + up/down aspects, drabbit + duck/rabbit faces.

462. I can look for him when he is not there, but not hang him when he is not there.

One might want to say: "But he must be around, if I am looking for him." – Then he must also be around if I don't find him, and even if he doesn't exist at all.

To rehearse. The (PI 201) thesis of the *Investigations* is that identity is paradox, called the rule, as neither of opposite cases + existing as both qua either.

Comment. Per PI 462: whatever the empirical sense or nonsense to do with looking for someone or hanging someone, the grammatical (lawful) threefold case is that of paradox + faces as the threefold case of look-for + looking-for/looked-for aspects, also hang + hanging/hanged aspects.

Games: paradox + faces (an variants, as per the Comment); per analogies, ladder + up/down aspects, drabbit + duck/rabbit faces.

*463. "You were looking for **him**? You couldn't even have known if he was there!" – But this problem **really does** arise when one looks for something in mathematics. One can ask, for example, how was it possible so much as to **look** for the trisection of an angle?*

To rehearse. The (PI 201) thesis of the *Investigations* is that identity is paradox, called the rule, as neither of opposite cases + existing as both qua either.

Comment. Per PI 463: to look for something – whether a person or the trisection of an angle – is grammatically (lawfully) a looking-for case as paradoxically a looked-for caser.

Games: paradox + faces; look-for + looking-for/locked-for cases; per analogies, ladder + up/down aspects, drabbit + duck/rabbit faces.

464. What I want to teach is: to pass from unobvious nonsense to obvious nonsense.

To rehearse. The (PI 201) thesis of the *Investigations* is that identity is paradox, called the rule, as neither of opposite cases + existing as both qua either.

Comment. Per PI 464: grammatically (lawfully), paradox is to faces; as per PI 43, word is to meaning/use cases; as nonsense is to unobvious/obvious cases.

Games: paradox + faces; word + meaning/use cases; nonsense + unobvious/obvious cases; per analogies, ladder + up/down aspects, drabbit + duck/rabbit faces.

465. "An expectation is so made that whatever happens has to accord with it, or not.

"If someone now asks: then is what is the case determined, give or take a yes or no, by an expectation or not – that is, is it determined in what sense the expectation would be satisfied by an event, no matter what happens? – then one has to reply: "Yes, unless the expression of the expectation is indefinite, for example, if it contains a disjunction of different possibilities."

To rehearse. The (PI 201) thesis of the *Investigations* is that identity is paradox, called the rule, as neither of opposite cases + existing as both qua either.

Comment. Per PI 465: the grammar (law sense) of the text is this; an expectation case, like a satisfaction case, as a paradox case, has its verb/noun senses – cf. meaning/expression aspects – qua paradox faces, each sense qua face as an eclipsing/eclipsed – accordant/conflicting, yes/no – case; here the faces as mutually eclipsing thereby are mutually determinative; from which, the either/or (eclipsing/eclipsed, determining/determined) face of paradox is its or/either (eclipsed/eclipsing, determined/determining) face .

Games: paradox + faces; expectation + expecting/expected aspects; per analogies, ladder + up/down aspects, drabbit + duck/rabbit faces.

*466. What does man think for? What is it good for? – Why does he make boilers according to **calculations**, and not leave the thickness of their walls to chance? After all, it is only a fact of experience that boilers made according to these calculations do not explode so often. But, just as having once been burnt, he would do anything rather than put his hand into a fire, so too he would do anything rather than not calculate for a boiler. – However, since we are not interested in causes, we shall say: human beings do in fact think: this is how they proceed, for example, when they make a boiler. – Now, can't a boiler produced in this way explode? Oh, yes.*

To rehearse. The (PI 201) thesis of the *Investigations* is that identity is paradox, called the rule, as neither of opposite cases + existing as both qua either.

Comment. Per PI 466 whatever the empirical-sense talk, such as to do with experience or causality, the grammatical (lawful) threefold talk of paradox + faces is the PI 466 talk of language + thinking/expression aspects.

Games: paradox + faces; per 43, word + meaning/use cases; human life + thinking/doing aspects; per analogies, ladder + up/down aspects, drabbit + duck/rabbit faces.

467. Does man think, then, because he has found that thinking pays? – Because he thinks it advantageous to think?

(Does he bring his children up because he has found it pays?)

To rehearse. The (PI 201) thesis of the *Investigations* is that identity is paradox, called the rule, as neither of opposite cases + existing as both qua either.

Comment. Per PI 467: whatever the empirical-sense talk, such as to do with experience or causality, the grammatical (lawful) threefold talk of paradox +

faces is the PI 467 talk of thinking + thinking/thinking – verb-sense/noun-sense – cases.

Games: paradox + faces; thinking + thinking/thinking – verb-sense/noun-sense, thinking/expression – cases; per analogies, child-rearing + verb/noun senses; per other analogies, ladder + up/down aspects, drabbit + duck/rabbit faces.

*468. How could one find out **why** he thinks?*

To rehearse. The (PI 201) thesis of the *Investigations* is that identity is paradox, called the rule, as neither of opposite cases + existing as both qua either.

Comment. Per PI 468: to discover why a man thinks is to (grammatically qua lawfully) understand that his thinking (verb sense) is paradoxically his thinking (noun sense); paradox is to faces; as per PI 43, word is to meaning/use cases; as thinking is to thinking/thinking – verb-sense/noun-sense, thinking/expression, thinking/doing – cases.

Games: paradox + faces; coincidence + distinct cases; word + meaning/use cases; thinking + thinking/thinking – verb-sense/noun-sense (and parallels) – cases; per analogies, ladder + up/down aspects, drabbit + duck/rabbit faces.

469. And yet one may say that thinking has been found to pay. That there are fewer boiler explosions than there used to be, now that we no longer go by hunches in deciding the thickness of the walls, but make such-and-such calculations instead. Or, ever since each calculation done by one engineer got checked by another.

To rehearse. The (PI 201) thesis of the *Investigations* is that identity is paradox, called the rule, as neither of opposite cases + existing as both qua either.

Comment. Per PI 469: rather than empirical talk of engineering, the grammatical (lawful) talk is threefold as that of paradox + faces as the threefold case of thinking + thinking/thinking – verb-sense/noun-sense – cases.

Games: paradox + face; thinking + thinking/thinking – verb-sense/noun-sense – cases; per analogies, ladder + up/down aspects, drabbit + duck/rabbit faces.

*470. So **sometimes** one thinks because it has been found to pay.*

To rehearse. The (PI 201) thesis of the *Investigations* is that identity is paradox, called the rule, as neither of opposite cases + existing as both qua either.

Comment. Per PI 470: whether or not it has been found by experience that thinking pays, whether always or even sometimes, the grammatical threefold case – threefold lawful; case – is that of paradox + faces as the threefold case of thinking + thinking/thinking – verb-sense/noun-sense – cases.

Games: paradox + face; thinking + thinking/thinking – verb-sense/noun-sense, thinking/expression, thinking/doing – cases; per analogies, ladder + up/down aspects, drabbit + duck/rabbit faces.

471. Often it is only when we suppress the question "Why?" that we become aware of those important facts, which then, in the course of our investigations, lead to an answer.

To rehearse. The (PI 201) thesis of the *Investigations* is that identity is paradox, called the rule, as neither of opposite cases + existing as both qua either.

Comment. Per PI 471: grammatically (lawfully), logic and experience, considered as paradox faces, facilitate grasping identity as paradox rather than onefold-only consistency sense: paradox is to faces; as per PI 43, word is to meaning/use – logical/empirical – cases.

Games: paradox + faces; per PI 43, word + meaning/use – logical/empirical – cases; per analogies, ladder + up/down aspects, drabbit + duck/rabbit faces.

*472. The character of the belief in the uniformity of nature can perhaps be seen most clearly in the case in which what is expected is something we fear. Nothing could induce me to put my hand into a flame – even though it is **only in the past** that I have burnt myself.*

To rehearse. The (PI 201) thesis of the *Investigations* is that identity is paradox, called the rule, as neither of opposite cases + existing as both qua either.

Comment. Per PI 472: grammatically (lawfully) – not logically, not empirically – uniformity talk is identity-as-paradox talk (see PI 208); by which, fire causally qua paradoxically burns; paradox is to faced; as present is to past/future cases; as fire is to has-burnt/will-burn cases; as uniformity is to cause/effect cases; here, the case of what has been is causally qua paradoxically the case of what will be.

Games: paradox + faces; uniformity + cause/effect cases; present qua coincidence + past/future cases qua distinct cases; per PI 215 sameness + same/ same cases; per analogies, ladder + up/down aspects, drabbit + duck/rabbit faces.

473. The belief that fire will burn me is of the same kind as the fear that it will burn me.

To rehearse. The (PI 201) thesis of the *Investigations* is that identity is paradox, called the rule, as neither of opposite cases + existing as both qua either.

Comment. Per PI 473: in terms of grammar qua law sense, a face of a paradox case is a corresponding other face; as per PI 43, the meaning of a word is its use; as the verb-sense aspect of fire, or burning, or believing, or fearing, is its noun-sense aspect.

Games: paradox + faces; word (fire qua burning, belief, fear) + meaning/use – verb-sense/noun-sense cases; per analogies, ladder + up/down aspects, drabbit + duck/rabbit faces.

474. I shall get burnt if I put my hand in the fire – that is certainty.

That is to say, here we see what certainty means. (Not just the meaning of the word "certainty" but also what certainty amounts to.)

To rehearse. The (PI 201) thesis of the *Investigations* is that identity is paradox, called the rule, as neither of opposite cases + existing as both qua either.

Comment. Per PI 474: the empirical-sense fire talk converts for its grammar (law) as follows; paradox is to faces; as fire is to burning/burning – verb/noun, cf. cause/effect – cases; from which, the paradox-face cases, per each language game, are certainly one another qua being paradoxically one another cf. per analogy, the up/down aspects of a ladder qua paradox case, and where the certainty case is the paradox case.

Games: paradox + faces; per PI 43, word + meaning/use cases; certainty + certainly-connected cases; culture + language/deed cases; fire + causal-burning/burning-effect cases; per analogies, ladder + up/down aspects, drabbit + duck/rabbit faces.

475. On being asked for the reasons for a supposition, one calls them to mind. Does the same thing happen here as when one considers what may have been the causes of an event?

To rehearse. The (PI 201) thesis of the *Investigations* is that identity is paradox, called the rule, as neither of opposite cases + existing as both qua either.

Comment. Per PI 475: in terms of grammar qua law sense, a reason for a supposition, like a cause for an event, is a paradox face referenced to a counterpart face.

Games: paradox + faces; word + meaning/use – cf. reason/supposition, cause/effect, logical-sense/empirical-sense – cases; per analogies, ladder + up/down aspects, drabbit + duck/rabbit faces.

476. A distinction should be made between the object of fear and the cause of fear.

So a face which inspires fear or delight (the object of fear or delight) is not on that account its cause, but – one might say – its target.

To rehearse. The (PI 201) thesis of the *Investigations* is that identity is paradox, called the rule, as neither of opposite cases + existing as both qua either.

Comment. Per PI 476: the grammar (law talk) presents as follows; fearfulness or delight (cf. face, event, target) is to fearing/feared or delighting-in/delighted-in (cause/effect, targeting/targeted) cases; as paradox is to faces; as per PI 43, word is to meaning/use – subject/object – cases.

Games: paradox + faces; word (fear, delight, target) + meaning/expression – verb-sense/noun-sense, subject/object, cause/effect – cases; per analogies, ladder + up/down aspects, drabbit + duck/rabbit faces.

477. "Why do you believe that you will burn yourself on the hotplate?" – Have you reasons for this belief, and do you need reasons?

To rehearse. The (PI 201) thesis of the *Investigations* is that identity is paradox, called the rule, as neither of opposite cases + existing as both qua either.

Comment. Per PI 477: grammatically (lawfully), there is a believing (or reasoning) case because there is a believed (or reasoned) case.

Games: paradox (belief, reason) + faces (believing/believed, reasoning/reasoned cases); per PI 43, word + meaning/use cases; per analogies, ladder + up down aspects, drabbit + duck/rabbit faces.

478. What kind of reason have I to assume that my finger will feel a resistance when it touches the table? What kind of reason for believing that this pencil will not pierce my hand without hurting it? — When I ask this, a hundred reasons present themselves, each drowning out the voice of the others. "But I have experienced it myself innumerable times, often heard of similar experiences; if it were not so, it would ...; and so forth."

To rehearse. The (PI 201) thesis of the *Investigations* is that identity is paradox, called the rule, as neither of opposite cases + existing as both qua either.

Comment. Per PI 478: for the grammar qua law sense, the reason for anything is its expression.

Games: paradox (reason, belief, assumption) + (verb-sense/noun-sense) faces i.e. reason + reasoning/reasoned, reasoning/expression, cases (and parallels); per PI 43, word + meaning/use cases; per analogies, ladder + up down aspects, drabbit + duck/rabbit faces.

479. The question "For what reasons do you believe this?" might mean: "From what reasons are you now deriving it (have you just derived it)?" But it might also mean: "With hindsight, what reasons can you give me for this

To rehearse. The (PI 201) thesis of the *Investigations* is that identity is paradox, called the rule, as neither of opposite cases + existing as both qua either.

Comment. Per PI 479: grammatically (lawfully), reasons for belief, whether as a talk giving out in logical terms, empirical terms, or everyday-discourse terms, presents grammatically as the threefold talk of reason for belief + verb-sense/noun-sense – reasoning/expression – talk.

Games: paradox + faces; per PI 43, word + meaning/use cases; reason (whether logical or empirical for, say, belief) + reasoning/reasoned cases; per analogies, ladder + up down aspects, drabbit + duck/rabbit faces.

*480. So one could actually take "reasons" for a belief to mean only what a person had said to himself before he arrived at the belief – the calculation that he actually carried out. If someone now asks, "But how **can** previous experience be a reason for the supposition that such-and-such will occur later on?", the answer is: What general concept have we of reasons for this kind of supposition? This sort of statement about the past is simply what we call a reason for supposing that this will happen in the future. – And if one is surprised at our playing such a game, I appeal to the **effect** of a past experience (to the fact that a burnt child fears the fire).*

To rehearse. The (PI 201) thesis of the *Investigations* is that identity is paradox, called the rule, as neither of opposite cases + existing as both qua either.

Comment. Per PI 480: the grammar qua law sense – in terms of assorted language games, each as a threefold grammar case – is this: a past aspect of a present case is its future aspect; as a reasoning (cf. self-talk) aspect of a reason case is its reasoned (cf. expression) aspect; as a believing aspect of a belief cased is its believed aspect; as a mental-process aspect of a belief case is its enactment aspect; as a supposing aspect of a supposition case is its supposed aspect; as a face of paradox is its corresponding other face; as a causal aspect of a nexus is its effected case.

Games: paradox + faces; per PI 43, word + meaning/use cases; reason + reasoning/reasoned – reasoning/expression – cases; nexus + cause/effect cases; belief + believing/believed cases; supposition + supposing/supposed cases; present fear + past/later-on fear-cases; talk + self/public talk-cases; calculation + calculating/calculated cases; per analogies, ladder + up down aspects, drabbit + duck/rabbit faces.

*481. If anyone said that information about the past couldn't convince him that something would happen in the future, I wouldn't understand him. One might ask him: What do you expect to be told, then? What sort of information do you call a reason for believing this? What do you call "convincing"? In what kind of way do you expect to be convinced? – If **these** are not reasons, then what are* reasons? – *If you say that these are not reasons, then you must surely be able to state what must be the case for us to be warranted in saying that there are reasons for our supposition.*

For note: here reasons are not propositions which logically imply what is believed.

But it is not as if one can say: less is needed for belief than for knowledge. – For this is not a matter of approximating to logical consequence.

To rehearse. The (PI 201) thesis of the *Investigations* is that identity is paradox, called the rule, as neither of opposite cases + existing as both qua either.

Comment. Per PI 481: logical-sense talk, like empirical-sense talk, converts for its grammar (law sense) as follows; the past aspect of a present case is its future aspect; as a reasoning aspect of a reason case is its reasoned aspect; as a convincing aspect of a conviction case is its convinced aspect; as a face of paradox is its counterpart face; as an informing aspect of an information case is its informed aspect; as a believing aspect of a belief case is its believed aspect; as a supposing aspect of a supposition case is its supposed aspect; whatever the threefold grammar qua games talk, each of its three members being the case warrants the other members being the case in that all three inhabit one another cf. per analogy the duck face of drabbit is its rabbit face, also the ascent aspect of a ladder is its descent aspect.

Games: paradox + faces (and variants, as peer the Comment); per analogies, ladder + up down aspects, drabbit + duck/rabbit faces.

482. We are misled by this way of putting it: "This is a good reason, for it makes the occurrence of the event probable" That is as if we had said something further about the reason, something which justified it as a reason; whereas to say that this reason makes the occurrence probable is to say nothing except that this reason comes up to a particular standard of good reasons – but that the standard has no ground.

To rehearse. The (PI 201) thesis of the *Investigations* is that identity is paradox, called the rule, as neither of opposite cases + existing as both qua either.

Comment. Per PI 483: grammatically (lawfully), paradox is to faces; as good (particular case, event, occurrence) is to reason/outcome – reason/probability – cases; as otherwise an ungrammatical case saying nothing because without ground qua justification there is the perspective (standard) of a good-reason case alongside – and not paradoxically – a good-outcome case cf. per analogy, drabbit-duck/drabbit-rabbit faces as not justified – not bonded paradoxically.

Games: paradox + faces; good + reason/outcome cases; per analogies, ladder + up down.

*483. A good reason is one that looks **like this**.*

To rehearse. The (PI 201) thesis of the *Investigations* is that identity is paradox, called the rule, as neither of opposite cases + existing as both qua either.

Comment. Per PI 483: referenced to the previous text, the grammar qua law sense is this: **this**-talk, like good-talk, is identity-as-paradox talk; paradox is to faces; as good is to reason/outcome cases; as **this** is to reason/outcome cases.

Games: paradox + faces; good, like **this** + reason + reason/outcome cases; per analogies, ladder + up down aspects, drabbit + duck/rabbit faces.

*484. One would like to say: "It is a good reason only because it makes the occurrence **really** probable." Because it, so to speak, really has an influence on the event; as it were an empirical one.*

To rehearse. The (PI 201) thesis of the *Investigations* is that identity is paradox, called the rule, as neither of opposite cases + existing as both qua either.

Comment. Per PI 484: further to the previous two texts, the grammar qua law sense – as the translation of empirical sense – is this; paradox is to faces; as good qua event, occurrence is to reason/outcome – reason/probability, reason/reality – cases; the reason paradox face influences – makes for – the event case, the good case, the paradox case, by being a counterpart for the outcome paradox face.

Games: paradox + faces; good (event, occurrence) + + reason/outcome – reason/probability, reason/reality – cases; per analogies, ladder + up/down aspects, drabbit + duck/rabbit faces.

485. Justification by experience comes to an end. If it did not, it would not be justification.

To rehearse. The (PI 201) thesis of the *Investigations* is that identity is paradox, called the rule, as neither of opposite cases + existing as both qua either.

Comment. Per PI 485: justification by experience comes to an end i.e. is ungrammatical in that the grammatical (lawful) case is that of justification by paradox; here, per analogy, the ladder's way-up is its way down not because it is experienced as being the case but because the up/down aspects are bonded paradoxically; given the one, thereby the other.

Games: paradox + faces; per PI 43, word + meaning/use cases; per analogies, ladder + up/down aspects, drabbit + duck/rabbit faces. r

*486. Does it **follow** from the sense impressions which I get that there is a chair over there? – How can a **proposition** follow from sense impressions? Well, does it follow from the propositions which describe the sense impressions? No. – But don't I infer that a chair is there from impressions, from sense-data? – I make no inference! – and yet I sometimes do. I see a photograph, for example, and say "So there must have been a chair over there", or again, "From what one can see here, I infer that there is a chair over there". That is an inference; but not one belonging to logic. An inference is* a transition to an assertion; and so also to the behaviour that corresponds to the assertion. 'I draw the consequences' not only in words, but also on deeds.

Was I justified in drawing these consequences? What is **called** a justification here? – How is the word "justification" used? Describe language-games! From these you will also be able to see the importance of being justified.

To rehearse. The (PI 201) thesis of the *Investigations* is that identity is paradox, called the rule, as neither of opposite cases + existing as both qua either.

Comment. Per PI 486: the grammar qua law talk is as follows; chair-sensing is to sensed-chair; as paradox face is to counterpart face; as mental-process is to reality; as thinking qua inferring (from another's behaviour) is to assertion qua inferred (the other's mental state; as per PI 43, word-meaning qua sentence-meaning is to word-use qua sentence-use; as the verb sense of transition is to its noun sense; from which, justification qua warrant obtains per each threefold language game (paradox + faces – and variants) in that all three members inhabit one another cf. ladder + up/down aspects such that any of the three members as the cases justifies (warrants) the other two members being the case.

Games: paradox + faces (and variants as per Comment; justification + mutually justifying cases; per analogies, ladder + up/down aspects, drabbit + duck/rabbit faces.

487. "I'm leaving the room because you tell me to."

"I'm leaving the room, but not because you tell me to."

Does this sentence **describe** a connection between my action and his order; or does it make the connection?

Can one ask: "How do you know that you do it because of this, or not because of this?" And is the answer perhaps: "I feel it"?

To rehearse. The (PI 201) thesis of the *Investigations* is that identity is paradox, called the rule, as neither of opposite cases + existing as both qua either.

Comment. Per PI 487: the sentence as a description is a threefold case of grammar (law); by which, connection is to connected cases; as paradox is to faces; as order is to ordering/behaviour aspects; the aspects are and are not connected in that they are paradoxically – not consistently, not contradictorily – connected.

Games: paradox + this/that faces; order + instruction/reaction cases; per analogies, ladder + up/down aspects, drabbit + duck/rabbit faces.

488. How do I judge whether it is so? By circumstantial evidence?

To rehearse. The (PI 201) thesis of the *Investigations* is that identity is paradox, called the rule, as neither of opposite cases + existing as both qua either.

Comment. Per PI 488: one judges it is so grammatically (lawfully) whereby judgement is to it/so cases; as paradox is to faces.

Games: paradox + faces; judgement + it/so cases; per analogies, ladder + up/down aspects, drabbit + duck/rabbit faces.

489. Ask yourself: On what occasion, for what purpose, do we say this?

What kinds of action accompany these words? (Think of a greeting.) In what kinds of setting will they be used; and what for?

To rehearse. The (PI 201) thesis of the *Investigations* is that identity is paradox, called the rule, as neither of opposite cases + existing as both qua either.

Comment. Per PI 489: the circumstance qua setting for word-meaning/word-use cases, or for language/deed cases, is grammatical (lawful); here, paradox is to faces; as word is to meaning/use cases; as culture is to language/deed cases.

Games: paradox + faces; per PI 43, word (greeting, say) + meaning/use – mental/behavioural – cases; culture + language/deed cases; per analogies, ladder + up/down aspects, drabbit + duck/rabbit faces.

490. How do I know that **this train of thought** has led me to this action? – Well, it is a particular picture: for example, of a calculation leading to a further experiment in an experimental investigation. It looks like **this** – and now I could describe an example.

To rehearse. The (PI 201) thesis of the *Investigations* is that identity is paradox, called the rule, as neither of opposite cases + existing as both qua either.

Comment. Per PI 490: in terms of grammar qua law sense; thinking leads to talking in that the two cases are paradoxically each other.

Games: paradox + faces; per PI 43, word + meaning/use – thinking/talking, calculation/experimentation – cases; particular case qua picture qua **this** + paired opposites; **this** + examples; **this** + look-alike cases cf. PI 215 sameness + same/same cases, per analogies ladder + up/down aspects, drabbit + duck/rabbit faces.

491. Not: "without language we could not communicate with one another" – but for sure: without language we cannot influence other human beings in such-and-such ways; cannot build roads and machines, and so on. And also: without the use of speech and writing, human beings could not communicate.

To rehearse. The (PI 201) thesis of the *Investigations* is that identity is paradox, called the rule, as neither of opposite cases + existing as both qua either.

Comment. Per PI 491: the grammar (law) reads as follows; paradox is to faces; as communication is to communicants; as human culture is to language/deed cases; as per PI 43, word is to meaning/use cases; from which, there is no paradox face without its counterpart face; likewise, there is no language case without its deed case; per analogy, there is no way-up aspect of a ladder without this as a paradoxically way-down aspect.

Games: paradox + faces; communication + communicants; culture + language/deed cases; word + meaning/use cases; per analogies, ladder + up/down aspects, drabbit + duck/rabbit faces.

492. To invent a language could mean to invent a device for a particular purpose on the basis of the laws of nature (or consistently with them); but it also has the other sense, analogous to that in which we speak of the invention of a game.

Here I am saying something about the grammar of the word "language", by connecting it with the grammar of the word "invent".

To rehearse. The (PI 201) thesis of the *Investigations* is that identity is paradox, called the rule, as neither of opposite cases + existing as both qua either.

Comment. Per PI 492: per nature, mind is to body; as per particular case, point or purpose is to enactment; as per language qua wordage, meaning is to use; as per game, move-making case is to made-move cases; as per invention, inventing aspect is to invented aspect; here the assorted language games qua cases of grammar (law) show that the language case and the invention case are connected as variant paradox-case cases.

Games: paradox + faces (and variants, as per the Comment); per analogies, ladder + up/down aspects, drabbit + duck/rabbit faces.

493. One says, "The cock calls the hens by crowing" – but isn't all this already based on a comparison with our language? – Don't we see all this quite differently if we imagine the crowing to set the hens in motion by some kind of physical causation?

*But if it were shown how the words "Come to me" act on the person addressed so that, finally, given certain conditions, the muscles of his legs are innervated, and so on – would that sentence thereby lose the character of a **sentence** for us?*

To rehearse. The (PI 201) thesis of the *Investigations* is that identity is paradox, called the rule, as neither of opposite cases + existing as both qua either.

Comment. Per PI 493: the grammar qua law sense is this; language is as much to do with logical sense as with empirical sense; from which, where the sentence case as a paradox case loses its character of grammar is where either of the logical/empirical cases – cf. cock-call/hen-bedlam, order/muscle-motion – obtain alone.

Games: paradox + faces; per PI 43, word qua language + meaning/use – logical-sense/empirical-sense – cases; per analogies, ladder + up/down aspects, drabbit + duck/rabbit faces.

*494. I want to say: it is **above all** the apparatus of our ordinary language, of our word-language, that we call "language"; and then other things by analogy or comparability with it.*

To rehearse. The (PI 201) thesis of the *Investigations* is that identity is paradox, called the rule, as neither of opposite cases + existing as both qua either.

Comment. Per PI 494: grammatically (lawfully), paradox is to faces; as per PI 43, word is to meaning/use cases – which threefold case is primarily (cf. Above all) called language; as culture is to language/deed cases; here, the language games are variants (as analogously, comparably) of the threefold grammar of identity-as-paradox + identical faces.

Games: paradox + faces; per PI 43, word + meaning/use cases; culture + language/deed cases; per analogies, ladder + up/down aspects, drabbit + duck/rabbit faces.

495. Clearly, I can establish by experience that a human being (or animal) reacts to one sign as I want him to, and to another not. That, for example, a human being goes to the right at the sign " → à " – and goes to the left at the sign "ß → "; but does not react to the sign "o → " as to " ← m", and so on.

I don't even need to make up a case, I just have to consider what is actually so: namely, that I can direct a person who has learned only English, only by using English. (For here I am looking at learning English as adjusting a mechanism to respond to a certain kind of influence; and it may be all one to us whether someone has learned the language, or was perhaps from birth constituted to react to sentences in English like a normal person who has learned English.)

To rehearse. The (PI 201) thesis of the *Investigations* is that identity is paradox, called the rule, as neither of opposite cases + existing as both qua either.

Comment. Per PI 495: grammatically (lawfully), paradox (neutral arrow) is to faces (left/right arrows); as per PI 43, word qua language (say, English) is to meaning/use cases and as culture is to language/deed cases; as per mechanism (cf. threefold grammar), adjustment (balancing) is to influence/response cases.

Games: paradox + faces; per whatever the language construction, word + meaning/use cases; per analogies, ladder + up/down aspects, drabbit + duck/rabbit faces.

496. Grammar does not tell us how language must be constructed in order to fulfil its purpose, in order to have such-and-such an effect on human beings. It only describes, and in no way explains, the use of signs.

To rehearse. The (PI 201) thesis of the *Investigations* is that identity is paradox, called the rule, as neither of opposite cases + existing as both qua either.

Comment. Per PI 496: from PI 495, grammar (law) qua the threefold case of paradox + faces (and variants) describes, and neither prescribes nor explains, each language case, whatever its construction.

Games: paradox + faces; per whatever the language construction, word + meaning/use – logical/empirical, prescriptive/explanatory – cases; per analogies, ladder + up/down aspects, drabbit + duck/rabbit faces.

*497. The rules of grammar may be called "arbitrary", if that is to mean that the **purpose** of grammar is nothing but that of language.*

*If someone says, "If our language had not this grammar, it could not express these facts" – it should be asked what "**could**" means here.*

To rehearse. The (PI 201) thesis of the *Investigations* is that identity is paradox, called the rule, as neither of opposite cases + existing as both qua either.

Comment. Per PI 497: the grammar qua law sense is this; the interpretation of rule is its counterpart interpretation; the purposeful aspect of language is its arbitrary aspect; as the logical sense of could is its empirical sense; as the expressing aspect of facticity is its expressed aspect.

Games: paradox + faces; rule + interpretations; per PI 43, word + meaning/use cases; language + private/public – logical/empirical, purposeful/arbitrary – cases; per analogies, ladder + up/down aspects, drabbit + duck/ rabbit faces.

498. When I say that the orders "Bring me sugar!" and "Bring me milk!" have a sense, but not the combination "Milk me sugar", this does not mean that the utterance of this combination of words has no effect. And if its effect is that the other person stares at me and gapes, I don't on that account call it an order to stare at me and gape, even if that was precisely the effect that I wanted to produce.

To rehearse. The (PI 201) thesis of the *Investigations* is that identity is paradox, called the rule, as neither of opposite cases + existing as both qua either.

Comment. Per PI 498: grammatically (lawfully), a human agreement case is to different cultures; as culture is to language/deed cases; as language qua wordage is to meaning/use cases; from which, the case of an order not to do with gaping but disagreeably connected with gaping is ungrammatical.

Games: paradox + faces; human form of life as an agreement case + language/deed cases; per analogies, ladder + up/down aspects, drabbit + duck/rabbit faces.

499. To say "This combination of words has no sense" excludes it from the sphere of language, and thereby bounds the domain of language. But when one draws a boundary, it may be for various kinds of reason. If I surround an area with a fence or a line or otherwise, the purpose may be to prevent someone from getting in or out; but it may also be part of a game and the players are supposed, say, to jump over the boundary; or it may show where the property of one person ends and that of another begins; and so on. So if I draw a boundary-line, that is not yet to say what I am drawing it for.

To rehearse. The (PI 201) thesis of the *Investigations* is that identity is paradox, called the rule, as neither of opposite cases + existing as both qua either.

Comment. Per PI 499: the grammar qua law talk reads as follows; whatever the logical reason for, or the empirical explanation of, a boundary case, its grammar qua law sense is that of an identity-as-paradox case, as neither of its faces; here, paradox is to faces; as boundary is to mutually bounding cases; where language qua wordage is the boundary, its mutually bounding cases are the meaning/use cases.

Games: paradox + faces; per PI 43, word + meaning/use cases; boundary + mutually bounding cases; per PI 201, neither face and coincidence of faces + faces; per analogies, ladder + up/down aspects, drabbit + duck/rabbit faces.

500. When a sentence is called senseless, it is not, as it were, its sense that is senseless. Rather, a combination of words is being excluded from the language, withdrawn from circulation.

To rehearse. The (PI 201) thesis of the *Investigations* is that identity is paradox, called the rule, as neither of opposite cases + existing as both qua either.

Comment. Per PI 500: the grammatical (lawful) talk is this; a senseless case is an ungrammatical case; otherwise, as grammatical (lawful), sense is to senseless (not sense); as per PI 43, meaning is to use (not meaning); as paradox face is to counterpart face.

Games: paradox + faces; word + meaning/use – meaning/not-meaning, meaning/meaningless, sense/expression, sense/not-sense, sense/senseless – cases; per analogies, ladder + up/down aspects, drabbit + duck/rabbit faces.

501. *"The purpose of language is to express thoughts." – So presumably the purpose of every sentence is to express a thought. Then what thought is expressed, for example, by the sentence "It's raining"?*

To rehearse. The (PI 201) thesis of the *Investigations* is that identity is paradox, called the rule, as neither of opposite cases + existing as both qua either.

Comment. Per PI 501: the grammar (law sense) presents as follows; the purposeful aspect of language is its expression aspect; as the face of a paradox is its counterpart face; as per PI 43, the meaning of a word is its use; as the thought qua thinking (expressing) aspect of a sentience (here, "It's raining") is its utterance (expressed) aspect.

Games: paradox + faces; word qua sentence + meaning/use – thinking/ enacted, expressing/expressed – cases; per analogies, ladder + up/down aspects, drabbit + duck/rabbit faces.

502. *Asking what the sense is. Compare:*

> *"This sentence has a sense." – "What sense?"*
> *"This sequence of words is a sentence." – "What sentence?"*

To rehearse. The (PI 201) thesis of the *Investigations* is that identity is paradox, called the rule, as neither of opposite cases + existing as both qua either.

Comment. Per PI 592: grammatically (lawfully), by PI 43, the meaning qua sense of a word is its expression qua use; as the face of a paradox is its counterpart face; from which, the sentence "*This sentience has a sense*" has its sense qua meaning as paradoxically its expression qua use; the sentence "*This sequence of words is a sentence.*" is for its sequencing aspect qua meaning paradoxically its sequenced aspect qua expression qua use;

Games: paradox + faces; word (wordage, sentence, "*This sentience has a sense*", "*This sequence of words is a sentence.*") + meaning/use – sense/expression, sequencing/sequenced – cases; per analogies, ladder + up/down aspects, drabbit + duck/rabbit faces.

*503. If I give anyone an order, I feel it to be **quite enough** to give him signs. And I'd never say: these are just words, and I've got to get behind the words. Equally, when I've asked someone something, and he gives me an answer (that is, a sign), I am content – that's what I expected – and I don't object: but that's a mere answer.*

To rehearse. The (PI 201) thesis of the *Investigations* is that identity is paradox, called the rule, as neither of opposite cases + existing as both qua either.

Comment. Per PI 503: the grammar qua law sense is this; when a sign qua a word is used it is never merely a use but (per PI 43) is paradoxically a meaning such that the word case is a paradox case; giving an order or answering a request is sufficiently a word-meaning case as paradoxically a word use case cf. a ladder is sufficiently a way up as paradoxically a way down.

Games: paradox + faces; word (order) + meaning/use – ordering/ordered, cf. addressing/answer – cases; per analogies, ladder + up/down aspects, drabbit + duck/rabbit faces.

*504. But if someone says, "How am I to know what he means – I see only his signs?", then I say, "How is **he** to know what he means, he too has only his signs?"*

To rehearse. The (PI 201) thesis of the *Investigations* is that identity is paradox, called the rule, as neither of opposite cases + existing as both qua either.

Comment. Per PI 504: the text presents its grammatical (lawful) sense as follows; it invites the response that to see a sign used is to know it meaning because the meaning/use cases are paradoxically one another, with the sign case as the paradox case; one understands that, grammatically, the sign-meaning case is paradoxically its sign-use case, whether the sign-language is one's own or another's.

Games: paradox + faces; per PI 43, sign qua word + meaning/use cases; sign + this/that cases i.e. signing/signed, own/another's cases; per analogies, ladder + up/down aspects, drabbit + duck/rabbit faces.

*505. Must I understand an order before I can act on it? – Certainly, otherwise you wouldn't know what you had to do! – But from **knowing** to doing is surely a further step!*

To rehearse. The (PI 201) thesis of the *Investigations* is that identity is paradox, called the rule, as neither of opposite cases + existing as both qua either.

Comment. Per PI 505: grammatically (lawfully), the understanding an order case is paradoxically the case of enacting it – knowing is paradoxically doing.

Games: paradox + faces; order + understanding/enactment cases i.e. knowing/doing case; per PI 43, word + meaning/use cases; culture + language/deed cases; per analogies, ladder + up/down aspects, drabbit + duck/rabbit faces.

506. *The absent-minded man who at the order "Right turn!" turns left, and then, clutching his forehead, says "Oh! right turn", and does a right turn. – What has struck him? An interpretation?*

To rehearse. The (PI 201) thesis of the *Investigations* is that identity is paradox, called the rule, as neither of opposite cases + existing as both qua either.

Comment. What strikes the man is that he is confusing different language games, much as if he confuses football and cricket by bowling the cricket ball at the goal mouth. Absent-mindedly, he takes the right-turn case to be a left-turn case. Coming to his senses, he employs a right-turn movement to mean a right-sense case. From PI 43, the meaning of a word ("right", order, rule) is its enactment.

Games: paradox (word, order, rule) + faces qua interpretations; right + meaning/movement – meaning/turn – cases; per analogies, ladder + up/down aspects, drabbit + duck/rabbit faces.

507. *"I am not merely saying this, I mean something by it." – When one considers what is going on in us when we **mean** (and don't merely say) words, it seems to us as if there were something coupled to these words, which otherwise would run idle. – As if they, so to speak, engaged with something in us.*

To rehearse. The (PI 201) thesis of the *Investigations* is that identity is paradox, called the rule, as neither of opposite cases + existing as both qua either.

Comment. Per PI 507: in terms of grammar qua law sense; per 43, word is never merely utterance but is meaning/use cases coupled paradoxically as thereby one another, where word is the paradox case; either of the meaning/use cases, if obtaining alone, is an idle case as ungrammatical.

Games: paradox + faces; word + meaning/use cases; per analogies, ladder + up/down aspects, drabbit + duck/rabbit faces.

508. I utter the sentence "The weather is fine"; but the words are, after all, arbitrary signs – so let's put "a b c d" in their place. But now, when I read this, I can't connect it, without more ado, with the above sense. I am not used, I might say, to saying "a" instead of "the", "b" instead of "weather", and so on. But I don't mean by this that I am not used to making an immediate association between the word "the" and "a"; rather, that I am not used to using "a" **in the place** of "the" – and therefore in the sense of "the". (I don't know this language.)

(I am not used to Fahrenheit measures of temperature. That's why such a specification of temperature '**says**' nothing to me.)

To rehearse. The (PI 201) thesis of the *Investigations* is that identity is paradox, called the rule, as neither of opposite cases + existing as both qua either.

Comment. Per PI 508: the grammar (law) converts the empirical sense of the text as follows; paradox is to faces; as human form of life is to cultures; as culture is to language/deed cases; as per PI 43, language (word-language, letter-language, Fahrenheit language, and so on) is to meaning/use cases.

Games: paradox + faces; human life + cultures; culture + language/deed cases; language (word, letter) + meaning/use cases; per analogies, ladder + up/down aspects, drabbit + duck/rabbit faces.

509. What if we asked someone, "In what sense are these words a description of what you see?" – and he answers: "I **mean** this by these words." (Perhaps he was looking at a landscape.) Why is this answer "I **mean** this ..." no answer at all?

How does one **mean**, with words, what one sees before one?

Suppose I said "a b c d" and meant thereby: the weather is fine. For as I uttered these signs, I had the experience normally had only by someone who, year in, year out, used "a" in the sense of "the", "b" in the sense of "weather", and so on. – Does "a b c d" now say: the weather is fine?

What should be the criterion for my having had **that** experience?

To rehearse. The (PI 201) thesis of the *Investigations* is that identity is paradox, called the rule, as neither of opposite cases + existing as both qua either.

Comment. Per PI 509: grammatically (lawfully), the language aspect of human life is the extra-linguistic aspect; as the face of paradox is to its counterpart face; as per PI 43, the meaning of a word-language is its use; here, the human language may be that of some foreign human tribe living life as all humans do but – in place of a word-language – using a letter-language.

Games: paradox + faces; human life + cultures; culture + language/deed cases; language (word, letter) + meaning/use cases; per analogies, ladder + up/down aspects, drabbit + duck/rabbit faces.

510. *Try to do the following:* **say** *"It's cold here", and* **mean** *"It's warm here". Can you do it? – And what are you doing as you do it? And is there only one way of doing it?*

To rehearse. The (PI 201) thesis of the *Investigations* is that identity is paradox, called the rule, as neither of opposite cases + existing as both qua either.

Comment. Per PI 510: the grammar (law sense) of the text is this; where some foreign human tribe speaks of cold to mean warn in the way in which the rest of mankind speaks of cold to mean cold, the grammar qua law sense is (per PI 43) that the meaning of a word as its use, and where the language is paradoxically what's done in terms of living the everyday human life.

Games: paradox + faces; human life + cultures; culture + language/deed cases; language (word, letter) + meaning/use cases; per analogies, ladder + up/down aspects, drabbit + duck/rabbit faces.

511. *What does "discovering that an utterance doesn't make sense" mean? – And what does it mean to say, "If I mean something by it, surely it must make sense"? – If I mean something by it? – If I mean* **what** *by it?! – One wants to say: a sentence that makes sense is one which one can not merely say, but also think.*

To rehearse. The (PI 201) thesis of the *Investigations* is that identity is paradox, called the rule, as neither of opposite cases + existing as both qua either.

Comment. Per PI 511: grammatically (lawfully), an utterance without sense is a paradox-face case without – as distinct from – its corresponding other paradox-face case; to mean *If I mean something by it, surely it must make sense* is to speak it; here, the non-italicised meaning case is paradoxically its expression case qua the speaking case; a sentence which is a thinking-qua-meaning case is paradoxically (not merely) a speaking case.

Games: paradox + faces; per PI 43, word (sentience) + meaning/use – sense/expression – cases; per analogies, ladder + up/down aspects, drabbit + duck/rabbit faces.

512. It looks as if one could say: "Word-language allows of nonsensical combinations of words, but the language of imagining does not allow us to imagine anything nonsensical." – Hence, too, the language of drawing doesn't allow nonsensical drawings? Suppose they were drawings from which bodies were to be modelled. In this case, some drawings make sense, some not. – What if I imagine nonsensical combinations of words?

To rehearse. The (PI 201) thesis of the *Investigations* is that identity is paradox, called the rule, as neither of opposite cases + existing as both qua either.

Comment. Per PI 512: in terms of grammar qua law sense, from PI 43, the meaning of a wordage (a combination-of-words) is its use (nonsense qua not-meaning); as a face of paradox is its corresponding other face (not the face to which it corresponds); a distinct aspect of a coincidence case (paradox, word, imagination, drawing) is its distinct coincidental aspect; whatever the game, it allows of distinct case as cases in coincidence; where there are not both of the sense/not-sense i.e. meaning/use distinct aspects, the case is senseless qua ungrammatical; too, in that human life is its language as paradoxically its everyday extra-linguistic activity, the language as distinct from as well as coincidental with the activity is a grammatical case whereas either of the two alone is nonsensical qua ungrammatical.

Games: paradox + faces; coincidence + distinct cases; word + meaning/use – sense/not-sense – cases; language (as word, as imagination, as drawing) + sense/not-sense cases; per analogies, ladder + up/down aspects, drabbit + duck/rabbit faces.

513. Consider the following form of expression: "The number of pages in my book is equal to a solution of the equation $x^3 + 2x - 3 = 0$." Or: "The number of my friends is n, and $n^2 + 2n + 2 = 0$." Does this sentence make sense? This cannot be seen immediately. From this example one can see how it can come about that something looks like a sentence which we understand, and yet makes no sense.

(This throws light on the concepts of understanding and of meaning something.)

To rehearse. The (PI 201) thesis of the *Investigations* is that identity is paradox, called the rule, as neither of opposite cases + existing as both qua either.

Comment. Per PI 513: the grammatical (lawful) sense is this; by PI 43, the meaning of a word is its use; as the face of a paradox case is its corresponding other face, as the meaning of a mathematical equation is its expression; as the verb-sense of understanding is its noun-sense; as non-apparency of a paradox case is its apparency; per game, the flanking cases as paradox-face case are immediately qua coincidentally connected as well as are not immediately connected by being distinct cases.; from which, grammatically, the onefold sense of identity as consistency – signed by A = A – is nonsense in that identity is paradox (here, as the threefold case of identity-as-paradox + identical faces, signed by '=' + A/A cases cf. per analogy, drabbit + duck/rabbit faces..

Games: paradox + faces; word + meaning/use – meaning/not-meaning, sense/nonsense, looks-like-sense/not-understandable, verb-sense-understanding/noun-sense-understanding – cases; per analogies, ladder + up/down aspects, drabbit + duck/rabbit faces.

514. A philosopher says that he understands the sentence "I am here", that he means something by it, thinks something – even though he doesn't call to mind in the least how, on what occasions, this sentence is used. And if I say "A rose is red in the dark too", you virtually see this red in the dark before you.

To rehearse. The (PI 201) thesis of the *Investigations* is that identity is paradox, called the rule, as neither of opposite cases + existing as both qua either.

Comment. Per PI 514: the text reads grammatically (lawfully) as follows; just as (per PI 43) the meaning of a word is its use, so (per PI 514) the meaning of the sentence "I am here" – like that of the sentence "A rose is red in the dark room" – is saying it; here, it matters not where/when it is said – empirically – nor whether or not such talk conduces to imaginative cases in the mind's-eye; what matters for an investigating philosopher is the grammar.

Games: paradox + faces; word (say, either of the PI 514 sentences) + meaning/use – thinking/use, understanding/use – cases; per analogies, ladder + up/down aspects, drabbit + duck/rabbit faces.

515. Two pictures of a rose in the dark. One is quite black; for the rose is not visible. In the other, it is painted in full detail and surrounded by black. Is one of them right, the other wrong? Don't we talk of a white rose in the dark and of a red rose in the dark? And don't we nevertheless say that they can't be distinguished in the dark?

To rehearse. The (PI 201) thesis of the *Investigations* is that identity is paradox, called the rule, as neither of opposite cases + existing as both qua either.

Comment. Per PI 515: picture talk is identity-as-paradox talk; grammatically qua lawfully – whatever the logical or empirical case – the unseen (cf. indistinguishable) aspect of a darkness case is its seen (distinguishable) aspect; as per PI 43, the meaning of a word is its use; as a face of paradox is its corresponding other face; the PI 515 empirical and everyday talk is the raw material for analytical treatment, which translates it into grammatical talk; another reading of the PI 514-PI 515 texts concerning the rose in darkness is this: just as in the threefold grammar there is the paradox case and its faces; so, in the darkness case, it contains the rose case and its invisible/visible aspects.

Games: paradox + faces; darkness case + unseen/seen cases; per PI 43, word + meaning/use cases; per analogies, ladder + up/down aspects, drabbit + duck/rabbit faces.

516. It seems clear that we understand the meaning of the question "Does the sequence 7777 occur in the development of π?" It is an English sentence; it can be shown what it means for 415 to occur in the development of π; and similar things. Well, our understanding of that question reaches just so far, one may say, as such explanations reach.

To rehearse. The (PI 201) thesis of the *Investigations* is that identity is paradox, called the rule, as neither of opposite cases + existing as both qua either.

Comment. Per PI 516: grammatically (lawfully) – not logically, not empirically – talk of a non-doable (either easily or not at all) case as a doable case is talk as a paradox case, the faces of which are the non-doable/doable cases.

Games: paradox + face; talk + non-doable/doable cases; per analogies, ladder + up/down aspects, drabbit + duck/rabbit faces.

517. The question arises: Can't we be mistaken in thinking that we understand a question?

*For some mathematical proofs do lead us to say that we **cannot** imagine something which we believed we could imagine. (For example, the construction of a heptagon.) They lead us to revise what counts as the domain of the imaginable.*

202   IDENTITY AS PARADOX

To rehearse. The (PI 201) thesis of the *Investigations* is that identity is paradox, called the rule, as neither of opposite cases + existing as both qua either.

Comment. Per PI 517: this text is a variant of the previous text; grammatically (lawfully) – not logically, not empirically – talk of a non-doable (either easily or not at all) case as a doable case is talk as a paradox case, the faces of which are the non-doable/doable cases.

Games: paradox + face; talk + non-doable/doable – cf. unimageable/imaginable – cases; per analogies, ladder + up/down aspects, drabbit + duck/rabbit faces.

*518. Socrates to Theaetetus: "And if someone imagines, mustn't he imagine **something**?" – Th.: "Yes, he must." – Soc.: "And if he imagines something, mustn't it be something real?" – Th.: "Apparently."*

And mustn't someone who is painting be painting something – and someone who is painting something be painting something real? – Well, tell me what the object of painting is: the picture of the man (for example), or the man whom the picture portrays?

To rehearse. The (PI 201) thesis of the *Investigations* is that identity is paradox, called the rule, as neither of opposite cases + existing as both qua either.

Comment. Per PI 518: grammatically (lawfully), a paradox is to its faces; as a picture (particular case, portrait, painting, imagination) is to its verb/noun senses; as man (particular case) is to on-canvas/real, subject/object, per PI 304 – Nothing/Something – cases.

Games: paradox + faces; per PI 216, identity + identical cases; man + subject/object – on-canvas/real-life, Nothing/Something – cases; per analogies, ladder + up/down aspects, drabbit + duck/rabbit faces.

*519. One wants to say that an order is a picture of the action that was carried out on the order; but also that it is a picture of the action that **is to be** carried out on the order.*

To rehearse. The (PI 201) thesis of the *Investigations* is that identity is paradox, called the rule, as neither of opposite cases + existing as both qua either.

Comment. Per PI 519: the grammar (law sense) is this; picture talk is identity-as-paradox talk; per PI 43, the meaning of a word is its use; as the face of a paradox is its counterpart face; as the out-picturing aspect of a picture is its out-pictured aspect; as the ordering (the to-be-enacted) aspect of an order is its ordered (enacted) aspect.

Games: paradox + faces; picture + out-pictures; order + ordering/enactment cases; word + meaning/use cases; per analogies, ladder + up/down aspects, drabbit + duck/rabbit faces.

520. "Even if one conceives of a proposition as a picture of a possible state of affairs, and says that it shows the possibility of the state of affairs, still, the most that a proposition can do is what a painting or relief or film does; and so it can, at any rate, not present what is not the case. So does what is, and what is not, called (logically) possible depend wholly on our grammar – that is, on what it permits?" – But surely that is arbitrary! – Is it arbitrary? – It is not every sentence-like formation that we know how to do something with, not every technique that has a use in our life; and when we are tempted in philosophy to count something quite useless as a proposition, that is often because we have not reflected sufficiently on its application.

To rehearse. The (PI 201) thesis of the *Investigations* is that identity is paradox, called the rule, as neither of opposite cases + existing as both qua either.

Comment. Per PI 520: in terms of the grammar (law sense) the text presents as follows; the possibility of a proposition (like any other identity-as-paradox case such as painting, a relief, a film) is what it shows; a, per PI 43, the meaning of a word is what it shows i.e. a use; whether or not a logical or an empirical case admits of conflicting is/is-not viewpoints, the grammatical case is that it has to it corresponding opposite aspects as paradox faces; per these faces, each is to the other as a case of what-is is to the case of what-is-not; this says that the faces are distinct case which yet also coincide as the paradox case cf. ladder + – up/down aspects.

Games: paradox + faces; proposition + possibility/expression cases cf. per PI 43, word + meaning/use cases; per analogies, ladder + up/down aspects, drabbit + duck/rabbit faces.

521. Compare 'logically possible' with 'chemically possible'. One might perhaps call a combination chemically possible if a formula with the right valencies existed (e.g. $H - O - O - O - H$). Of course, such a combination need not exist; but even the formula HO_2 cannot have less than no combination corresponding to it in reality.

To rehearse. The (PI 201) thesis of the *Investigations* is that identity is paradox, called the rule, as neither of opposite cases + existing as both qua either.

Comment. Per PI 521: grammatically (lawfully), possibility is to logical/empirical – here, logical/chemical – cases; as paradox is to faces, as per PI 304, nothing is to Nothing/Something cases.

Games: paradox + faces; per PI 43, word + meaning/use cases; possibility + logical/empirical – logical/chemical – cases; neither (Nothing nor Something) + Nothing/Something cases; combination qua coincidence + distinct cases; per analogies, ladder + up/down aspects, drabbit + duck/rabbit faces.

522. If we compare a proposition to a picture, we must consider whether we are comparing it to a portrait (a historical representation) or to a genre-picture. And both comparisons make sense.

*When I look at a genre-picture, it 'tells' me something, even though I don't believe (imagine) for a moment that the people I see in it really exist, or that there have really been people in that situation. For suppose I ask, "**What** does it tell me, then?"*

To rehearse. The (PI 201) thesis of the *Investigations* is that identity is paradox, called the rule, as neither of opposite cases + existing as both qua either.

Comment. Per PI 522: grammatically (lawfully), picture talk is identity-as-paradox talk; paradox is to faces; as picture is to picturing/pictured cases; as per PI 43, word (proposition qua sentence) is to meaning/use cases; as portrait, like genre case, is to telling/told – out-picturing/out-pictured, out-picturing/not-out-picturing – cases; from which, what a paradox case tells out is its faces, each as a telling/told qua telling/not-telling – eclipsing/ eclipsed – case.

Games: paradox + faces; word (portrait, genre case, picture, proposition) + meaning/use cases; possibility + logical/empirical – non-historical/ historical, imagined/real – cases; per analogies, ladder + up/down aspects, drabbit + duck/rabbit faces.

*523. "A picture tells me itself" is what I'd like to say. That is, it's telling me something consists in **its** own structure, in its own forms and colours. (What would it mean to say "A musical theme tells me itself"?)*

To rehearse. The (PI 201) thesis of the *Investigations* is that identity is paradox, called the rule, as neither of opposite cases + existing as both qua either.

Comment. Per PI 523: for its grammar qua law sense the text says this; picture talk is identity-as-paradox talk, here exemplified by musical-theme talk, or a telling talk; by which, the 'it' aspect of the is case is the 'itself' aspect; as the face of paradox is the counterpart face; as the verb-sense aspect of a telling is its noun-sense aspect.

Games: identity-as-paradox + identical faces; per PI 43, word + meaning/use – cf. form/matter, form/content, form/construction – cases; picture + out-pictures; (per identity law stating of identity that 'it is itself') 'is' + 'it/itself' cases; telling + verb/noun senses; per analogies, ladder + up/down aspects, drabbit + duck/rabbit faces.

524. Don't take it as a matter of course, but as a remarkable fact, that pictures and fictitious narratives give us pleasure, absorb us.

("Don't take it as a matter of course" – that means: puzzle over this, as you do over some other things which disturb you. Then what is problematic will disappear, by your accepting the one fact as you do the other.)

((The transition from obvious nonsense to something which is unobvious))

To rehearse. The (PI 201) thesis of the *Investigations* is that identity is paradox, called the rule, as neither of opposite cases + existing as both qua either.

Comment. PI 524: the grammatical qua law sense of the text reads as follows; talk of picture + fictitious narratives is talk of identity-as-paradox + identical faces cf. drabbit + duck/rabbit faces; entertainment is to absorption/pleasure cases; as picture is to fictitious narratives; as paradox is to faces; as transition is to remarkable/matter-of-course cases; as nonsense is to unobvious/obvious cases cf. per PI 304, nothing (neither anything nor nothing) + Nothing/Something cases.

Games: paradox + faces; picture + fictitious narratives; entertainment + absorption/pleasure aspects; transition + remarkable/matter-of-course aspects; nonsense + unobvious/obvious cases; acceptance + one-fact/other-fact cases; per PI 304, nothing + Nothing/Something cases; per analogies, ladder + up/down aspects, drabbit + duck/rabbit faces.

525. "After he had said this, he left her as he did the day before." – Do I understand this sentence? Do I understand it just as I would if I heard it in the course of a report? If it stood alone, I'd say I don't know what it's about. But all the same, I'd know how this sentence might perhaps be used; I could even invent a context for it.

(A multitude of familiar paths lead off from these words in all directions.)

To rehearse. The (PI 201) thesis of the *Investigations* is that identity is paradox, called the rule, as neither of opposite cases + existing as both qua either.

Comment. Per PI 525: grammatically (lawfully), whether or not a sentence locates in an empirical context, it locates in a threefold grammatical context as a paradox case, the faces of which, per PI 43, are its meaning/use cases.

Games: paradox + faces; per PI 43, word (sentence) + meaning/use cases; per analogies, ladder + up/down aspects, drabbit + duck/rabbit faces.

526. What does it mean to understand a picture, a drawing? Here too there is understanding and not understanding. And here too these expressions may mean various kinds of thing. The picture is, say, a still-life; but I don't understand one part of it: I cannot see solid objects there, but only patches of colour on the canvas. – Or I see all the objects, but I am not familiar with them (they look like implements, but I don't know their use). – Perhaps, however, I know the objects, but, in another sense, do not understand the way they are arranged.

To rehearse. The (PI 201) thesis of the *Investigations* is that identity is paradox, called the rule, as neither of opposite cases + existing as both qua either.

Comment. Per PI 526: in terms of the grammar qua law sense of the text, understanding is to understanding/understanding cases; as understanding is to verb/noun senses or verb/not-verb senses; as understanding is to understanding/not-understanding cases; the foregoing language games are grammatical cases regardless of their being presented empirically.

Games: paradox + faces; picture + picturing/pictured cases; per PI 43, word (here, understanding) + meaning/use – understanding/understanding, verb-sense/noun-sense – cases; per analogies, ladder + up/down aspects, drabbit + duck/rabbit faces.

*527. Understanding a sentence in language is much more akin to understanding a theme in music than one may think. What I mean is that understanding a spoken sentence is closer than one thinks to what is ordinarily called understanding a musical theme. Why is just **this** the pattern of variation in intensity and tempo? One would like to say: "Because I know what it all means." But what does it mean? I'd not be able to say. As an 'explanation', I could compare it with something else which has the same rhythm (I mean the same pattern). (One says, "Don't you see, this is as if a conclusion were being drawn" or "This is, as it were, a parenthesis", and so on. How does one justify such comparisons? – There are very different kinds of justification here.)*

To rehearse. The (PI 201) thesis of the *Investigations* is that identity is paradox, called the rule, as neither of opposite cases + existing as both qua either.

Comment. Per PI 527: the grammatical (lawful) sense is this; whatever the empirical-sense identity (say, sentence or musical theme) and howsoever it is given an empirical-sense understanding (say, musically loud or soft, or linguistically a paraphrase or conclusion), the grammatical threefold case is that of understanding + understanding/understanding – verb-sense/noun-sense – cases as a threefold grammar of identity-as-paradox + identical faces cf. drabbit + duck/rabbit faces.

Games: paradox + faces; understanding + understanding/understood – verb-sense/noun-sense – cases; per analogies, ladder + up/down aspects, drabbit + duck/rabbit faces.

528. One might imagine people who had something not altogether unlike a language: vocal gestures, without vocabulary or grammar. ('Speaking with tongues'.)

To rehearse. The (PI 201) thesis of the *Investigations* is that identity is paradox, called the rule, as neither of opposite cases + existing as both qua either.

Comment. Per 528: grammatically (lawfully), the speaking-in-tongues case is that of divine/mundane communication; communication thus need not express in terms of conventional vocabulary or gesture; the case of communication is the grammatical case of paradox; the communicators are the paradox-face cases.

Games: paradox + faces; communication + communicators; understanding + understanding/understood – verb-sense/noun-sense – cases; per analogies, ladder + up/down aspects, drabbit + duck/rabbit faces.

529. "But what would the meaning of the sounds be in such a case?" – What is it in music? Though I don't at all wish to say that this language of vocal gestures would have to be compared to music.

To rehearse. The (PI 201) thesis of the *Investigations* is that identity is paradox, called the rule, as neither of opposite cases + existing as both qua either.

Comment. Per PI 529: the grammar (law sense) is this; whether the identity-as-paradox + faces threefold grammatical case exemplifies as a sound + making/made threefold case or as a music + making/made threefold case, it is, per PI 43, a threefold language (word) + meaning/use threefold case; here, meaning is paradoxically enactment.

Games: paradox + faces; language (cf. sound, music) + meaning/use cases; understanding + understanding/understood – verb-sense/noun-sense – cases; per analogies, ladder + up/down aspects, drabbit + duck/rabbit faces.

530. There might also be a language in whose use the 'soul' of the words played no part. In which, for example, we had no objection to replacing one word by a new, arbitrarily invented one.

To rehearse. The (PI 201) thesis of the *Investigations* is that identity is paradox, called the rule, as neither of opposite cases + existing as both qua either.

Comment. Per PI 530: the grammatical (lawful) sense presents as follows; language is to soul/use cases or soul/not-soul cases; as per PI 43, word (any word, agreed or arbitrary invention) is to meaning/use – meaning/not-meaning – cases; as paradox is to faces.

Games: paradox + faces; word + meaning/use cases; understanding + understanding/understood – verb-sense/noun-sense – cases; per analogies, ladder + up/down aspects, drabbit + duck/rabbit faces.

531. We speak of understanding a sentence in the sense in which it can be replaced by another which says the same; but also in the sense in which it cannot be replaced by any other. (Any more than one musical theme can be replaced by another.)

In the one case, the thought in the sentence is what is common to different sentences; in the other, something that is expressed only by these words in these positions. (Understanding a poem.)

To rehearse. The (PI 201) thesis of the *Investigations* is that identity is paradox, called the rule, as neither of opposite cases + existing as both qua either.

Comment. Per PI 531: whether a sentence is to be understood as that it can or cannot be replaced by another, by PI 43, it is grammatically (lawfully) its meaning as paradoxically its expression.

Games: paradox + faces; word + meaning/use cases; per analogies, ladder + up/down aspects, drabbit + duck/rabbit faces.

*532. Then has "understanding" two different meanings here? — I would rather say that these kinds of use of "understanding" make up its meaning, make up my **concept** of understanding.*

*For I **want** to apply the word "understanding" to all this.*

To rehearse. The (PI 201) thesis of the *Investigations* is that identity is paradox, called the rule, as neither of opposite cases + existing as both qua either.

Comment. PI 532: here, the grammar (law sense) reads as follows; the text further clarifies the PI 531 case of understanding as that of a concept qua meaning as paradoxically its expression qua use; to rehearse, the case of understanding may thrice role play as the threefold case, viz., grammar, as a paradox case, also as each of the paradox-face cases.

Games: paradox + faces; per PI 43, understanding as a word + understanding/ understanding cases i.e. meaning/use cases i.e. concept/expression cases cf. the variant verb-sense/noun-sense aspects of understanding qua a paradox case; per analogies, ladder + up/down aspects, drabbit + duck/rabbit faces.

*533. But in the second case, how can one explain the expression, communicate what one understands? Ask yourself: How does one **lead** someone to understand a poem or a theme? The answer to this tells us how one explains the sense here.*

To rehearse. The (PI 201) thesis of the *Investigations* is that identity is paradox, called the rule, as neither of opposite cases + existing as both qua either.

Comment. Per PI 533: in terms of grammar (law), in the second case, viz., word-use case such as to do with, say, a poem (see, PI 531), the meaning of such word-use is explained qua warranted by it being paradoxically the word-use.

Games: paradox + faces; per PI 43, wordage (say, a poem) + meaning/use cases; understanding + understanding/understanding – verb/noun – cases; per analogies, ladder + up/down aspects, drabbit + duck/rabbit faces.

*534. **Hearing** a word as having this meaning. How curious that there should be such a thing!*

*Phrased like **this**, emphasized like this, heard in this way, this sentence is the beginning of a transition to **these** sentences, pictures, actions.*

((A multitude of familiar paths lead off from these words in all directions.))

To rehearse. The (PI 201) thesis of the *Investigations* is that identity is paradox, called the rule, as neither of opposite cases + existing as both qua either.

Comment. Per PI 534: grammatically (lawfully), to say that a certain hearing pertains to a corresponding certain meaning – whether to do with language, music, or whatever – is to say that a certain paradox face is referenced to its counterpart face; in terms of assorted language games, **this** sentences (and parallels) is to **these** sentences (and parallels); as a paradox case in one game stands to paradox cases in other games.

Games: paradox (**this**) + faces; per PI 43, word (sentence, picture, action) + meaning/use cases; hearing + verb/noun senses; per analogies, ladder + up/down aspects, drabbit + duck/rabbit faces.

535. *What happens when we learn to **feel** the ending of a church mode as an ending?*

To rehearse. The (PI 201) thesis of the *Investigations* is that identity is paradox, called the rule, as neither of opposite cases + existing as both qua either.

Comment. Per PI 535: the grammar (law sense) of the text presents as follows; the verb-sense learning (or feeling) aspect of a learning (feeling) case is its noun-sense learning (feeling) case, as face of paradox is to counterpart face.

Games: paradox + faces; per PI 43, word cf. mode, ending + meaning/use cases; learning or feeling + verb/noun senses; per analogies, ladder + up/down aspects, drabbit + duck/rabbit faces.

536. I say: "I can think of this face (which gives an impression of timidity) as courageous too." We do not mean by this that I can imagine someone with this face perhaps saving someone's life (that, of course, is imaginable in connection with any face). I am speaking, rather, of an aspect of the face itself. Nor do I mean that I can imagine that this man's face might change so that it looked courageous in the ordinary sense, though I may very well mean that there is a quite definite way in which it can turn into a courageous face. The reinterpretation of a facial expression can be compared to the reinterpretation of a chord in music, when we hear it as a modulation first into this, then into that, key.

To rehearse. The (PI 201) thesis of the *Investigations* is that identity is paradox, called the rule, as neither of opposite cases + existing as both qua either.

Comment. Per PI 536: the grammatical sense (law sense) case – in conversion of the raw-material empirical sense – is this; paradox is to faces; as face is to expressions; as chord is to modulations; as per analogy, drabbit is to duck/rabbit faces.

Games: paradox + faces (and variants, as per the Comment); per analogies, ladder + up/down aspects, drabbit + duck/rabbit faces.

*537. It is possible to say "I read timidity in this face", but, at any rate, the timidity does not seem to be merely associated, outwardly connected, with the face; rather, fear is there, alive, in the features. If the features change slightly, we can speak of a corresponding change in the fear. If we were asked, "Can you think of this face as an expression of courage too?" – we should, as it were, not know how to lodge courage in these features. Then perhaps I say, "I don't know what it would mean if this is a courageous face." But what would an answer to such a question be like? Perhaps one says: "Yes, now I understand: the face is, as it were, indifferent to the outer world." So we have somehow read courage into the face. Now once more, one might say, courage **fits** this face. But **what** fits **what** here?*

To rehearse. The (PI 201) thesis of the *Investigations* is that identity is paradox, called the rule, as neither of opposite cases + existing as both qua either.

Comment. Per PI 537: the logical sense and the empirical sense of the text serves as raw material for conversion to grammatical (lawful) sense, as follows; the face as an indifference case is to its fear/courage expressions; as paradox is to faces; as per analogy, drabbit as neither of its faces is to its faces (as cases distinct from the drabbit case).

Games: paradox + faces (and variants, as per the Comment); per analogies, ladder + up/down aspects, drabbit + duck/rabbit faces

538. *There is a related case (though perhaps it will not seem so) when, for example, we Germans are surprised that in French the predicative adjective agrees with the substantive in gender, and when we explain it to ourselves by saying: they mean "der Mensch ist **ein guter**".*

To rehearse. The (PI 201) thesis of the *Investigations* is that identity is paradox, called the rule, as neither of opposite cases + existing as both qua either.

Comment. PI 538: the grammar qua law sense is this; paradox is to faces; as language is to different – French/German – expressions.

Games: paradox + faces; language + different French/German expressions; per analogies, ladder + up/down aspects, drabbit + duck/rabbit faces.

539. *I see a picture which represents a smiling face. What do I do if I take the smile now as a kind one, now as malicious? Don't I often imagine it with a spatial and temporal context of kindness or malice? Thus I might, when looking at the picture, imagine it to be of a smiler smiling down on a child at play, or again on the suffering of an enemy.*

This is in no way altered by the fact that I can also take the apparently genial situation and interpret it differently by putting it into a wider context. – If no special circumstances reverse my interpretation, I shall conceive a particular smile as kind, call it a "kind" one, react accordingly.

((Probability, frequency.))

To rehearse. The (PI 201) thesis of the *Investigations* is that identity is paradox, called the rule, as neither of opposite cases + existing as both qua either.

Comment. Per PI 539: grammatically (lawfully – not empirically as a, say, sense-making from frequent experience or probability perspective – the text runs as follows; picture is to picturing/pictured cases; as paradox is to faces; as per PI 43, word is to meaning/use cases; as face qua smile is to kind/malicious cases; as particular smile is to concept/reaction cases.

Games: paradox+ faces; word + meaning/use cases; picture + out-pictures; smile + kind/malicious case; particular case (here, a smile) + concept/reaction cases; per analogies, ladder + up/down aspects, drabbit + duck/rabbit faces.

*540. "Isn't it very peculiar that, without the institution of language and all its surroundings, I shouldn't be able to think that it will soon stop raining?" – Do you want to say that it is strange that you should be unable to say these words to yourself and **mean** them without those surroundings?*

Suppose someone were to point at the sky and come out with a number of unintelligible words. When we ask him what he means, he explains that the words mean "Thank heaven it'll soon stop raining". He even explains to us what the individual words mean. – I am assuming that he will, as it were, suddenly come to himself and say that the sentence was complete nonsense, but that when he uttered it, it had seemed to him like a sentence in a language he knew (perhaps even like a familiar quotation.) – What am I to say now? Didn't he understand the sentence as he was saying it? Wasn't the whole meaning there in the sentence?

To rehearse. The (PI 201) thesis of the *Investigations* is that identity is paradox, called the rule, as neither of opposite cases + existing as both qua either.

Comment. Per PI 540: the grammatical (lawful) case is this; where there is no language, or language as other than the shared human language, there is thereby no human thinking (understanding); just as without the case of paradox or a paradox without counterpart faces, there is no paradox-face case cf. per analogy, without either drabbit or drabbit without a duck face, there is no rabbit face.

Games: paradox + faces; per PI 43, word + meaning/use – thinking/speaking – cases; understanding + understanding/understanding – verb-sense/noun-sense – cases; language + – private/public – cases; culture + language-deeds cases; per analogies, ladder + up/down aspects, drabbit + duck/rabbit faces.

*541. But what did this understanding, and the meaning, consist in? He uttered the sounds in a cheerful voice perhaps, pointing to the sky while it was still raining but was already beginning to clear up; **later** he made a connection between his words and the English words.*

To rehearse. The (PI 201) thesis of the *Investigations* is that identity is paradox, called the rule, as neither of opposite cases + existing as both qua either.

Comment. Per PI 541: in terms of grammar qua law sense, as per the PI 540 Comment, the case of his utterance is grammatically (lawfully) understandable as ungrammatical, notwithstanding his initial non-awareness of this.

Games: as per PI 540.

*542. "But the point is, the words felt to him like the words of a language he knew well." – Yes; a criterion for it is his later saying just **that**. And now **don't** say: "The feel of the words in a language we know is of a quite particular kind." (What is the **expression** of this feeling?)*

To rehearse. The (PI 201) thesis of the *Investigations* is that identity is paradox, called the rule, as neither of opposite cases + existing as both qua either.

Comment. Per PI 542: the grammar (law sense) of the text is this; the PI 540 case is that of private language + feeling/babble cases but not cross-referenced to public language, hence not – as the babbler claimed – sufficing as language nor even at all grammatical; compare word-meaning/word-use cases as cross-referenced – paradoxical – cases; language feeling i.e. private language cf. word-meaning is paradoxically its expression i.e. public language cf. word-use.

Games: paradox + faces; language + private/public – feeling/expression cf. word-meaning/word-use – cases; per analogies, ladder + up/down aspects, drabbit + duck/rabbit faces.

543. Can't I say: a cry, a laugh, are full of meaning?

And that means, roughly: much can be gathered from them.

To rehearse. The (PI 201) thesis of the *Investigations* is that identity is paradox, called the rule, as neither of opposite cases + existing as both qua either.

Comment. Per PI 543: this text presents its grammar qua law sense as follows; language as meaning/use cross-referenced – paradoxical – cases need not be a verbal language in that it can be a language expressed by laughter or by crying.

Games: paradox + faces; per PI 43, language (verbal, crying, laughter) + meaning/use – meaning/expression – case; per analogies, ladder + up/down aspects, drabbit + duck/rabbit faces.

544. When longing makes me exclaim "Oh, if only he'd come!", the feeling gives the words 'meaning'. But does it give the individual words their meanings?

*But here one could also say that the feeling gave the words **truth**. And now you see how the concepts here shade into one another. (This recalls the question: what is the **sense** of a mathematical proposition?)*

To rehearse. The (PI 201) thesis of the *Investigations* is that identity is paradox, called the rule, as neither of opposite cases + existing as both qua either.

Comment. Per PI 544: grammatically (lawfully), from PI 43, the meaning aspect of each of the individual words of a sentence qua wordage is paradoxically a use aspect, its expression aspect; the felt-longing of a cry is its utterance; the telling of a truth-talk is its being told; the sense-making aspect of a sense case qua a mathematical proposition is its sense-made aspect.

Games: paradox + faces; language (word, wordage, sentence) + meaning/use – feeling/expression, telling/told – cases; per analogies, ladder + up/down aspects, drabbit + duck/rabbit faces.

*545. But when one says "I **hope** he'll come" – doesn't the feeling give the word "hope" its meaning? (And what about the sentence "I **no** longer hope he'll come"?) The feeling does perhaps give the word "hope" its special ring; that is, it is expressed in that ring. – If the feeling gives the word its meaning, then here "meaning" amounts to: **that which matters**. But why is the feeling what matters?*

Is hope a feeling? (Characteristic marks.)

To rehearse. The (PI 201) thesis of the *Investigations* is that identity is paradox, called the rule, as neither of opposite cases + existing as both qua either.

Comment. Per PI 545: the case of grammar qua law sense is this; the face of a paradox is its counterpart face; as per PI 43, the meaning of a word (sentence) is its us; as the verb-sense aspect of feel (hope, special-ring, no-hope, **that which matters**) is its noun sense aspect.

Games: paradox + faces; word + meaning/use cases; feel + verb/noun senses (and variants, as per Comment); per analogies, ladder + up/down aspects, drabbit + duck/rabbit faces.

546. *In this way, I'd like to say, the words "Oh, if only he'd come!" are charged with my longing. And words can be wrung from us – like a cry. Words can be **hard** to utter: those, for example, with which one renounces something, or confesses a weakness. (Words are also deeds.)*

To rehearse. The (PI 201) thesis of the *Investigations* is that identity is paradox, called the rule, as neither of opposite cases + existing as both qua either.

Comment. Per PI 546: the grammatical (lawful) talk is as follows; by PI 43, word (wordage, sentence) is to meaning/use – meaning/deed – cases; as paradox is to faces; as long (charge qua fill, wring, cry, hear, remembrance, confession) is to verb/noun senses.

Games: paradox + faces; word + meaning/use – meaning/verbal-deed – cases; long (and variants, as per Comment) + verb/noun senses; culture + language/deed – word/extra-linguistic-deed – cases; per analogies, ladder + up/down aspects, drabbit + duck/rabbit faces.

547. *Negating: a 'mental activity'. Negate something and observe what you are doing. – Do you perhaps inwardly shake your head? And if you do, is this process more deserving of our interest than, say, that of writing a sign of negation in a sentence? Do you now know the **essence** of negation?*

To rehearse. The (PI 201) thesis of the *Investigations* is that identity is paradox, called the rule, as neither of opposite cases + existing as both qua either.

Comment. Per PI 547: in terms of grammar qua law sense, by PI 43, negation as a word qua paradox case is its paradox faces qua negating/negated aspects – meaning/use, essence/expression, mental/behavioural, inward/ outward – aspects.

Games: paradox + faces; word + meaning/use cases; negation + verb/noun senses (and variants, as per Comment); per analogies, ladder + up/down aspects, drabbit + duck/rabbit faces.

*548. What is the difference between the two processes: wishing that something should happen and wishing that the same thing should **not** happen?*

*If one wanted to represent it pictorially, one might treat the picture of the event in different ways: cross it out, or put a line round it, and so on. But this strikes us as a **crude** method of expression. In word language we do indeed use the sign "not". This is like a clumsy expedient. One supposes that in **thought** it happens differently.*

To rehearse. The (PI 201) thesis of the *Investigations* is that identity is paradox, called the rule, as neither of opposite cases + existing as both qua either.

Comment. Per PI 548 grammar qua law: drawing from PI 215, a wish as a sameness case is its same/same aspects as its happening/not-happening – positive/negative – aspects; by which, paradox is to faces; as wish is to positive/negative aspects.

Games: paradox + faces; picture + out-pictures; per PI 43, word + meaning/use cases; wish + positive/negative aspects; sameness + same/same cases; per analogies, ladder + up/down aspects, drabbit + duck/rabbit faces.

549. "How can the word 'not' negate?" – "The sign 'not' indicates that you are to take what follows negatively." One would like to say: the sign of negation is our occasion for doing something – possibly something very complicated. It is as if the negation sign prompted us to do something. But what? That is not said. It is as if it only needed to be hinted at; as if we already knew. As if no explanation were needed, since we are already familiar with the matter anyway.

To rehearse. The (PI 201) thesis of the *Investigations* is that identity is paradox, called the rule, as neither of opposite cases + existing as both qua either.

Comment. Per PI 549 grammar qua law: the not-case is a distinction-case, a case distinct from a corresponding other case, as thereby not that other case, and which corresponding cases are exemplified by paradox faces, also by eclipsing/eclipsing paradox-face functions; to negate is to do something, viz., to see corresponding opposite cases qua mutually negating cases as complementary paradox faces.

Games: paradox + faces (where each face is not the other, and where, per face, each function is not the other); per analogies, ladder + up/down aspects, drabbit + duck/rabbit faces.

Notes on Negation

(a) *"The fact that three negations yield a negation again must already be contained in the single negation that I am using now." (The temptation to invent a myth of 'meaning'.) It looks as if it followed from the nature of negation that a double negation is an affirmation. (And there is something right about this. What? Our nature is connected with both.)*

(b) *There can be no debate about whether these or other rules are the right ones for the word "not" (I mean, whether they accord with its meaning). For without these rules, the word has as yet no meaning; and if we change the rules, it now has another meaning (or none), and in that case we may just as well change the word too.*

To rehearse. The (PI 201) thesis of the *Investigations* is that identity is paradox, called the rule, as neither of opposite cases + existing as both qua either.

Comment. Per notes (a) and (b) re: grammar qua law: an eclipsed paradox face existing as an eclipsed face is a negation case as that which is not the (eclipsing) face; what is not not-the-case, as a double-negative case, is an affirmative case (an eclipsing paradox face); what is not a double-negative case i.e. what is not an affirmative case (an eclipsing paradox face) is again a negative case (an eclipsed paradox face; paradox is to eclipsing/eclipsed – cf. affirmation/ negation – faces; as, per PI 201, rule is to accordant/conflicting cases; as, per PI 43, word is to mutually eclipsing meaning/use – meaning/ not-meaning – cases; as per PI 201, rule qua paradox is to ruled cases qua courses of action, each as a rule-following/ going-against-the-rule – eclipsing-face/eclipsed-face – functional action.

Games: paradox qua rule + mutually eclipsing (mutually substituting) cases; per example, word + meaning/use faces; per analogies, ladder + up/down aspects, drabbit + duck/rabbit faces.

550. Negating, one might say, is a gesture of exclusion, of rejection. But we use such a gesture in a great variety of cases!

To rehearse. The (PI 201) thesis of the *Investigations* is that identity is paradox, called the rule, as neither of opposite cases + existing as both qua either.

Comment. Per PI 550 grammar qua law: paradox-face cases mutually eclipse/negate/exclude/reject – and in variant ways e.g. word-meaning/word-use cases; grammatically, to gesture a case not to be the case is to render paradox-face cases as distinct cases, each not the other, yet coinciding as the paradox case.

Games: paradox + faces; word + meaning/use cases; mutual negation (and parallels) + mutually negating cases; per analogies, ladder + up/down aspects, drabbit + duck/rabbit faces.

*551. "Is the negation in 'Iron does not melt at 100 degrees Centigrade' the same as in 'Two times two is not five'?" Is this to be decided by introspection, by trying to see what we are **thinking** as we utter the two sentences?*

To rehearse. The (PI 201) thesis of the *Investigations* is that identity is paradox, called the rule, as neither of opposite cases + existing as both qua either.

Comment. Per PI 551 grammar qua law: from PI 215, sameness is to same/same cases; as paradox is to faces; as negation is to empirical/arithmetical negation cases; as, per PI 43, word is to meaning/use – cf. thinking/uttering – cases; whatever the negation case – logical or empirical – its meaning is paradoxically its use.

Games: paradox + faces; sameness + same/same cases; negation + arithmetical/empirical negation cases; word + meaning/use – cf. thinking/uttering – cases; per analogies, ladder + up/down aspects, drabbit + duck/rabbit faces.

552. What if I were to ask: does it become evident, while we are uttering the sentences "This rod is 1 metre long" and "Here is 1 soldier", that we mean different things by "1", that "1" has different meanings? – It does not become evident at all. – Say, for example, such a sentence as "1 metre is occupied by 1 soldier, and so 2 metres are occupied by 2 soldiers". Asked, "Do you mean the same by both 'ones'?", one would perhaps answer, "Of course I mean the same: one!" (Perhaps raising one finger.)

To rehearse. The (PI 201) thesis of the *Investigations* is that identity is paradox, called the rule, as neither of opposite cases + existing as both qua either.

Comment. Per PI 552 grammar qua law: from PI 215, sameness is to same/same cases; as oneness is to one/one cases; this last threefold grammatical case obtains whether to do with the rod or with the soldier – in either case, the meaning of the one is its use, as the face of a paradox is its counterpart face.

Games: paradox + faces; per PI 43, word + meaning/use cases; coincidence + different cases; oneness + one/one cases; sameness + same/same cases; per analogies, ladder + up/down aspects, drabbit + duck/rabbit faces.

*553. Now has "1" a different meaning when it stands for a measure and when it stands for a number? If the question is framed in **this** way, one will answer in the affirmative.*

To rehearse. The (PI 201) thesis of the *Investigations* is that identity is paradox, called the rule, as neither of opposite cases + existing as both qua either.

Comment. Per PI 553 grammar qua law: from PI 215, sameness is to same/same cases; as oneness is to one/one cases; this last threefold grammatical case obtains whether to do with the measure case or with the number case; from which, there are not different cases where oneness is the paradox case as well as difference as the one/one – number/measure – paradox-face cases.

Games: paradox + faces; per PI 43, word + meaning/use cases; coincidence + different cases; oneness + one/one cases; **this** + metre/number cases; sameness + same/same cases; per analogies, ladder + up/down aspects, drabbit + duck/rabbit faces.

554. We can easily imagine human beings with a 'more primitive' logic, in which something corresponding to our negation is applied only to certain sentences; perhaps to those that do not yet contain any negation. It would be possible to negate the sentence "He is going into the house", but a negation of the negated sentence would be senseless, or would count only as a repetition of the negation. Think of means of expressing negation different from ours: by the pitch of the uttered sentence, for instance. What would a double negation be like there?

To rehearse. The (PI 201) thesis of the *Investigations* is that identity is paradox, called the rule, as neither of opposite cases + existing as both qua either.

Comment. Per PI 554 grammar qua law: from PI 215 sameness is to same/same cases; as negation is to negation/negation – verb-sense/noun-sense cases; this last threefold grammatical case obtains whether to do with verbal language or with gestural language; here, the threefold grammar obtains howsoever empirical in kind is the negation case.

Games: paradox + faces; per PI 43, word + meaning/use cases; coincidence + different cases; negation + negation/negation – verbal-sense/noun-sense – cases; per PI 215, sameness + same/same cases; per analogies, ladder + up/down aspects, drabbit + duck/rabbit faces.

555. *The question of whether negation had the same meaning to these people as to us would be analogous to the question as to whether the figure "5" meant the same to people whose number series ended at 5 as to us.*

To rehearse. The (PI 201) thesis of the *Investigations* is that identity is paradox, called the rule, as neither of opposite cases + existing as both qua either.

Comment. Per PI 555 grammar qua law: by PI 43, the meaning of a word is its use in a language – be the language primitive or not primitive; by which, paradox is to faces; as word is to meaning/use cases; as 5 is to meaning/use cases; as negation is to negation/negation – verb-sense/noun-sense, negating/negated – cases.

Games: paradox + faces; word (5, negation) + meaning/use – cf. verb-sense/noun-sense – cases; per analogies, ladder + up/down aspects, drabbit + duck/rabbit faces.

556. *Imagine a language with two different words for negation, "X" and "Y". Doubling "X" yields an affirmation, doubling "Y" an emphatic negation. Apart from that, the two words are used similarly. – Now have "X" and "Y" the same meaning in sentences where they occur without being repeated? – One might give various answers to this.*

(a) *The two words have different uses. So they have different meanings. But sentences in which they occur without being repeated, and which are otherwise the same, have the same sense.*

(b) *The two words have the same function in language-games, except for this one difference, which is just an unimportant matter of custom. The use of the two words is taught in the same way, by means of the same actions, gestures, pictures, and so on; and in explanations of the words, the difference in the ways they are used is appended as something incidental, as one of the capricious features of the language. That's why we'll say: "X" and "Y" have the same meaning.*

(c) *We connect different images with the two negations. "X", as it were, turns the sense through 180°. And **that** is why two such negations restore the sense to its former position. "Y" is like shaking one's head. And just as one doesn't annul a shake of the head by shaking it again, so too one doesn't cancel one "Y" by a second one. And so even if in practice sentences with the two signs of negation come to the same thing, still "X" and "Y" express different ideas.*

To rehearse. The (PI 201) thesis of the *Investigations* is that identity is paradox, called the rule, as neither of opposite cases + existing as both qua either.

Comment. Per PI 556 grammar qua law: a grammar of the text's empirical-sense talk, also of its cases (a)-(c), run as follows: a face of paradox is its counterpart face; whether the word be X, or Y, or affirmation, or emphasis, per PI 43, the meaning of a word is its use; by PI 215, sameness as a paradox is its same/same faces cf. drabbit + duck/rabbit faces; from which, it is not X and Y that have the same meaning; rather, per any word case, it is its meaning/use case that have the word as the sameness case.

Games: paradox + faces; word + meaning/use cases; sameness + same/same cases; per analogies, ladder + up/down cases; drabbit + duck/rabbit faces.

*557. When I uttered the double negation, what constituted my meaning it as an emphatic negation and not as an affirmation? There is no answer running: "It consisted in the fact that …" In certain circumstances, instead of saying "This reiteration is meant as an emphasis", I can **pronounce** it as an emphasis. Instead of saying "The reiteration of the negation is meant to cancel it", I can, for example, insert brackets. – "Yes, but these brackets may themselves have different roles; for who says that they are to be taken as **brackets**?" No one does. And haven't you explained your own conception in turn by means of words? What the brackets mean lies in the technique of applying them. The question is: under what circumstances does it make sense to say "I meant …", and what circumstances warrant my saying "He meant …"?*

To rehearse. The (PI 201) thesis of the *Investigations* is that identity is paradox, called the rule, as neither of opposite cases + existing as both qua either.

Comment. Per PI 557 grammar qua law: whatever the empirical-sense talk, it translates grammatically as follows; the affirmation/emphasis words have different meanings because locating in different language games; per each of these words, and by PI 43, its meaning is paradoxically its use in a language (game); it is under grammatical circumstances that word-talk, in terms of meaning/use aspects, makes sense.

Games: paradox + faces; word + meaning/use cases; per analogies, ladder + up/down cases; drabbit + duck/rabbit faces.

*558. What does it mean to say that the "is" in "The rose is red" has a different meaning from the "is" in "Two times two is four"? If it is answered that it means that different rules are valid for these two words, the retort is that we have only **one** word here. – And if I attend only to the grammatical rules, these do allow the use of the word "is" in both kinds of context. – But the rule which shows that the word "is" has different meanings in these sentences is the one allowing us to replace the word "is" in the second sentence by the sign of equality, and forbidding this substitution in the first sentence.*

To rehearse. The (PI 201) thesis of the *Investigations* is that identity is paradox, called the rule, as neither of opposite cases + existing as both qua either.

Comment. Per PI 558 grammar qua law: the empirical-sense talk, like the mathematical-sense talk, translates grammatically as follows: paradox is to faces; as an "is" case is to the rose/red cases; as an "is" case is to the twice-two/four cases; as an '=' sign is to the twice-two/four cases; whatever the threefold grammatical case (language game), the "is" case is an identity-as-paradox case where the cases flanking the "is" case are identical case as paradox-face cases cf. per analogy, the ladder-ascent is a ladder-descent.

Games: paradox ("is", "=") + (rose/red, twice-two/four) faces; per analogies, ladder + up/down aspects, drabbit + duck/rabbit faces.

*559. One would like to speak of the function of a word in **this** sentence. As if the sentence were a mechanism in which the word had a particular function. But what does this function consist in? How does it come to light? For after all, nothing is hidden – we see the whole sentence! The function must come out in operating the calculus. ((Meaning-bodies.))*

To rehearse. The (PI 201) thesis of the *Investigations* is that identity is paradox, called the rule, as neither of opposite cases + existing as both qua either.

Comment. Per PI 559 grammar qua law: **this**-talk is identity-as-paradox talk, it is word talk as in the PI 43 threefold grammar of the word qua paradox as its meaning/use cases qua paradox faces; each face – each word-meaning case or word-use case – functions such that the faces are in continual mutual eclipse.

Games: paradox qua **this** + faces; word + meaning/use – meaning/body, mind/body – cases; mutual-eclipse activity + mutually eclipsing functions; per analogies, ladder + up/down aspects, drabbit + duck/rabbit faces.

560. "The meaning of a word is what an explanation of its meaning explains." That is, if you want to understand the use of the word "meaning", look for what one calls "an explanation of meaning".

To rehearse. The (PI 201) thesis of the *Investigations* is that identity is paradox, called the rule, as neither of opposite cases + existing as both qua either.

Comment. Per PI 560 grammar qua law: the face of a paradox is its corresponding other face; as per PI 43, the meaning of a word is its use; as the explaining aspect of an explanation is its what-it-is aspect quad its explained aspect; to look for the explanation of a meaning is to look for a case of meaning referenced to a threefold grammar; in mixed terms, this could be the grammar of meaning qua word + explaining/use aspects.

Games: paradox + faces; word + meaning/use cases; explanation + explanation/explanation cases i.e. verb-sense/noun-sense – explaining/ explained

– cases; understanding + understanding/understanding cases i.e. verb-sense/noun-sense, understanding/understood – cases; per analogies, ladder + up/down aspects, drabbit + duck/rabbit faces.

561. Now isn't it remarkable that I say that the word "is" is used with two different meanings (as copula and as sign of equality), and wouldn't want to say that its meaning is its use; its use, namely, as copula and as sign of equality?

One would like to say that these two kinds of use don't yield a single meaning; the union under one head, effected by the same word, is an inessential coincidence.

To rehearse. The (PI 201) thesis of the *Investigations* is that identity is paradox, called the rule, as neither of opposite cases + existing as both qua either.

Comment. Per PI 561 grammar qua law: whether a word-case be "is", or "coincides with", or "equates with", its meaning (per PI 43) is paradoxically its use, its variant meanings are its corresponding variant uses; by which, the word case is an identity-as-paradox case, with its meaning/use aspects as its identical paradox faces cf. per PI 216 and per the analogy of drabbit + duck/rabbit faces; to account two cases, viz., the copula and equality cases as the one "is" case – and in addition to call the 2-as-1 case and inessential coincidence – calls for the grammatical clarification as follows; the "is"/copula/equality cases obtain in assorted language games as talk of identity-as-paradox qua the coincidence of distinct paradox faces qua meaning/use – essence/expression – cases.

Games: paradox ("is", copula, equality) + faces; per PI 216, identity + identical cases; per PI 43, word + meaning/use – essence/expression – cases; coincidence + distinct cases; per analogies, ladder + up/down aspects, drabbit + duck/rabbit faces.

562. But how can I decide what is an essential, and what an inessential, coincidental, feature of the notation? Is there some reality lying behind the notation, to which its grammar conforms?

Let's think of a similar case in a game: in draughts a king is indicated by putting one piece on top of another. Now won't one say that it's inessential to the game for a king to consist of two pieces?

To rehearse. The (PI 201) thesis of the *Investigations* is that identity is paradox, called the rule, as neither of opposite cases + existing as both qua either.

Comment. Per PI 562 grammar qua law: given the notion that the meaning of a word is its use (so, PI 43), this translates as that the face of a paradox is its counterpart face i.e. (for example) the essential aspect of a coincidence case is its inessential qua not-essential qua expression aspect cf. per analogy, the piece of a draughts-game king is its other piece; the king models identity-as-paradox – the coincidence of opposites.

Games: paradox + faces; word + meaning/use cases; coincidence + distinct cases; king + two pieces; per analogies, ladder + up/down aspects, drabbit + duck/rabbit faces.

563. Let's say that the meaning of a piece is its role in the game. – Now let it be decided by lot, before a game of chess begins, which of the players gets white. For this, one player holds a king in each closed hand, while the other chooses one of the two hands, trusting to luck. Will it be counted as part of the role of the king in chess that it is used to draw lots in this way?

To rehearse. The (PI 201) thesis of the *Investigations* is that identity is paradox, called the rule, as neither of opposite cases + existing as both qua either.

Comment. Per PI 563 grammar qua law: whether in the pre-game ritual of drawing lots or the playing of the post-ritual game, the king is to meaning/use cases; as, per PI 43, word is to meaning/use cases; as paradox is to faces.

Games: paradox + faces; word (cf. king) + meaning/use cases; game + ritual/play cases; per analogies, ladder + up/down aspects, drabbit + duck/rabbit faces.

*564. So I am inclined to distinguish between essential and inessential rules in a game too. The game, one would like to say, has not only rules but also a **point**.*

To rehearse. The (PI 201) thesis of the *Investigations* is that identity is paradox, called the rule, as neither of opposite cases + existing as both qua either.

Comment. Per PI 564 grammar qua law: the point or purpose of a rule qua game is its activity; as per PI 43, the essential qua meaningful aspect of a word is its inessential (opposite of essential) qua practice or use aspect.

Games: paradox + faces; rule + purpose/enactment aspects; word + meaning/ use − essence/expression, essential/inessential, essential/not-essential, meaning/ not-meaning − cases; per analogies, ladder + up/down aspects, drabbit + duck/rabbit faces.

565. What's the point of using the same word? In the calculus we don't make use of any such sameness of sign! − Why the same chess piece for both purposes? − But what does it mean here to speak of "making use of the sameness of sign"? For isn't it a single use, if we actually use the same word?

To rehearse. The (PI 201) thesis of the *Investigations* is that identity is paradox, called the rule, as neither of opposite cases + existing as both qua either.

Comment. Per PI 565 grammar qua law: by PI 215, sameness is same/same cases cf. as drabbit is duck/rabbit faces; as paradox is face/face cases; as the same chess piece is its different meaning/use cases; as per PI 43, word is meaning/use − purpose/use, point/use − cases; as sign is same/same cases qua sign-making/sign-made cases; from which, in all such grammatical talk, sameness is paradox, not singleness qua consistency.

Games: paradox + faces; word + meaning/use − point/use, purpose/use − cases; sameness + same/same cases; per analogies, ladder + up/down aspects, drabbit + duck/rabbit faces.

*566. And now it looks as if the use of the same word or the same piece had a **purpose** – if the sameness is not coincidental, inessential. And as if the purpose were that one should be able to recognize the piece and know how to play. – Are we talking about a physical or a logical possibility here? If the latter, then the sameness of the piece is part of the game.*

To rehearse. The (PI 201) thesis of the *Investigations* is that identity is paradox, called the rule, as neither of opposite cases + existing as both qua either.

Comment. Per PI 566 grammar qua law: the text presents in deliberate confusion of empirical-sense and logical-sense terms grammatically translating as that sameness is paradox not singleness sense; by which, paradox is to faces; as, per PI 43, word is to meaning/use – purpose/enactment – cases; as, per PI 215, sameness is to same/same cases cf., per analogy, as drabbit is to duck/rabbit faces; as coincidence is to essential/inessential – meaning/expression – cases.

Games: paradox + faces; sameness + same/same cases; word + meaning/use – essence/expression, essential/inessential, essential/not-essential, meaning/not-meaning, purpose/expression – cases; per analogies, ladder + up/down aspects, drabbit + duck/rabbit faces.

567. But, after all, the game is supposed to be determined by the rules! So, if a rule of the game prescribes that the kings are to be used for drawing lots before a game of chess, then that is an essential part of the game. What objection might one make to this? That one does not see the point of this prescription. Perhaps as one likewise wouldn't see the point of a rule by which each piece had to be turned around three times |before one moved it. If we found this rule in a board-game, we'd be surprised and would speculate about the purpose of the rule. ("Was this prescription meant to prevent one from moving without due consideration?")

To rehearse. The (PI 201) thesis of the *Investigations* is that identity is paradox, called the rule, as neither of opposite cases + existing as both qua either.

Comment. Per PI 567 grammar qua law: logical and empirical talk runs grammatically as follows; the king in the pre-play case, like the king is the play case, is the rule, the aspects of which are the purpose/enactment cases cf. per PI 43, the word as meaning/use cases, also per PI 215, sameness + same/same cases cf. drabbit + duck/rabbit faces.

Games: paradox + faces; rule + interpretations; word + meaning/use cases; sameness + same/same cases; king + essential/inessential – meaning/ material, purpose/enactment – cases; per analogies, ladder + up/down aspects, drabbit + duck/rabbit faces.

568. If I understand the character of the game aright, I might say, then this isn't an essential part of it.

((Meaning – a physiognomy.))

To rehearse. The (PI 201) thesis of the *Investigations* is that identity is paradox, called the rule, as neither of opposite cases + existing as both qua either.

Comment. Per PI 568 grammar qua law: meaning is paradoxically expression (physiognomy); as verb-sense understanding is noun-sense understanding; as this case of meaning qua essential case is its counterpart expression qua not-meaning, not-essential, case.

Games: paradox + faces; per PI 43, word + meaning/use cases; game-part + essential/inessential – meaning/expression, essence/expression, essential/ inessential, essential/not-essential, meaning/not-meaning – cases; per analogies, ladder + up/down aspects, drabbit + duck/rabbit faces.

*569. Language is an instrument. Its concepts are instruments. Now perhaps one thinks that it can make no **great** difference **which** concepts we employ. As, after all, it is possible to do physics in feet and inches as well as in metres and centimetres; the difference is merely one of convenience. But even this is not true* if, for instance, calculations in some system of measurement demand more time and trouble than we can afford.

To rehearse. The (PI 201) thesis of the *Investigations* is that identity is paradox, called the rule, as neither of opposite cases + existing as both qua either.

Comment. Per PI 569 grammar qua law: instrument is to meaning/employment cases; as, per PI 43, word is to meaning/use cases; as paradox is to its paired faces; each case of meaning, each concept, pairs with its own case of employment in that the meaning/employment cases are paradoxically each other cf. the up/down aspects of a ladder; per language of physics, imperial/metric cases are bonded paradoxically.

Games: paradox + faces; word + meaning/use – concept/application – cases; per analogies, ladder + up/down aspects, drabbit + duck/rabbit faces.

570. Concepts lead us to make investigations. They are the expression of our interest and direct our interest.

To rehearse. The (PI 201) thesis of the *Investigations* is that identity is paradox, called the rule, as neither of opposite cases + existing as both qua either.

Comment. Per PI 570 grammar qua law: language is to concept/employment – directing/directed – cases; as, per PI 43, word is to meaning/use cases; as paradox is to faces; as investigation is to interest/expression cases.

Games: paradox + faces; word + meaning/use – directing-concept/directed-employment cf. interest/expression – cases; per analogies, ladder + up/down aspects, drabbit + duck/rabbit faces.

571. A misleading parallel: psychology treats of processes in the mental sphere, as does physics in the physical.

Seeing, hearing, thinking, feeling, willing, are not the subject matter of psychology **in the same sense** *as that in which the movements of bodies, the phenomena of electricity, and so forth are the subject matter of physics. You can see this from the fact that the physicist sees, hears, thinks about and informs us of these phenomena, and the psychologist observes the utterances (the behaviour) of the subject.*

To rehearse. The (PI 201) thesis of the *Investigations* is that identity is paradox, called the rule, as neither of opposite cases + existing as both qua either.

Comment. Per PI 571 grammar qua law: psychology is to mind/body cases; as physicist is to meaning/matter cases; as paradox is to faces; as per PI 43, word is to meaning/expression – meaning/use – cases.

Games: paradox + faces; word + meaning/use cases; per PI 215, sameness + same/same case; science + psychology/physics cases; language + logic/empiricism – mind/body, meaning/matter – cases; per analogies, ladder + up/down aspects, drabbit + duck/rabbit faces.

572. Expectation is, grammatically, a state; like being of an opinion, hoping for something, knowing something, being able to do something. But in order to understand the grammar of these states, it is necessary to ask: "What counts as a criterion for anyone's being in such a state?" (States of hardness, of weight, of fitting.)

To rehearse. The (PI 201) thesis of the *Investigations* is that identity is paradox, called the rule, as neither of opposite cases + existing as both qua either.

Comment. Per PI 572 grammar qua law: state is to its expression; as per PI 43, meaning is to use; as paradox face is to counterpart face; per each paradox + faces threefold language game, in that its three members inhabit one another cf. ladder + up/down aspects each member as the case is the criterion for the other two members being the case.

Games: paradox + faces; person + state/expression – cf. mind/body, mental/behavioural – cases; per analogies, ladder + up/down aspects, drabbit + duck/rabbit faces.

573. To have an opinion is a state. – A state of what? Of the soul? Of the mind? Well, what does one say has an opinion? Mr N.N., for example. And that is the correct answer.

*One should not expect to be enlightened by the answer to **that** question. Other questions that go deeper are: What, in particular cases, do we regard as criteria for someone's being of such-and-such an opinion? When do we say that he reached this opinion at that time? When that he has altered his opinion? And so on. The picture that the answers to these questions give us shows **what** gets treated grammatically as a **state** here.*

To rehearse. The (PI 201) thesis of the *Investigations* is that identity is paradox, called the rule, as neither of opposite cases + existing as both qua either.

Comment. Per PI 573 grammar qua law: from PI 572, what gets treated grammatically as a state qua paradox face and, as thereby a criterion for a state case, is its expression qua counterpart face, as well as the person case as the paradox case.

Games: paradox i.e. picture i.e. particular case + faces; person + state/ expression – mind/body, mental/behavioural – cases; per PI 43, word (language) + meaning/use (private/public) – meaning/expression – cases; per analogies, ladder + up/down aspects, drabbit + duck/rabbit faces.

574. A sentence, and hence in another sense a thought, can be the 'expression' of belief, hope, expectation, etc. But believing is not thinking. (A grammatical remark.) The concepts of believing, expecting, hoping are less different in kind from one another than they are from the concept of thinking.

To rehearse. The (PI 201) thesis of the *Investigations* is that identity is paradox, called the rule, as neither of opposite cases + existing as both qua either.

Comment. Per PI 574 grammar qua law: per PI 43, wording qua sentence qua expression (here, in terms of thinking or attitude qua attitude of belief or hope or expectation etc.) is to verb/noun senses (say, hope/hope, hoping/

hoping, hoping/hoped) qua meaning/use cases; by which, the attitude qua attitude cases are less different in kind from one another than from the thinking case, and such that believing, say, is not thinking; nonetheless, thinking, belief, hope, expectation, make for assorted language games – cases of threefold grammar – commonly bespeaking identity as paradox.

Games: paradox + faces; word + meaning/use cases; sentence qua expression (per thinking or attitude) + expressing/expressed – thinking/thinking, believing/believing, hoping/hoping, expecting/expecting, verb-sense/noun-sense – cases; per analogies, ladder + up/down aspects, drabbit + duck/rabbit faces.

575. When I sat down on this chair, of course I believed it would bear me. The thought of its collapsing never crossed my mind.

But: "In spite of everything that he did, I held fast to the belief..." Here there is thought, and perhaps a recurrent struggle to maintain an attitude.

To rehearse. The (PI 201) thesis of the *Investigations* is that identity is paradox, called the rule, as neither of opposite cases + existing as both qua either.

Comment. Per PI 575 grammar qua law: paradox is to faces; as belief, like thinking, is to verb/noun sense

Games: paradox + faces; per PI 43, word + meaning/use cases; chair-belief case qua attitude case + verb/noun senses; thinking case + verb/noun senses; per analogies, ladder + up/down aspects, drabbit + duck/rabbit faces.

576. I look at a burning fuse, excitedly watching the flame approach the explosive. Perhaps I don't think anything at all, or have lots of disjointed thoughts. This is certainly a case of expecting.

To rehearse. The (PI 201) thesis of the *Investigations* is that identity is paradox, called the rule, as neither of opposite cases + existing as both qua either.

Comment. Per PI 576 grammar qua law: paradox is to faces; as expectation is to verb/noun senses; as thinking case is to verb/noun senses; as per PI 43, word is to meaning/use cases; per analogies, ladder + up/down aspects, drabbit + duck/rabbit faces.

*577. We say "I'm expecting him" when we believe that he'll come, though his coming does not **occupy** our thoughts. (Here "I'm expecting him" would mean "I'd be surprised if he didn't come" – and that will not be called a description of a state of mind.) But we also say "I'm expecting him" when it is supposed to mean: I'm eagerly awaiting him. We could imagine a language in which different verbs were consistently used in these cases. And similarly, more than one verb where we speak of 'believing', 'hoping', and so on. The concepts of such a language would perhaps be more suitable for understanding psychology than are the concepts of our language.*

To rehearse. The (PI 201) thesis of the *Investigations* is that identity is paradox, called the rule, as neither of opposite cases + existing as both qua either.

Comment. Per PI 577 grammar qua law: with respect to ordinary language as well as a psychological language, all of which serves as raw material for grammatical treatment, paradox is to faces; as expectation, like belief (and parallels), is to verb/noun senses; as per PI 43, also PI 574, word is to meaning/use cases.

*578. Ask yourself: What does it mean to **believe** Goldbach's conjecture? What does this belief consist in? In a feeling of certainty as we state, hear or think the conjecture? (That would not interest us.) And what are the characteristics of this feeling? Why, I don't even know how far the feeling may be caused by the conjecture itself.*

Am I to say that belief is a colour tone of our thoughts? Where does this idea come from? Well, there is a tone of believing, as of doubting.

I should like to ask: how does the belief engage with this conjecture? Let us look and see what are the consequences of this belief, where it takes us. "It makes me search for a proof of the conjecture." — Very well; and now let us look and see what your searching really consists in! Then we shall know what believing the conjecture amounts to.

To rehearse. The (PI 201) thesis of the *Investigations* is that identity is paradox, called the rule, as neither of opposite cases + existing as both qua either.

Comment. Per PI 578 grammar qua law: paradox is to faces; as per PI 43 wording (belief re: Goldbach's conjecture) is to meaning/use – believing/believed cases; as thinking is to verb/noun senses; as certainty-feeling is to verb/noun senses; as nexus is to cause/effect cases; as colour tone is to toning/toned – belief/thinking cases; as conjecture-belief is to search/proof cases.

Games: paradox + faces; per PI 43, word (say, belief) + meaning/use cases; per analogies, ladder + up/down aspects, drabbit + duck/rabbit faces.

579. A feeling of confidence. How is it manifested in behaviour?

To rehearse. The (PI 201) thesis of the *Investigations* is that identity is paradox, called the rule, as neither of opposite cases + existing as both qua either.

Comment. Per PI 579 grammar qua law: paradox is to faces; as per PI 43, word (say, confidence) is to meaning/use – feeling/behaviour – cases; here, the feeling aspect (cf. a mental aspect) is paradoxically a behavioural aspect (cf. a physical aspect).

Games: paradox + faces (and variants, as per the Comment); per analogies, ladder + up/down aspects, drabbit + duck/rabbit faces.

580. An 'inner process' stands in need of outward criteria.

To rehearse. The (PI 201) thesis of the *Investigations* is that identity is paradox, called the rule, as neither of opposite cases + existing as both qua either.

Comment. Per PI 580 grammar qua law: the meaning of a word is its use (as per PI 43); the inner process qua paradox face of a paradox is its outward expression qua counterpart face; here, as cross-referenced – paradoxical – cases, each of the paradox-face cases as the case is the criterion (warrant, justification) for the other being the case cf. per analogy, the up/down aspects of a ladder.

Games: paradox + faces; word + meaning/use cases; language + inner-process/outer-behaviour – private/public – cases; per analogies, ladder + up/down aspects, drabbit + duck/rabbit faces.

*581. An expectation is embedded in a situation, from which it arises. The expectation of an explosion may, for example, arise from a situation in which an explosion **is to be expected**.*

To rehearse. The (PI 201) thesis of the *Investigations* is that identity is paradox, called the rule, as neither of opposite cases + existing as both qua either.

Comment. Per PI 581 grammar qua law: the paradox, like its faces, pertains to (is embedded in) the threefold grammar case; expectation, like expecting/expected aspects, is embedded in grammatical language as its situation.

Games, cases of threefold grammar: paradox + faces; expectation + verb/noun senses; per analogies, ladder + up/down aspects, drabbit + duck/rabbit faces.

582. If, instead of saying "I expect the explosion any moment now", someone whispered "It'll go off in a moment", then his words do not describe a feeling, although they and their tone may be a manifestation of it.

To rehearse. The (PI 201) thesis of the *Investigations* is that identity is paradox, called the rule, as neither of opposite cases + existing as both qua either.

Comment. Per PI 582 grammar qua law: paradox is to faces; as per PI 43, word is to meaning/use cases; as his-words qua expectation is to verb/noun senses; as thinking, like feeling, is to verb/noun senses; as manifestation is to manifesting/manifested cases; as expectation is to thinking/feeling cases.

Games: paradox + faces; per PI 43, word (expectation) + meaning/use cases (and parallels, as per the Comment); per analogies, ladder + up/down aspects, drabbit + duck/rabbit faces.

583. "But you talk as if I weren't really expecting, hoping, **now** – when I thought I was. As if what were happening **now** had no deep significance." – What does it mean to say "What is happening now has significance" or "has deep significance"? What is a **deep** feeling? Could someone have a feeling of ardent love or hope for one second – **no matter what** preceded or followed this second? – What is happening now has significance – in these surroundings. The surroundings give it its importance. And the word "hope" refers to a phenomenon of human life. (A smiling mouth **smiles** only in a human face.)

To rehearse. The (PI 201) thesis of the *Investigations* is that identity is paradox, called the rule, as neither of opposite cases + existing as both qua either.

Comment. Per PI 583 grammar qua law: the significance aspect of a deep case qua an event case is its outcome aspect; as a face of paradox is its counterpart face; as per PI 43, the meaning cf. verb sense of a word (say, hope, long, expectation, happening, event, thinking, feeling) is its use cf. noun sense; as the past aspect of the now is its future aspect; whatever the variant language game, its threefold grammar is the context for its three member-cases; whatever the threefold case it is a human language game.

Games: paradox + faces; word + meaning/use cases (and variants, as per the Comment); per analogies, ladder + up/down aspects, drabbit + duck/rabbit faces.

584. Now suppose I sit in my room and hope that N.N. will come and bring me some money, and suppose one minute of this state could be isolated, cut out of its context; would what happen in it then not be hoping? – Think, for example, of the words which you may utter in this time. They are no longer part of this language. And in different surroundings the institution of money doesn't exist either.

A coronation is the picture of pomp and dignity. Cut one minute of this proceeding out of its surroundings: the crown is being placed on the head of the king in his coronation robes. – But in different surroundings, gold is the cheapest of metals, its gleam is thought vulgar. There the fabric of the robe is cheap to produce. A crown is a parody of a respectable hat. And so on.

To rehearse. The (PI 201) thesis of the *Investigations* is that identity is paradox, called the rule, as neither of opposite cases + existing as both qua either.

Comment. Per PI 584 grammar qua law: a word is a word – not a mere sound or scribble – where it is used, as thereby paradoxically meaningful, in a language game; out of that context, it having not that use, hence not that meaning, it is a mere sound or scrobble; likewise, freed from pertaining to grammar, a jumble of sounds is nonsense; variant language games – cases of threefold grammar – coincide in bespeaking identity-as-paradox in assorted ways.

Games: paradox + faces; per PI 433, word + meaning/use cases; culture + language/deed cases; per analogies, ladder + up/down aspects, drabbit + duck/rabbit faces.

*585. When someone says "I hope he'll come", is this a **report** about his state of mind, or a **manifestation** of his hope? – I may, for example, say it to myself. And surely I am not giving myself a report. It may be a sigh; but it need not be. If I tell someone, "I can't keep my mind on my work today; I keep on thinking of his coming" – **this** will be called a description of my state of mind.*

To rehearse. The (PI 201) thesis of the *Investigations* is that identity is paradox, called the rule, as neither of opposite cases + existing as both qua either.

Comment. Per PI 585 grammar qua law: a paradox-face case warrants (makes manifest) a corresponding other paradox-face case; as a report case warrants a state-of-mind – say, a hope – case; as a word-use case warrants a word-meaning case (so, PI 43); as description qua expression of a thinking case warrants that thinking – state of mind – case.

Games: paradox + faces; word (cf. sentence) + meaning/use – state-of-mind/description, hoping/report, hoping/manifestation – cases.

586. *"I've heard he is coming; I've been expecting him all day." This is a report on how I have spent the day. – In conversation, I come to the conclusion that a particular event is to be expected, and I draw this conclusion in the words "So now I must expect him to come". This may be called the first thought, the first act, of this expectation. – The exclamation "I'm expecting him – I'm longing to see him!" may be called an act of expecting. But I can utter the same words as the result of self-observation, and then they might amount to: "So, after all that has happened, I'm still expecting him with longing." It all depends on what led up to these words.*

To rehearse. The (PI 201) thesis of the *Investigations* is that identity is paradox, called the rule, as neither of opposite cases + existing as both qua either.

Comment. Per PI 586 grammar qua law: assorted language games qua cases of threefold grammar are as follows; from PI 43, word qua sentence qua expectation-talk qua particular-event-talk qua exclamation is to meaning/report – expecting/expected, first-thought/first-act, longing/expression, exclaiming/exclaimed, self-observation/utterance – cases; as paradox is to faces.

Games: paradox + faces (and variants – as per Comment); per analogies, ladder + up/down aspects, drabbit + duck/rabbit faces.

587. *Does it make sense to ask "How do you know that you believe that?" – and is the answer: "I find it out by introspection"?*

*In **some** cases it will be possible to say some such thing, in most not.*

It makes sense to ask, "Do I really love her, or am I only fooling myself?", and the process of introspection is the calling up of memories, of imagined possible situations, and of the feelings that one would have if...

To rehearse. The (PI 201) thesis of the *Investigations* is that identity is paradox, called the rule, as neither of opposite cases + existing as both qua either.

Comment. Per PI 587 grammar qua law: in analysis of empirical-sense talk, any of the targeted, so to say, introspective cases of feeling, loving, fooling, memorising, fantasising, believing, or knowing, is nothing real (grammatical) other than as paradoxically its enactment, just as, per PI 43, word-meaning is nothing other than paradoxically word-use; any such case is partly the case as necessarily grammatical but otherwise is not the case as sufficiently grammatical; each of the cases as a paradox-face is necessarily but not sufficiently the threefold identity-as-paradox + faces gramma as, for example, the paradox + faces, or feeling + feeling/feeling, qua verb-sense/noon-sense, cases.

Games: paradox + faces; per PI 43, word + meaning/use – cf. introspection/expression – cases; per analogies, ladder + up/down aspects, drabbit + duck/rabbit faces.

588. "I'm in two minds whether to go away tomorrow." (This may be called a description of a state of mind.) – "Your arguments don't convince me; now as before it is my intention to go away tomorrow." Here one is tempted to call the intention a feeling. The feeling is one of a certain rigidity, of irrevocable decision. (But here too there are many different characteristic feelings and attitudes.) – I am asked: "How long are you staying here?" I reply: "Tomorrow I'm going away; it's the end of my holidays." – But, by contrast, I say, at the end of a quarrel, "All right! Then I'll go tomorrow!" – I make a decision.

To rehearse. The (PI 201) thesis of the *Investigations* is that identity is paradox, called the rule, as neither of opposite cases + existing as both qua either.

Comment. Per PI 588 grammar qua law: the intention case in one instance is the report of a mind-state whereas in another intense it is the expression of feeling (whatever the shade) or of a decision; the state-of-mind report is one of indecision; from which, the text presents as assorted language games, each bespeaking identity as paradox, See Games, next.

Games: identity-as-paradox + faces; per PI 43, word + meaning/use cases; indecision, like decision, like intention, like feeling + verb/noun senses; per analogies, ladder + up/down aspects, drabbit + duck/rabbit faces.

589. *"In my heart I've decided it." And one is even inclined to point to one's breast as one says it. Psychologically, this way of speaking should be taken seriously. Why should it be taken less seriously than the statement that faith is a state of the soul? (Luther: "Faith is under the left nipple.")*

To rehearse. The (PI 201) thesis of the *Investigations* is that identity is paradox, called the rule, as neither of opposite cases + existing as both qua either.

Comment. Per PI 589 grammar qua law: the psychological talk and religious talk translates grammatically as follows; the face of paradox is to its counterpart face; as per PI 43, the meaning of a word is its use; as the deciding aspect of a serious case qua the sentence case is to its heart-pointing behaviour aspect; as the soul-state aspect of a serious case qua faith is to its heart-behaviour (cf. under-left-nipple location) aspect.

Game: paradox + face (and variants, as per the Comment); per analogies, ladder + up/down aspects, drabbit + duck/rabbit faces.

590. *Someone might learn to understand the meaning of the expression "seriously __meaning__ what one says" by a gesture of pointing at the heart. But now one must ask: "What shows that he has learnt it?"*

To rehearse. The (PI 201) thesis of the *Investigations* is that identity is paradox, called the rule, as neither of opposite cases + existing as both qua either.

246 IDENTITY AS PARADOX

Comment. Per PI 590 grammar qua law: what shows that a noun-sense learning case is so is its paradoxical verb-sense learning case; paradox is to faces; as learning is to verb/noun senses; as per PI 43, word is to meaning/use cases; as the meaning aspect of a serious case is its gesture aspect.

Game: paradox + faces; per PI 43, wording + meaning/use cases; learning + verb/noun senses; seriousness + meaning/gesture cases; per analogies, ladder + up/down aspects, drabbit + duck/rabbit faces.

*591. Am I to say that any one who has an intention has an experience of tending towards something? That there are particular experiences of 'tending'? — Remember this case: if one urgently wants to make some remark, some objection, in a discussion, it often happens that one opens one's mouth, draws a breath, and holds it; if one then decides to let the objection drop, one lets one's breath out. The experience of what goes on here seems to be an experience of a tendency to say something. An observer will realize that I wanted to say something and then thought better of it. In **this** situation, that is. — In a different one, he would not interpret my behaviour in this way, however characteristic of the intention to speak it may be in the present situation. And is there any reason for assuming that this same experience could not occur in some quite different situation in which it has nothing to do with any 'tending'?*

To rehearse. The (PI 201) thesis of the *Investigations* is that identity is paradox, called the rule, as neither of opposite cases + existing as both qua either.

Comment. Per PI 591 grammar qua law: per PI 215, sameness is to different same/same cases cf. as drabbit is to duck/rabbit faces; as same behaviour is to non-intention/intention cases; as intention is to intending/intended cases.

Games: paradox qua **this** qua particular case + faces; sameness behaviour + same/same – non-intention/intention – cases; intention + verb/noun senses; per analogies, ladder + up/down aspects, drabbit + duck/rabbit faces

*592. "But when you say 'I intend to go away', you surely mean it! Here again it just is the mental act of meaning that gives the sentence life. If you merely repeat the sentence after someone else, say in order to mock his way of speaking, then you utter it without this act of meaning." – When we are doing philosophy, it may sometimes look like that. But let's think up really **different** situations and conversations, and the ways in which that sentence is uttered in them. – "I always discover a mental undertone; perhaps not always the **same** one." – And was there no undertone there when you repeated the sentence after someone else? And how is the 'undertone' now to be separated from the rest of the experience of speaking?*

To rehearse. The (PI 201) thesis of the *Investigations* is that identity is paradox, called the rule, as neither of opposite cases + existing as both qua either.

Comment. Per PI 592 grammar qua law: the *Investigations* philosophy treats with the three cases of identity-as-paradox + corresponding faces; these, per PI 43, are the cases of language (word) + meaning/use cases; in whatever way a sentence is uttered in a language case the utterance is paradoxically its meaning; a sentence is not merely said; it is meaningfully said; if I repeat a saying meant by its creator passionately, I mean what I say as, for example, a mimicry; such is the grammar.

Games: paradox + faces; (per PI 215) sameness + same/same cases; (per PI 43) word (sentence) + meaning/use cases; per analogies, ladder + up/down aspects, drabbit + duck/rabbit faces.

593. A main cause of philosophical diseases – one-sided diet: one nourishes one's thinking with only one kind of example.

To rehearse. The (PI 201) thesis of the *Investigations* is that identity is paradox, called the rule, as neither of opposite cases + existing as both qua either.

Comment. Per PI 593 grammar qua law: it is a grammatical disease – hence an ungrammatical case – to deem a sentence to be meaningful where used in one-only way; different language situations call for a same-sentence case to have its different meaning/use cases according to that language case in which it features; in whatever way a sentence is uttered in a language case the utterance is paradoxically its meaning.

Games: paradox + faces; (per PI 43) sentence (word) + meaning/use cases; (per PI 215) sameness + same/same cases; per analogies, ladder + up/down aspects, drabbit + duck/rabbit faces.

594. "But the words, significantly uttered, have, after all, not only a surface, but also a dimension of depth!" After all, something different does take place when they are uttered significantly from when they are merely uttered. – How I express this is not the point. Whether I say that in the first case they have depth; or that something goes on in me, in my mind, as I utter them; or that they have an atmosphere – it always comes to the same thing.

"Well, if we all agree about that, won't it be true?"

(I cannot accept the other person's testimony, because it is not **testimony**. It only tells me what he is **inclined** to say.)

To rehearse. The (PI 201) thesis of the *Investigations* is that identity is paradox, called the rule, as neither of opposite cases + existing as both qua either.

Comment. Per PI 594 grammar qua law: the depth dimension of a sentence is its surface dimension; as, per PI 43, the meaning of a word is its use; as the face of paradox is its counterpart face; in all such cases of threefold talk, the agreement principle is not one of either logic or empiricism but of grammar (law); by PI 594, a sentence is grammatical in being its meaning/use dimensions as paradoxically one another and is not grammatical if one-dimensionally used without meaning; for the human form of life – its language – its threefold grammar as paradox + faces is that of agreement + agreed cases; a word cannot merely be said, without meaning – any more than a ladder can be an ascent without being a descent cf. inclining is to saying, as testimony-giving is testimony-expression, as ladder-ascent is ladder-descent.

Games: paradox + faces; per PI 43, word + meaning/use – cf. depth/surface – cases; per analogies, ladder + up/down aspects, drabbit + duck/rabbit faces.

595. It is natural for us to say a sentence in such-and-such a context, and unnatural to say it in isolation. Are we to say that there is a particular feeling accompanying the utterance of every sentence whose utterance comes naturally to us?

To rehearse. The (PI 201) thesis of the *Investigations* is that identity is paradox, called the rule, as neither of opposite cases + existing as both qua either.

Comment. Per PI 595 grammar qua law: per language context, it is grammatical for a sentence to have its unnatural/natural – meaning/use – aspects and ungrammatical for it to have one of these only in isolation; the understanding, here, for the philosopher, is grammatical, not logical or empirical; it is to do with identity law, identity grammar; the unnatural is the not-natural, the distinct from the natural; compare meaning as not-use i.e. distinct from use; also use as meaningless, not-meaningful i.e. distinct from meaning; again, the talk is grammatical.

Games: paradox + faces; (per PI 43) word qua sentence + meaning/use – unnatural/natural, cf. concept/expression – cases; per analogies, ladder + up/down aspects, drabbit + duck/rabbit faces.

596. The feeling of 'familiarity' and of 'naturalness'. It is easier to come across a feeling of unfamiliarity and of unnaturalness. Or, **feelings**. For not everything that is unfamiliar to us makes an impression of unfamiliarity upon us. And here one has to consider what we call "unfamiliar". If a boulder lies on the road, we know it for a boulder, but perhaps not for the one which has always been lying there. We recognize a man, say, as a man, but not as an acquaintance. There are feelings of long-standing familiarity: they are sometimes manifest in a particular way of looking or by the words "The same old room!" (which I occupied many years before and, now returning, find unchanged). Equally, there are feelings of strangeness: I stop short, look at the object or man questioningly

or suspiciously, and say "I find it all strange". — But the existence of this feeling of strangeness does not give us a reason for saying that every object which we know well and which does not seem strange to us gives us a feeling of familiarity. — It is as if we thought that the space once filled by the feeling of strangeness must surely be filled by **something***. The space for these kinds of atmosphere is there, and if one of them is not filling it, then another is.*

To rehearse. The (PI 201) thesis of the *Investigations* is that identity is paradox, called the rule, as neither of opposite cases + existing as both qua either.

Comment. Per PI 596 grammar qua law: paradox face is to paradox face; as familiar is to strange; as unfamiliar is to familiar; as unnatural is to natural; as feeling is to expression; ass, per PI 43, word-meaning is to word-use; from which, according to the language-game variant, the paradox face is the counterpart paradox face; the feeling is the expression; the word-meaning is the word-use; the unfamiliar i.e. unnatural is the familiar i.e. natural; whatever the variant cases of paradox faces which present themselves for consideration, these are spaces that live in one another cf. the ladder-ascent/ladder-descent aspects.

Games: paradox + faces; per PI 43, word + meaning/use – feeling/expression, strange/familiar, unfamiliar/familiar, unnatural/natural cases; per analogies, ladder + up/down aspects, drabbit + duck/rabbit faces.

597. Germanisms will creep into the speech of a German who speaks English well, even though he does not first construct the German expression and then translate it into English. This will make him speak English **as if he were translating** *'unconsciously' from German. So too, we often think in a way that makes it seem as if our thinking were grounded in a thought-schema, as if we were translating from a more primitive mode of thought into our own.*

To rehearse. The (PI 201) thesis of the *Investigations* is that identity is paradox, called the rule, as neither of opposite cases + existing as both qua either.

Comment. Per PI 597 grammar qua law: paradox is to faces; as coincidence is to distinctly different cases (say, unconscious/conscious, German/English, alternative ways of putting things).

Games: paradox + faces; per PI 43, word + meaning/use – feeling/expression – cases; Germanism + German/English – unconscious/conscious, unfamiliar/familiar – aspects; translation activity + translating/translated aspects cf. PI 201 – paradox as a substitution activity whereby paradox-face cases interchange; per analogies, ladder + up/down aspects, drabbit + duck/rabbit faces.

598. *When we do philosophy, we are inclined to hypostatize feelings where there are none. They serve to explain our thoughts to us.*

*"**Here** the explanation of our thinking requires a feeling!" It is as if our conviction answered to this demand.*

To rehearse. The (PI 201) thesis of the *Investigations* is that identity is paradox, called the rule, as neither of opposite cases + existing as both qua either.

Comment. Per PI 598 grammar qua law: the logical and/or empirical sense given out in the text translates grammatically as follows; to hypostatize feelings is, in variant terms, to express meaning – where the meaning/expression – cf. thinking/feeling, thought/explanation – cases are paradox-face cases; where taken as distinct cases, each thereby as not the other, there is no feeling aspect in the thinking aspect, and vice versa.

Games: paradox + faces; per PI 43, word qua sentence + meaning/use – thinking/speaking, thinking/feeling, meaning/expression, – cases; conviction + convincing/convinced cases; expression + expressing/expressed cases; per analogies ladder + up/down aspects, drabbit + duck/rabbit faces.

599. *In philosophy no inferences are drawn. "But it must be like this!" is not a philosophical proposition. Philosophy only states what everyone concedes to it.*

To rehearse. The (PI 201) thesis of the *Investigations* is that identity is paradox, called the rule, as neither of opposite cases + existing as both qua either.

Comment. Per PI 599 grammar qua law: *Investigations* philosophy finds for grammar qua law not as prescription but as description – of what plainly is the case.

Games: paradox + faces; exclamation + thought/expression cases; per analogies, ladder + up/down aspects, drabbit + duck/rabbit faces.

*600. Does everything that we do not find conspicuous make an impression of inconspicuousness? Does what is ordinary always make the **impression** of ordinariness?*

To rehearse. The (PI 201) thesis of the *Investigations* is that identity is paradox, called the rule, as neither of opposite cases + existing as both qua either.

Comment. Per PI 600 grammar qua law: whatever the logical case or the empirical-sense case, the grammatical cases – each as threefold – are as follows; paradox is to faces; as per PI 43, word is to meaning/use – cf. inconspicuous/conspicuous, non-ordinary/ordinary, inconspicuous/ordinary – cases qua impressions.

Games: paradox + face (and variants, as per the Comment); per analogies, ladder + up/down aspects, drabbit + duck/rabbit faces.

*601. When I talk about this table – do I **remember** that this object is called a "table"?*

To rehearse. The (PI 201) thesis of the *Investigations* is that identity is paradox, called the rule, as neither of opposite cases + existing as both qua either.

Comment. Per PI 601 grammar qua law: table-talk is to remembering/remembering – verb-sense/noun-sense – cases; as per PI 43, word is to meaning/use cases; what gives the table-word its meaning cf. memorising aspect is paradoxically its use cf. memorised aspect.

Games: paradox + faces; word + meaning/use cases; table-talk + remembrance/remembrance – verb-sense/noun-sense – case; per analogies, ladder + up/down aspects, drabbit + duck/rabbit faces.

602. Asked "Did you recognize your desk when you entered your room this morning?" – I'd no doubt say "Certainly!" And yet it would be misleading to say that any recognizing had occurred. Of course, the desk was not strange to me; I wasn't surprised to see it, as I would have been if another one had been standing there, or some unfamiliar object.

To rehearse. The (PI 201) thesis of the *Investigations* is that identity is paradox, called the rule, as neither of opposite cases + existing as both qua either.

Comment. Per PI 602 grammar qua law: per desk, recognition is to recognition/recognition – verb-sense/noun-sense – cases; as, identity-as-paradox is to identical faces cf. drabbit + duck/rabbit faces; here, it is misleading (ungrammatical) to speak of either of the verb/noun senses of recognition without the other as its paradoxical case cf. drabbit as a duck face with no rabbit face; too, the certainty qua recognition case as a paradox case, as neither of – as distinct from – the verb/noun aspects, has for its faces the verb/noun aspects.

Games: paradox + faces; per PI 43, word + meaning/use cases; (per desk) recognition + recognition/recognition – recognising/recognised – cases; per analogies, ladder + up/down aspects, drabbit + duck/rabbit faces.

603. No one will say that every time I enter my room, my long familiar surroundings, there occurs an act of recognition of all that I see and have seen hundreds of times before.

To rehearse. The (PI 201) thesis of the *Investigations* is that identity is paradox, called the rule, as neither of opposite cases + existing as both qua either.

Comment. Per PI 603 grammar qua law: paradox face is to counterpart paradox face; as, per PI 43, word-meaning is to word-use; as, per 596, the unfamiliar case is to the familiar case; as a, per PI 603 (cf. PI 602), the recognition case qua verb-sense case is to the recognition case qua noun-sense case; to rehearse, the philosopher's task is to translate logical or empirical cases into grammatical cases; his concern is to investigate identity law, identity grammar; logical and empirical cases are the raw material for grammatical treatment.

Games: paradox + faces; word + meaning/use – unfamiliar/familiar, recognition/recognition qua verb-sense/noun-sense – cases; per analogies, ladder + up/down aspects, drabbit + duck/rabbit faces.

604. It is easy to misconceive what is called "recognizing"; as if recognizing always consisted in comparing two impressions with one another. It is as if I carried a picture of an object with me and used it to identify an object as the one represented by the picture. Our memory seems to us to be the agent of such a comparison, by preserving a picture of what has been seen before, or by allowing us to look into the past (as if down a spyglass).

To rehearse. The (PI 201) thesis of the *Investigations* is that identity is paradox, called the rule, as neither of opposite cases + existing as both qua either.

Comment. Per PI 604 grammar qua law: picture talk is identity-as-paradox talk; recognition implying the comparison of two case side by side, as it were, is a misconception (not grammatical) in that the case of paired opposites is that of cases as paradoxically – coincidentally – one another cf. the ladder's way-up/way-down aspects; grammatically, memory is not a go-between mental recognition and external object or between past and present – rather, and as assorted language games, each bespeaking identity as paradox, identity-as-paradox qua memory, like identity-as-paradox as recognition, is its verb/noun senses as its paradox faces.

Games: identity-as-paradox + identical faces; picture qua recognition + recognition/recognition – recognising/recognised, verb/noun – cases; memory + subjective/objective cases; per analogies, ladder + up/down aspects, drabbit + duck/rabbit faces.

*605. Indeed, it is not so much as if I were comparing the object with a picture set beside it, but as if the object **coincided** with the picture. So I see only one thing, not two.*

To rehearse. The (PI 201) thesis of the *Investigations* is that identity is paradox, called the rule, as neither of opposite cases + existing as both qua either.

Comment. Per PI 605 grammar qua law: picture talk in the grammatical sense is identity-as-paradox talk; grammatically, per paradox case, a face is paradoxically a (thereby counterpart) face; as, per a recognition case, a verb-sense recognition case is coincidentally a noun-sense recognition case cf. drabbit as picture with its duck/rabbit coincidental faces – drabbit is neither two side-by-side identities nor a onefold-only identity but is a double-aspect (double-faced) identity-as-paradox qua coincidence case as a mutual-eclipse activity case (so, PI 201).

Games: paradox + faces; coincidence + distinct cases; recognition + verb/noun aspects; see, too, PI 604; per analogies, ladder + up/down aspects, drabbit + duck/rabbit faces.

*606. We say "The expression in his voice was **genuine**". If it was spurious, we think of another one, as it were behind it. – **This** is the face he shows the world; inwardly he has another one. – But this does not mean that when his expression is **genuine**, he has two identical faces.*

(("A quite particular expression."))

To rehearse. The (PI 201) thesis of the *Investigations* is that identity is paradox, called the rule, as neither of opposite cases + existing as both qua either.

Comment. Per PI 606 grammar qua law: the ordinary language of the text translates grammatically as follows; voice is to genuineness/expression (or otherwise spuriousness/expression) cases; as paradox is to faces; as **this** qua particular case is to inner/outer cases; the genuine-talk case is not a two-faced talk; rather, the voice is two faces as the genuine/spurious cases.

Games: identity-as-paradox + identical faces; per PI 43, word + meaning/use cases; face + hidden/presenting, spurious/genuine, cases; coincidence + different (distinct) cases; per analogies, ladder + up/down aspects, drabbit + duck/rabbit faces.

*607. How does one guess the time? I don't mean by clues, such as the position of the sun, the brightness of the room, and the like. – One asks oneself, say, "What time can it be?", pauses a moment, perhaps imagines a clock face, and then says a time. – Or one considers various possibilities, thinks first of one time, then of another, and in the end stops at a particular one. That's the sort of thing one does. – But isn't the hunch accompanied by a feeling of conviction; and doesn't that mean that it now accords with an inner clock? – No, I don't read the time off from any clock; there is a feeling of conviction inasmuch as I say a time to myself **without** a feeling of doubt, with calm assurance. – But doesn't something click as I say the time, stopping at a number? And I'd never have spoken of 'a feeling of conviction' here, but would have said: I considered a while and then plumped for its being quarter past five. – But what did I go by? I might perhaps have said "just by feeling", which only means that I relied on a hunch. – But surely you must at least have put yourself in a particular state of mind in order to guess the time; and you don't take just any old idea of what time it is as giving the correct time! – To repeat: I **asked** myself "I wonder what time it is" That is, I did not, for example, read this sentence in a story, or quote it as someone else's utterance; nor was I practising the pronunciation of these words; and so on. **These** were not the circumstances of my saying the words. – But then, **what** were the circumstances? – I was thinking about my breakfast, and wondering whether it would be late today. These were the kind of circumstances. – But do you really not see that you were in a state of mind which, though intangible, is characteristic of guessing the time, as if you were surrounded by an atmosphere characteristic of doing so. – Yes; what was characteristic was that I said to* myself "I wonder what time it is" – And if this sentence has a particular atmosphere, how am I to separate it from the sentence itself? It would never have occurred to me to think that the sentence had such an aura, if I had not thought of how one might say it differently – as a quotation, as a joke, as practice in elocution, and so on. And **then** all at once I wanted to say – then all at once it seemed to me – that I must after all have **meant** the words somehow specially; differently, that is, from in those other cases. The picture of the special atmosphere forced itself upon me; I virtually see the atmosphere before me – so long, that is, as I do not look at what, according to my memory, really happened.

And as for the feeling of certainty: I sometimes say to myself, "I am sure it's ... o'clock", and in a more or less confident tone of voice, and so on. If you ask me the **reason** for this certainty, I have none.

If I say: I read it off from an inner clock – that is a picture, and all that corresponds to it is that I estimated the time. And the purpose of the picture is to assimilate this case to the other one. I am reluctant to acknowledge two different cases here.

To rehearse. The (PI 201) thesis of the *Investigations* is that identity is paradox, called the rule, as neither of opposite cases + existing as both qua either.

Comment. Per PI 607 grammar qua law: picture talk is identity-as-paradox talk; PI 607 issues in a great deal of logical-sense talk and empirical-sense talk implying that, philosophically, the focus needs to be on making grammatical sense of the talk; the case at the fore is that of how the time might be judged, and as to how that is done; grammatically, telling the time means saying the time; as the face of a paradox is the counterpart face; as per PI 43, the meaning of a word is using it.

Games (include): paradox + faces; word + meaning/use – cf. mental/physical, aura/expression, atmosphere/application – cases; time-telling + verb/noun aspects; time + question/answer cases; now (as neither past nor future) + both past/future cases; deliberation + starting/ending cases; conviction + feeling/felt cases; calm assurance + feeling/speaking cases; per analogies, ladder + up/down aspects, drabbit + duck/rabbit faces.

608. *The idea of the intangibility of that mental state in estimating the time is of the greatest importance. Why is it **intangible**? Isn't it because we refuse to count what is tangible about our state as part of the specific state which we are postulating?*

To rehearse. The (PI 201) thesis of the *Investigations* is that identity is paradox, called the rule, as neither of opposite cases + existing as both qua either.

Comment. Per PI 608 grammar qua law: specific-talk is identity-as-paradox talk; intangible/tangible cases qua mental-state/expression cases are paradox faces, hence inseparables cf. drabbit + duck/rabbit faces; the grammar thus is threefold, with each of its three members distinct from the others yet also indwelling the others; here, the tangible alone is accounted insufficiently identity as paradox.

Games: paradox (cf. specific case) + faces; per PI 43, word + meaning/use – cf. intangible/tangible, mental-state/expression – cases; per analogies, ladder + up/down aspects, drabbit + duck/rabbit faces.

609. *The description of an atmosphere is a special application of language, for special purposes.*

((Interpreting 'understanding' as atmosphere; as a mental act. One can fabricate an atmosphere apropos anything. 'An indescribable character.'))

To rehearse. The (PI 201) thesis of the *Investigations* is that identity is paradox, called the rule, as neither of opposite cases + existing as both qua either.

Comment. Per PI 609 grammar qua law: special-talk is identity-as-paradox talk; atmosphere is to solidity; as paradox-face is to paradox face; as mental-process is to behaviour; as intangibility is to tangibility; as, per PI 43, word-meaning is to word-use; as verb-sense understanding is to noun-sense understanding; as indescribable is to describable; from which, language atmosphere is paradoxically language description qua language application – its special purpose is thus to function as a paradoxical case.

Games: paradox (cf. special case) + faces; word + meaning/use – atmosphere/solidity – cases; per analogies, ladder + up/down aspects, drabbit + duck/rabbit faces.

*610. Describe the aroma of coffee! – Why can't it be done? Do we lack the words? And **for what** are words lacking? – But where do we get the idea that such a description must, after all, be possible? Have you ever felt the lack of such a description? Have you tried to describe the aroma and failed?*

((I am inclined to say: "These notes say something glorious, but I do not know what." These notes are a powerful gesture, but I cannot put anything side by side with it that will serve as an explanation. A grave nod. James: "We lack the words." Then why don't we introduce new ones? What would have to be the case for us to be able to?))

To rehearse. The (PI 201) thesis of the *Investigations* is that identity is paradox, called the rule, as neither of opposite cases + existing as both qua either.

Comment. Per PI 610 grammar qua law: the face of a paradox case is its counterpart face; as, per PI 43, the meaning of a word is its use; as, per PI 610, the describing aromatic aspect of an aroma description is its described aromatic aspect; as the glory aspect of the notes is the sound aspect; as the graveness aspect of a nod is its behavioural aspect; whatever the logical-sense or the empirical-sense to be made of the aroma case as challenging for language, its grammatical sense is clear – the verb-sense smelling aspect (paradox face) of a case of smelling (paradox case) is its noun-sense smelling (corresponding paradox face) aspect.

Games: paradox + faces; word (say, coffee) + meaning/use – aroma/liquid – cases; aroma description + describing/described aspects; notes + glory/ sound cases; per analogies, ladder + up/down aspects, drabbit + duck/rabbit faces.

611. "Willing – wanting – too is merely an experience," one would like to say (the 'will' too only 'idea'). It comes when it comes, and I cannot bring it about.

*Not bring it about? – Like **what**? What can I bring about, then? What am I comparing it with when I say this?*

To rehearse. The (PI 201) thesis of the *Investigations* is that identity is paradox, called the rule, as neither of opposite cases + existing as both qua either.

Comment. Per PI 611 grammar qua law: the idea of willing is its experience; as the bringing something about aspect of the will is its what is brought about aspect; as the verb sense aspect of willing is its noun-sense aspect; a, per PI 43, the meaning of a word is its use; as the face of paradox is its corresponding other face; from which, that paradox-face cases come and go is their grammatical lot (function) as mutually eclipsing cases.

Games: paradox + faces; word (say, will) + meaning/use – will/behaviour cf. idea/happening – cases; will + verb/noun senses; per analogies, ladder + up/down aspects, drabbit + duck/rabbit faces.

*612. I wouldn't say of the movement of my arm, for example, that it comes when it comes, and so on. And this is the domain in which it makes sense to say that something doesn't simply happen to us, but that we **do** it. "I don't need to wait for my arm to rise – I can raise it." And here I am making a contrast between the movement of my arm and, say, the fact that the violent thudding of my heart will subside.*

To rehearse. The (PI 201) thesis of the *Investigations* is that identity is paradox, called the rule, as neither of opposite cases + existing as both qua either.

Comment. Per PI 612 grammar qua law: voluntary arm movement cf. will movement is to raising/raised – doing/done, willing/willed – cases; as involuntary heartbeat is to rising/subsiding cases; as paradox is to faces; as per PI 43, word is to meaning/use cases.

Games: paradox + faces; word + meaning/use cases; will + willing/willed cases; arm-movement + doing/done cases; heartbeat + rising/subsiding cases; per analogies, ladder + up/down aspects, drabbit + duck/rabbit faces.

613. In the sense in which I can ever bring about anything (such as stomach-ache through overeating), I can also bring about wanting. In this sense, I bring about wanting to swim by jumping into the water. I suppose I was trying to say: I can't want to want; that is, it makes no sense to speak of wanting to want. "Wanting" is not the name of an action, and so not of a voluntary one either. And my use of a wrong expression came from the fact that one is inclined to think of wanting as an immediate non-causal bringing about. But a misleading analogy lies at the root of this idea; the causal nexus seems to be established by a mechanism connecting two parts of a machine. The connection may be disrupted if the mechanism malfunctions. (One thinks only of the normal ways in which a mechanism goes wrong, not, say, of cog-wheels suddenly going soft, or penetrating each other, and so on.)

To rehearse. The (PI 201) thesis of the *Investigations* is that identity is paradox, called the rule, as neither of opposite cases + existing as both qua either.

Comment. Per PI 613 grammar qua law: the case of wanting is not the case of an action but is the case of a mutual activity of wanting/wanting – verb-sense/noun-sense – activities; wanting is to wanting/wanting cases; as paradox is to faces; as connectivity is to connected cases; without such connectivity, there is no paradox case, hence no threefold paradox + faces grammar; the mechanism talk is misleading if it is taken that the connected cases are, so to say, side by side rather than, grammatically, going proxy for paradox-face cases connected coincidentally – cf. the up/down aspects of a ladder.

Games: paradox + faces; want cf. will + verb/noun senses; connectivity + connected cases; nexus + cause/effect cases; coincidence + distinct cases; mutual-eclipse activity + participants qua mutually eclipsing cases; per analogies, ladder + up/down aspects, drabbit + duck/rabbit faces.

614. When I raise my arm 'voluntarily', I don't make use of any means to bring the movement about. My wish is not such a means either.

To rehearse. The (PI 201) thesis of the *Investigations* is that identity is paradox, called the rule, as neither of opposite cases + existing as both qua either.

Comment. Per PI 614 grammar qua law: arm-raising willingly is to arm-raising willingly; as verb-sense willing is to noun-sense willing; as paradox-face case is to counterpart paradox-face case; as (per a variant language game) verb-sense wish is to noun-sense wish; where cases coincide – cf. up/down aspects of a ladder – no means feature to connect the cases as though they were, so to say, side-by-side cases; to contrast the will/wish cases is to call attention to these as distinct language-game cases but which coincide as exemplary language games commonly bespeaking the threefold grammar of identity-as-paradox + identical faces cf. drabbit + duck/rabbit faces.

Games: paradox + faces; coincidence + coincidental cases; will cf. wish + will/will cf. wish/wish cases qua verb/noun senses; per analogies, ladder + up/down aspects, drabbit + duck/rabbit faces.

615. *"Willing, if it is not to be a sort of wishing, must be the action itself. It mustn't stop anywhere short of the action." If it is the action, then it is so in the ordinary sense of the word; so it is speaking, writing, walking, lifting a thing, imagining something. But it is also striving, trying, making an effort – to speak, to write, to lift a thing, to imagine something, and so on.*

To rehearse. The (PI 201) thesis of the *Investigations* is that identity is paradox, called the rule, as neither of opposite cases + existing as both qua either.

Comment. Per PI 615 grammar qua law: paradox is to faces; as wish or will is the verb/noun senses; as will is to striving/deed cases; whatever the logical-sense or empirical-sense language of the text, it converts grammatically such that whatever the language game, it bespeaks identity as paradox.

Games: paradox + faces; will as a coincidence case + will/will distinct cases i.e. verb-sense/noun-sense cases or willing/expression cf. striving/deed cases; per analogies, ladder + up/down aspects, drabbit + duck/rabbit faces.

*616. When I raise my arm, I have **not** wished it to rise. The voluntary action excludes this wish. It is, however, possible to say: "I hope I shall draw the circle faultlessly." And that is to express a wish that one's hand should move in such-and-such a way.*

To rehearse. The (PI 201) thesis of the *Investigations* is that identity is paradox, called the rule, as neither of opposite cases + existing as both qua either.

Comment. Per PI 616 grammar qua law: a paradox-face case of a paradox case is its corresponding other paradox-face case; as a voluntary (willing) aspect of the will case (raise the arm) is a voluntary (willed) enactment case; as a wishing aspect of a wish case (to draw faultlessly) is a wished (expression) case; the games-talk of will and the games-talk of wish are distinct cases, each thereby excluding the other, yet where they also commonly bespeak the threefold paradox + faces grammar.

Games: paradox + faces; arm-raising + verb-sense/noun-sense cases; will + mind-state/enactment cases; faultless circle-drawing + wishing/wishing − verb/noun, mental-process/expression − cases; per analogies, ladder + up/down aspects, drabbit + duck/rabbit faces.

*617. If we cross our fingers in a special way, we are sometimes unable to move a particular finger when someone tells us to do so, if he only **points** to the finger — merely shows it to the eye. However, if he touches it, we **can** move it. One would like to describe this experience as follows: we are unable to **will** to move the finger. The case is quite different from that in which we are not able to move the finger because someone is, say, holding it. One is now inclined to describe the former case by saying: one can't find any point of application for the will until the finger is touched. Only when one feels the finger can the will know where it is to engage. − But this way of putting it is misleading. One would like to say: "How am I to know where I am to catch hold with the will, if the feeling does not indicate the place?" But then how do I know to what point I am to direct the will when the feeling **is** there?*

It is experience that shows that in this case the finger is, as it were, paralysed until we feel a touch on it; it could not have been known a priori.

To rehearse. The (PI 201) thesis of the *Investigations* is that identity is paradox, called the rule, as neither of opposite cases + existing as both qua either.

Comment. Per PI 617 grammar qua law: whatever logical or empirical factors which impede a willing case being a willed case, the grammatical case is that of the willing/willed cases being inseparables in that they are paradoxically one another cf. the up/down aspects of a ladder.

Games: paradox + faces; will + willing/willed cases; per analogies, ladder + up/down aspects, drabbit + duck/rabbit faces.

618. One imagines the willing subject here as something without any mass (without any inertia), as a motor which has no inertia in itself to overcome. And so it is only mover, not moved. That is: one can say "I will, but my body does not obey me" – but not: "My will does not obey me." (Augustine)

But in the sense in which I can't fail to will, I can't try to will either.

To rehearse. The (PI 201) thesis of the *Investigations* is that identity is paradox, called the rule, as neither of opposite cases + existing as both qua either.

Comment. Per PI 618 grammar qua law: PI 618 speaks neither of the will as a paradox case nor its willed aspect as a paradox face but only of the willing aspect as the counterpart paradox face; the will-and-willed – paradox-and-face – cases are implied; per PI 43, word (cf. the will, movement) is to meaning/use – cf. willing/willed, doing/done, mover/moved, moving/moved, verb-sense-movement/noun-sense-movement, energy/mass, – cases; as paradox is to faces; in that, per analogy, the ascent aspect of a ladder can neither fail nor strive to be its corresponding descent aspect; so, the willing aspect of the will can neither fail nor strive to be its corresponding willed aspect; talk of the body disobeying the will is grammatical talk of the willed aspect as distinct from the willing aspect; obedience talk would be coincidence talk as that of the aspects coinciding as the will qua paradox.

Games: paradox + faces (and variants, as per the Comment); per analogies, ladder + up/down aspects, drabbit + duck/rabbit faces.

619. And one might say: "It is only inasmuch as I can never try to will that I can always will."

To rehearse. The (PI 201) thesis of the *Investigations* is that identity is paradox, called the rule, as neither of opposite cases + existing as both qua either.

Comment. Per PI 619 grammar qua law: it is only in that, grammatically, willing/willed cases are paradoxically (cf. always, ever without trying) each other – cf. ladder-ascent as ladder-descent – that it is ungrammatical nonsense to say that each of the willing/willed cases try to be one another.

Games: paradox + faces; will + willing/willed cases; per analogies, ladder + up/down aspects, drabbit + duck/rabbit faces.

*620. **Doing** itself seems not to have any experiential volume. It seems like an extensionless point, the point of a needle. This point seems to be the real agent – and what happens in the realm of appearances merely consequences of this doing. "I **do**" seems to have a definite sense, independently of any experience.*

To rehearse. The (PI 201) thesis of the *Investigations* is that identity is paradox, called the rule, as neither of opposite cases + existing as both qua either.

Comment. Per PI 620 grammar qua law: distinct from empirical – experiential – talk which is the raw material for grammatical analysis, the grammatical talk is this; paradox (extensionless needle point cf. neither of its faces) is to faces cf. PI 304, as nothing is to Nothing/Something cases; as per PI 43, word (doing,) is to meaning/use – doing/doing qua verb/noun, moving/moved, mover/moved, agent/consequences – cases.

Games: paradox + faces; doing (*extensionless* needle-point) + doing/doing – verb-sense/noun-sense, agency/consequences – cases; per analogies, ladder + up/down aspects, drabbit + duck/rabbit faces.

621. But there is one thing we shouldn't overlook: when 'I raise my arm', my arm rises. And now a problem emerges: what is left over if I subtract the fact that my arm rises from the fact that I raise my arm?

((Are the kinaesthetic sensations my willing?))

To rehearse. The (PI 201) thesis of the *Investigations* is that identity is paradox, called the rule, as neither of opposite cases + existing as both qua either.

Comment. Per PI 621 grammar qua law: to subtract the raised-arm case from the arm-raising case is to subtract one paradox-face case from the corresponding other paradox-face case – what is left over i.e. what is a third member of the paradox + faces grammar is the arm-raise paradox case; talk of kinaesthetic sensations is empirical talk as the raw material for translation into threefold-grammar talk; the talk of (translated) kinaesthetic movements and talk of the will are cases of assorted language games – see Games, next.

Games: paradox + faces; arm-raise + arm-raising/raised-arm cases; will + willing/willed cases; per analogies, ladder + up/down aspects, drabbit + duck/rabbit faces.

*622. When I raise my arm, I don't usually **try** to raise it.*

To rehearse. The (PI 201) thesis of the *Investigations* is that identity is paradox, called the rule, as neither of opposite cases + existing as both qua either.

Comment. Per PI 622 grammar qua law: grammatically, the arm-raising/raised-arm cases locate in the threefold grammar of paradox + faces as the threefold case of arm-raise + arm-raising/raised-arm – verb-sense/noun-sense, agency/enactment – cases; in this games-talk, effort talk does not feature cf. effort talk is irrelevant in the language game whereby ladder-ascent is effortlessly qua paradoxically ladder descent; effort talk locates in the variant threefold grammar of try + verb-sense/noun-sense aspects; yet all variant games commonly bespeak identity as paradox; too, see PI 618 on paradox faces in mutual eclipse requires no trying.

Games: paradox + faces; arm-raise case, like try case + verb/noun senses; per analogies, ladder + up/down aspects, drabbit + duck/rabbit faces.

623. *"I want to get to that house at all costs." – But if there is no difficulty about it,* **can** *I strive at all costs to get to the house?*

To rehearse. The (PI 201) thesis of the *Investigations* is that identity is paradox, called the rule, as neither of opposite cases + existing as both qua either.

Comment. Per PI 623 grammar qua law: the faces of paradox as paradoxically one another thereby don't strive to be each other; just as the house reaching/reached aspects (of the house-reach case) are each other, hence – grammatically – no strife case obtains.

Games: paradox + faces; house-reach + reaching/reached cases; per analogies, ladder + up/down aspects, drabbit + duck/rabbit faces.

624. *In the laboratory, when subjected to an electric current, for example, someone with his eyes shut says "I am moving my arm up and down" – though his arm is not moving. "So", we say, "he has the special feeling of making that movement." – Move your arm to and fro with your eyes shut. And now try, while you do so, to talk yourself into the idea that your arm is staying still and that you are only having certain strange feelings in your muscles and joints!*

To rehearse. The (PI 201) thesis of the *Investigations* is that identity is paradox, called the rule, as neither of opposite cases + existing as both qua either.

Comment. Per PI 624 grammar qua law: where logical-sense talk and empirical-sense talk translate into grammatical talk, each of the cases of stillness as movement, and movement as stillness, is the case of a paradox-face as its corresponding other paradox-face; empirically speaking, the stillness/movement cases do not coincide; logically speaking, the cases are contradictories; grammatically, however, the cases are complementary paradox-face cases; to say that an arm at rest is a swinging arm is to say that here, grammatically speaking, the arm case is a paradox case, the faces of which are the movement/stillness aspects.

Games: paradox + faces; arm + movement/stillness cases; per analogies, ladder + up/down aspects, drabbit + duck/rabbit faces.

625. *"How do you know that you've raised your arm?" – "I feel it." So what you recognize is the feeling? And are you certain that you recognize it right? – You're certain that you've raised your arm; isn't this the criterion, the measure, of recognizing?*

To rehearse. The (PI 201) thesis of the *Investigations* is that identity is paradox, called the rule, as neither of opposite cases + existing as both qua either.

Comment. Per PI 625 grammar qua law: just as there is the certainty of the paradox case where there are its paradox-face cases; so, there is the grammatical certainty of the arm-raising case where there are its verb-sense/noun-sense – feeling/enactment – cases; in any threefold games-talk case, in that the three members live in one another – cf. the ladder + up/down aspects threefold case – each of the three members as the case thereby is the criterion qua warrant for the other two members certainly being the case.

Games: paradox + faces; certainty of raising + verb-sense/noun-sense cases of raising; arm-raising + feeling/enactment cases; feeling, also recognition, also knowledge + verb-sense/noun-sense cases; per analogies, ladder + up/down aspects, drabbit + duck/rabbit faces.

626. "When I touch this object with a stick, I have the sensation of touching in the tip of the stick, not in the hand that holds it." When someone says "The pain isn't here in my hand, but in my wrist", this has the consequence that the doctor examines the wrist. But what difference does it make if I say that I feel the hardness of the object in the tip of the stick or in my hand? Does what I say mean "It's as if I had nerve endings in the tip of the stick?" **In what way** is it like that? – Well, I am at any rate inclined to say, "I feel the hardness and so forth in the tip of the stick". What goes with this is that when I touch the object, I look not at my hand but at the tip of the stick; that I describe what I feel by saying "I feel something hard and round there" – not "I feel a pressure against the tips of my thumb, middle finger, and index finger ..." If, for example, someone were to ask me, "What are you now feeling in the fingers that hold the probe?", I might reply: "I don't know – I feel something hard and rough **over there**".

To rehearse. The (PI 201) thesis of the *Investigations* is that identity is paradox, called the rule, as neither of opposite cases + existing as both qua either.

Comment. Per PI 626 grammar qua law: the thrust of the considerable empirical-sense talk and logical-sense talk translates grammatically as follows: stick-tip is to hand/object cases; as touch is to touching/touched, feeling/over-there – cases; as paradox is to faces.

Games: paradox + faces; stick-tip + hand/object cases; feel (sensation, hardness, roundness) + feeling/felt – over-here/over-their – cases; touch + touching/touched cases; per analogies, ladder + up/down aspects, drabbit + duck/rabbit faces.

627. Consider the following description of a voluntary action: "I form the decision to pull the bell at 5 o'clock; and when it strikes 5, my arm makes this movement." – Is that the correct description, and not **this** one: "... and when it strikes 5, I raise my arm"? – One would like to supplement the first description: "And lo and behold! my arm goes up when it strikes 5." And this "lo and behold!" is precisely what doesn't belong here. I do **not** say "Look, my arm is going up!" when I raise it.

270   IDENTITY AS PARADOX

To rehearse. The (PI 201) thesis of the *Investigations* is that identity is paradox, called the rule, as neither of opposite cases + existing as both qua either.

Comment. Per PI 627 grammar qua law: paradox is to faces; as bell-ring is to bell-ringing/rung-bell cases; here, as grammatical cases of talk, the empirical exclamatory talk is irrelevant, thus not featuring.

Games: bell-pull + pulling/pulled cases; voluntary arm-lift + lifting/lifted cases; decision + deciding/decided cases; per analogies, ladder + up/down aspects, drabbit + duck/rabbit faces.

628. *So one might say: voluntary movement is marked by the absence of surprise. And now I don't mean you to ask "But **why** isn't one surprised here?"*

To rehearse. The (PI 201) thesis of the *Investigations* is that identity is paradox, called the rule, as neither of opposite cases + existing as both qua either.

Comment. Per PI 628 grammar qua law: by the perspective of PI 627, and concerning the surprise-talk case, in that the arm-raising/arm-raising – verb-sense/noun-sense – aspects are coincidental paradox-face cases, there is thereby an absence of surprise in the two aspects being connected; compare, there is no surprise in there being a ladder's way-up aspect being its way-down aspect for the up/down aspects coincide; this said, where empirical exclamatory talk obtains, say, elsewhere than as to do with voluntary cases, it translates grammatically as that paradox is to faces, as surprise is too verb/noun senses.

Games: paradox + faces; voluntary movement, like non-voluntary movement + verb/noun aspects; per analogies, ladder + up/down aspects, drabbit + duck/rabbit faces.

629. *When people talk about the possibility of foreknowledge of the future, they always overlook the case of predicting one's voluntary movements.*

To rehearse. The (PI 201) thesis of the *Investigations* is that identity is paradox, called the rule, as neither of opposite cases + existing as both qua either.

Comment. Per PI 629 grammar qua law: talk of voluntary movement having to it verb-sense + noun-sense cases is talk of a paradox case having to it paradox-face cases; in variant terms, this is talk of knowledge having to it the before/after cases, foreknowledge/outcome cases, or is talk of voluntary movement having to it intention/enactment cases i.e. prediction/outcome cases; a foreknowledge language game and a voluntary-movement language game are to be seen as variant language games bespeaking the grammar of identity-as-paradox; the variant language games thereby have kinship.

Games: paradox + faces; voluntary movement qua knowledge + prediction/outcome cases; per analogies, ladder + up/down aspects, drabbit + duck/rabbit faces.

630. Consider these two language-games:

(a) *Someone gives someone else the order to make particular movements with his arm, or to assume particular bodily positions (gymnastics instructor and pupil). And a variant of this language-game is this: the pupil gives himself orders and then carries them out.*

(b) *Someone observes certain regular processes – for example, the reactions of different metals to acids – and thereupon makes predictions about the reactions that will occur in certain cases.*

There is an evident kinship between these two language-games, and also a fundamental difference. In both, one might call the spoken words "predictions". But compare the training which leads to the first technique with the training for the second one!

To rehearse. The (PI 201) thesis of the *Investigations* is that identity is paradox, called the rule, as neither of opposite cases + existing as both qua either.

Comment. Per PI 630 grammar qua law: paradox is to faces; as kinship qua language game is to kin/kin – (a)/(b) exemplar – cases; whatever the empirical-sense talk to do with differing trainings for (a) and (b), the two exemplar language games are fundamentally qua grammatically different in respect of being distinct paradox faces qua distinct exemplars.

Games: paradox + faces; language game + exemplars; training + (a)/(b) cases; voluntary movement + willing/willed cases; reaction-observation + prediction/outcome cases; prediction + predicting/predicted cases; per analogies, ladder + up/down aspects, drabbit + duck/rabbit faces.

631. *"I'm going to take two powders now, and in half an hour I shall be sick." – It explains nothing to say that in the first case I am the agent, in the second merely the observer. Or that in the first case I see the causal connection from inside, in the second from outside. And much else to the same effect.*

Nor is it to the point to say that a prediction of the first kind is no more infallible than one of the second kind.

It wasn't on the basis of observations of my behaviour that I said I was going to take two powders. The antecedents of this statement were different. I mean the thoughts, actions, and so on which led up to it. And it can only be misleading to say: "The only essential presupposition of your utterance was precisely your decision."

To rehearse. The (PI 201) thesis of the *Investigations* is that identity is paradox, called the rule, as neither of opposite cases + existing as both qua either.

Comment. Per PI 631 grammar qua law: cases of paradox faces are as follows: medication/nausea, agency/observation, first/second, predicting/predicted, deciding/decided cf. intending/intended, inside/outside cf. thinking/doing, cause/effect, antecedent/consequent, essential/behavioural cf. PI 43, word-meaning/word-use, presupposition/enactment; from which, the focus is not upon empirical talk but on its translation in terms of threefold paradox + faces grammar (law); per paradox-face cases (and parallels), they connect infallibly in that they are paradoxically, hence inseparably, one another cf. the up/down aspects of a ladder – from which, explanation is irrelevant of how opposites – if taken as side-by-side cases – can be connected; the meaning (essential qua deciding) aspect of a word (sentence, decision) is not the decision case but a use (utterance, decided outcome, expression) aspect.

Games: paradox + faces (and variants, as per Comment); infallible connectivity + paired-opposites cases – example: utterance qua (say) decision cf. intention + medication/nausea aspects; per analogies, ladder + up/down aspects, drabbit + duck/rabbit faces.

632. I do not want to say that in the case of the expression of intention "I am going to take two powders" the prediction is a cause – and its fulfilment the effect. (Perhaps a physiological investigation could determine this.) So much, however, is true: we can often predict a man's actions from his expression of a decision. An important language-game.

To rehearse. The (PI 201) thesis of the *Investigations* is that identity is paradox, called the rule, as neither of opposite cases + existing as both qua either.

Comment. Per PI 632 grammar qua law: the empirical talk translates grammatically as follows; paradox is to faces; as per PI 43, word (utterance) is to meaning/use – cf. predicting/predicted, cause/effect, predicting/fulfilment, predicting/enactment, intending/intended, intending/expressed, deciding/decided, deciding/expression, thinking/action – aspects; each case of paired opposites is integral to the important threefold language game of paradox + faces as a threefold identity-as-paradox + identical paradox faces grammar (law) cf. per analogy, drabbit + duck/rabbit faces.

Games: paradox + faces (and variants, as per Comment); per analogies, ladder + up/down aspects, drabbit + duck/rabbit faces.

633. "You were interrupted a while ago; do you still know what you were going to say?" – If I do know now, and say it, does that mean that I had already thought it before, only not said it? No. Unless you take the certainty with which I continue the interrupted sentence as a criterion of the thought's already having been completed at that time. – But, to be sure, the situation and the thoughts I had already contain all sorts of things to help the sentence on.

To rehearse. The (PI 201) thesis of the *Investigations* is that identity is paradox, called the rule, as neither of opposite cases + existing as both qua either.

Comment. Per PI 633 grammar qua law: per PI 43, a word is its meaning/use aspects (whether or not the aspects are temporally-interrupted cases); as a paradox is to its faces; here, the meaning/use paradox-face cases warrant – make certain, are the criterion for – one another being the case cf. per analogy, the up/down aspects of the ladder as the warrant for each other as the case; where one privately thinks a word without saying it, that thinking – that word-meaning – nevertheless is referenced to the public use of that meaning as a use featuring in the public shared human language.

Games: paradox + faces; word + meaning/use aspects; interruption + interrupting/interrupted cases; per analogies, ladder + up/down aspects, drabbit + duck/rabbit faces.

634. When I continue the interrupted sentence and say that **this** *was how I had been going to continue it, this is similar to elaborating a train of thought from brief notes.*

Then don't I **interpret** *the notes? Was only one continuation possible in these circumstances? Of course not. But I didn't* **choose** *between these interpretations. I* **remembered** *that I was going to say this.*

To rehearse. The (PI 201) thesis of the *Investigations* is that identity is paradox, called the rule, as neither of opposite cases + existing as both qua either.

Comment. Per PI 634 grammar qua law: paradox is to faces; as, per PI 43, word (sentence, **this** case) is to meaning/use – cf. brief-notes/elaboration, earlier/

later, thinking/saying, interpreting/interpreted, remembering/ remembered – aspects; temporal talk is discounted other than as raw material for translating into identity grammar (law); what is said is paradoxically – not chosen i.e. not optionally – its meaning.

Games: paradox + faces; continuation + notes/elaboration aspects; interpretation activity + interpreting/interpreted aspects; per analogies, ladder + up/down aspects, drabbit + duck/rabbit faces.

635. "I was going to say ..." – You remember various details. But not even all of them together show this intention. It is as if a snapshot of a scene had been taken, but only a few scattered details of it were to be seen: here a hand, there a bit of a face, or hat – the rest is dark. And now it is as if I knew quite certainly what the whole picture represented. As if I could read the darkness.

To rehearse. The (PI 201) thesis of the *Investigations* is that identity is paradox, called the rule, as neither of opposite cases + existing as both qua either.

Comment. Per PI 635 grammar qua law: a going-to-say case is to gist/expansion – details/whole, darkness/light, remembering/remembered, scatterings/composition – aspects; as paradox case is to faces; the empirical then/now case is translated into a grammatical (identity-lawful) paradox-faces case such that the then/now aspects are one another cf. per analogy the ladder's up/down aspects; variants are these – paradox + faces; per PI 43, word + meaning/use cases; snapshot + pieces/whole cases.

Games: paradox + faces; picture + parts/whole cases; going-to-say case + darkness/light aspects (and variants); per analogies, ladder + up/down aspects, drabbit + duck/rabbit faces.

636. These 'details' are not irrelevant in the sense in which other circumstances, which I can also remember, are irrelevant. But if I tell someone "For a moment I was going to say ...", he doesn't learn those details from this, nor need he guess them. He needn't know, for instance, that I had already opened my mouth to speak. But he **can** 'fill out the picture' in this way. (And this ability is part of understanding what I tell him.)

To rehearse. The (PI 201) thesis of the *Investigations* is that identity is paradox, called the rule, as neither of opposite cases + existing as both qua either.

Comment. Per PI 636 grammar qua law: the going-to-say case is to details/elaboration cases; as information is to informer/informed cases; as context-awareness is to relevance details.

Games: paradox + faces; was-going-to-say + detail/expansion cases; information + informer-remembered/listener-surmised cases; per analogies, ladder + up/down aspects, drabbit + duck/rabbit faces.

637. "*I know exactly what I was going to say!*" And yet I didn't say it. — And yet I don't read it off from some other process which took place then and which I remember.

Nor am I **interpreting** that situation and its antecedents, which, after all, I neither consider nor judge.

To rehearse. The (PI 201) thesis of the *Investigations* is that identity is paradox, called the rule, as neither of opposite cases + existing as both qua either.

Comment. Per PI 637 grammar qua law: the unsaid case is to the said case; as paradox face is to counterpart paradox face; nothing other than a paradox face makes for its counterpart being the counterpart cf. nothing makes for a ladder-ascent aspect than its paradoxical ladder-descent aspect.

Games: paradox + faces; the going-to-say case + unsaid/said aspects; per analogies, ladder + up/down aspects, drabbit + duck/rabbit faces.

638. *How does it come about that, in spite of this, I am inclined to see an interpretation in saying "For a moment I was going to deceive him"?*

"How can you be certain that, for a moment, you were going to deceive him? Weren't your actions and thoughts much too rudimentary?"

For may the evidence not be too scanty? Yes, when one follows it up, it seems extraordinarily scanty; but isn't this because one is taking no account of the background of this evidence? If, for a moment, I intended to pretend to someone that I was unwell, that required an antecedent context.

If someone says "For a moment ...", is he really only describing a momentary process?

But not even the entire background was my evidence for saying "For a moment ..."

To rehearse. The (PI 201) thesis of the *Investigations* is that identity is paradox, called the rule, as neither of opposite cases + existing as both qua either.

Comment. Per PI 638 grammar qua law: talk of what is momentary, scanty, rudimentary, and the like, is empirical-sense talk as raw material for translation into grammatical terms; paradox is to faces; as deceit is to deceiving/deceived cases; here, the whole grammatical background qua context is the threefold case of identity-as-paradox + identical faces cf. drabbit + duck/rabbit faces; what warrants – gives certainty to – any of the three members of the threefold case being the case is the other two members cf. per analogy, ladder + up/down aspects; here, each of the three lives in the other two such that all three are inseparables.

Games: paradox + faces; per PI 43, word + meaning/use cases; moment cf. the now + past/future cases; deceit, like intention, like interpretation + verb-sense/noun-sense aspects; deceit + language/deed aspects; per analogies, ladder + up/down aspects, drabbit + duck/rabbit faces.

639. *Meaning something, one wants to say,* **develops**. *But there is a mistake in this too.*

To rehearse. The (PI 201) thesis of the *Investigations* is that identity is paradox, called the rule, as neither of opposite cases + existing as both qua either.

Comment. Per PI 639 grammar qua law: it is mistaken (ungrammatical) to say that word-meaning develops empirically towards something qua word-use; rather, meaning/use cases as paradox faces inhabit one another – cf. per analogy, the up/down aspects of a ladder – whereby they develop as mutually eclipsing faces.

Games: paradox + faces; per PI 43, word + meaning/use cases; mutual development activity + mutually eclipsing faces; per analogies, ladder + up/down aspects, drabbit + duck/rabbit faces.

640. "This thought links up with thoughts which I have had before." – How does it do so? Through a **feeling** of such a link? But how can a feeling really link these thoughts? – The word "feeling" is very misleading here. But it is sometimes possible to say with certainty, "This thought is connected with those earlier ones", even though one is unable to point out the connection. Perhaps one will succeed later.

To rehearse. The (PI 201) thesis of the *Investigations* is that identity is paradox, called the rule, as neither of opposite cases + existing as both qua either.

Comment. Per PI 640 grammar qua law: paradox is to faces; as thought is to this/earlier cases; as link (connection) is to linked (connected cases; a variant language game is that whereby feeling is to earlier/later cases.; no paradox case shows itself – can be pin pointed – other than in terms of its mutually eclipsing faces; it is the mutual-eclipse activity case (so, 201); per each threefold grammar of paradox + faces, the faces are ever and always instantaneously linked paradoxically cf. per analogy, the up/down ladder aspects; here, in that all three members of the paradox + faces case inhabit one another, they thereby give certainty of being the case to one another.

Games: paradox and faces; thought (cf. feeling) + this/earlier cases; per analogies, ladder + up/down aspects, drabbit + duck/rabbit faces.

641. "Even if I had uttered the words 'Now I'm going to deceive him', my intention would have been no more certain than it already was." – But if you had uttered those words, would you necessarily have meant them seriously? (So, the most explicit expression of intention is by itself insufficient evidence of intention.)

To rehearse. The (PI 201) thesis of the *Investigations* is that identity is paradox, called the rule, as neither of opposite cases + existing as both qua either.

Comment. Per PI 641 grammar qua law: the face of a paradox is its counterpart face; as per PI 43, the meaning (here, verb-sense intention) of a word (intention) is its use (noun-sense intention) cf. per analogy, the ascent aspect of a ladder is its descent aspect; the empirical talk of the text thus translates grammatically such that paradox-face cases inhabit one another and thereby give certainty to one another's existence; each face without the other is an insufficient – thus ungrammatical (unlawful) – case.; talk of word-meaning seriously is talk of meaning paradoxically (word-use).

Games: paradox + faces; word + meaning/use cases; intention + verb/noun sense – intending/intended – cases; per analogies, ladder + up/down aspects, drabbit + duck/rabbit faces.

642. "At that moment I hated him." – What happened here? Didn't it consist in thoughts, feelings and actions? And if I were to rehearse that moment to myself, I'd assume a particular expression, think of certain happenings, breathe in a particular way, arouse certain feelings in myself. I might think up a conversation, a whole scene in which that hatred flared up. And I might act this scene with feelings approximating those of a real incident. That I have actually been through something of the sort will naturally help me to do so.

To rehearse. The (PI 201) thesis of the *Investigations* is that identity is paradox, called the rule, as neither of opposite cases + existing as both qua either.

Comment. Per PI 642 grammar qua law: the assorted empirical talk of this text translates into threefold grammatical talk; paradox is to faces; as hate wordage is to meaning/use cases; as hate is to language/deed cases.

Games: paradox + faces; per PI 43, word such as hate + meaning/use – cf. thinking/acting – cases; hate + language/action cases; hate + verb/noun language cases; per analogies, ladder + up/down aspects, drabbit + duck/rabbit faces.

643. If I now become ashamed of this incident, I am ashamed of the whole thing: of the words, of the poisonous tone, and so on.

To rehearse. The (PI 201) thesis of the *Investigations* is that identity is paradox, called the rule, as neither of opposite cases + existing as both qua either.

Comment. Per PI 643 grammar qua law: whole thing is to threefold grammar; as incident is to identity-as-a-paradox case; as shame-word is to tone/expression paradox faces; as (per PI 43) word is to meaning/use case.

Games: paradox faces; word + meaning/use cases; shame + tone/expression cases; per analogies, ladder + up/down aspects, drabbit + duck/rabbit faces.

*644. "I'm not ashamed of what I did then, but of the intention which I had." – And didn't the intention lie **also** in what I did? What justifies the shame? The whole background of the incident.*

To rehearse. The (PI 201) thesis of the *Investigations* is that identity is paradox, called the rule, as neither of opposite cases + existing as both qua either.

Comment. Per PI 644 grammar qua law: whole background is to threefold grammar; as shame case is to identity-as-paradox case; as shame is to language/deed – intention/enactment – aspects qua paradox faces; per each case of threefold grammar its three members justify one another being the cases in that they indwell (lie in) one another cf. ladder + up/down aspects.

Games: paradox faces; shame + language/deed – also intention/enactment – cases; per analogies, ladder + up/down aspects, drabbit + duck/rabbit faces.

*645. "For a moment I was going to ..." That is, I had a particular feeling, an inner experience; and I remember it. — And now remember **quite precisely**! Then the 'inner experience' of intending seems to vanish again. Instead, one remembers thoughts, feelings, movements and also connections with earlier situations.*

It is as if one had altered the adjustment of a microscope: one did not see before what is now in focus.

To rehearse. The (PI 201) thesis of the *Investigations* is that identity is paradox, called the rule, as neither of opposite cases + existing as both qua either.

Comment. Per PI 645 grammar qua law: the "*For a moment I was going to ...*" utterance (cf. sentence) qua paradox case has to it intentional/remembrance aspects qua paradox faces in mutual eclipse – here, as a case of eclipsing/eclipsed – presenting/vanishing – faces; talk of remembering-precisely is talk is remembering-paradoxically – paradox is to faces; as precision qua remembrance is to remembering/remembered aspects.

Games: paradox + faces; per PI 43, word + meaning/use cases; utterance + intention/remembrance cases; per analogies, ladder + up/down aspects, drabbit + duck/rabbit faces.

646. "Well, that only shows that you have adjusted your microscope wrongly. You were supposed to examine a particular slice of the preparation, and now you are looking at a different one."

There is something right about this. But suppose that (with a certain adjustment of the lenses) I did remember a particular sensation; what allows me to say that it is what I call the "intention"? It might be that (for example) a particular tickle accompanied every one of my intentions.

To rehearse. The (PI 201) thesis of the *Investigations* is that identity is paradox, called the rule, as neither of opposite cases + existing as both qua either.

Comment. Per PI 646 grammar qua law: the previous-text *"For a moment I was going to ..."* utterance qua paradox case has to it intentional/remembrance aspects qua paradox faces; grammatically, whatever the intention detail, it is a remembrance detain, and vice versa, in that the intention/remembrance cases live in one another as paradoxically each other cf. drabbit + duck/rabbit faces where the duck-beak detail is the rabbit-ears detail; particular-talk is paradox-talk, and where different particular qua paradox cases occur in variant language games, commonly bespeaking identity-as-paradox.

Games: paradox + faces; per PI 43, word + meaning/use cases; utterance + intention/remembrance cases; per analogies, ladder + up/down aspects, drabbit + duck/rabbit faces.

647. What is the natural expression of an intention? – Look at a cat when it stalks a bird; or a beast when it wants to escape.

(((Connection with propositions about sensations.))

To rehearse. The (PI 201) thesis of the *Investigations* is that identity is paradox, called the rule, as neither of opposite cases + existing as both qua either.

Comment. Per PI 647 grammar qua law: the empirical-sense talk translates grammatically as follows; sensation is to its sensing/sensed aspects; as paradox is to its faces; as intention is to its verb-sense/noun-sense, thinking/enactment – intending/intended, inner-process/natural-expression – cases.

Games: paradox + faces; per PI 43, word (sentence, proposition) + meaning/use cases; sensation + sensing/sensed cases; intention + mental-process/natural-expression cases; per analogies, ladder + up/down aspects, drabbit + duck/rabbit faces.

*648. "I no longer remember the words I used, but I remember my intention precisely; I wanted my words to calm him down." What does my memory **show** me;*

what does it bring before my mind? Suppose it did nothing but suggest those words to me! – and perhaps others which fill out the picture still more exactly. – ("I don't remember my words any more, but I certainly remember their spirit.")

To rehearse. The (PI 201) thesis of the *Investigations* is that identity is paradox, called the rule, as neither of opposite cases + existing as both qua either.

Comment. Per PI 648 grammar qua law: the empirical-sense talk of the text runs grammatically as follows; the face of a paradox is its counterpart face; by PI 43, the meaning of a word is its is use cf. per analogy, the ascent aspect of a ladder is its descent aspect; from which, it is ungrammatical to say that any word-meaning (intention, remembering) obtains but with inexact or absent expression (intended aspect, remembered aspect); exactitude-talk is paradox-talk – paradox is to faces, as exactness is to cases connected exactly qua paradoxically cf. the ladder analogy.

Games: paradox + faces; word + meaning/use – essence/expression, intention/expression – cases; per analogies, ladder + up/down aspects, drabbit + duck/rabbit faces.

649. "So if someone has not learned a language, is he unable to have certain memories?" Of course – he cannot have linguistic memories, linguistic wishes or fears, and so on. And memories and suchlike in language are not mere threadbare representations of the **real** experiences; for is what is linguistic not an experience?

To rehearse. The (PI 201) thesis of the *Investigations* is that identity is paradox, called the rule, as neither of opposite cases + existing as both qua either.

Comment. Per PI 649 grammar qua law: any case of meaning (memory, thinking, feeling, and so on) is not threadbare reality qua language i.e. is not an aspect of language without a paradoxical use aspect (this, from PI 43); too, paradox is to faces; as reality is to (say) anti-reality/pro-reality – cf. mental/behavioural – cases.

Games: paradox + faces; word in a language (say, memory, intention) + meaning/use cases, mental-process/utterance cases, verb-sense/noun-sense cases, and so on; human form of life + language/reality cases; per analogies, ladder + up/down aspects, drabbit + duck/rabbit faces.

650. We say a dog is afraid his master will beat him; but not: he is afraid his master will beat him tomorrow. Why not?

To rehearse. The (PI 201) thesis of the *Investigations* is that identity is paradox, called the rule, as neither of opposite cases + existing as both qua either.

Comment. Per PI 650 grammar qua law: we say, per 43, that the meaning of a word is its use but not that the meaning of a word is its use tomorrow; grammatically, word-meaning is (paradoxically) word-use, and where the empirical (temporal) reference to tomorrow is irrelevant; likewise, a fearing aspect of fear is (paradoxically) its feared aspect, to which grammar the empirical (temporal) reference to tomorrow is irrelevant.

Games: paradox + faces; word + meaning/use cases; fear + fearing/feared aspects; per analogies, ladder + up/down aspects, drabbit + duck/rabbit faces.

651. "I remember that I would have been glad then to stay still longer." – What picture of this desire comes before my mind? None at all. What I see in my memory allows no conclusion as to my feelings. And yet I remember quite clearly that they were there.

To rehearse. The (PI 201) thesis of the *Investigations* is that identity is paradox, called the rule, as neither of opposite cases + existing as both qua either.

Comment. Per PI 651 grammar qua law: picture talk is identity-as-paradox talk; paradox is to faces; as remembrance, like wish, like feeling, is to it verb/noun senses; the remembering and feeling cases pertain to different language games.

Games: paradox + faces; per PI 43, word + meaning/use cases; remembrance, feeling, wish + verb/noun senses; per analogies, ladder + up/down aspects, drabbit + duck/rabbit faces.

652. *"He sized him up with a hostile glance and said ..." The reader of the story understands this; he has no doubt in his mind. Now you say: "Very well, he supplies the meaning, he guesses it." – Generally speaking, no. Generally speaking, he supplies nothing, guesses nothing. – But it is also possible that the hostile glance and the words later prove to have been pretence, or that the reader is kept in doubt whether they are so or not, and so that he really does guess at a possible interpretation. – But then the main thing he guesses is a context. He says to himself, for example: the two men affecting such hostility here are in reality friends, and so forth.*

(("If you want to understand the sentence, you have to imagine the psychological significance, the states of mind involved."))

To rehearse. The (PI 201) thesis of the *Investigations* is that identity is paradox, called the rule, as neither of opposite cases + existing as both qua either.

Comment. Per PI 652 grammar qua law: the empirical-sense talk and logical-sense talk of the text is raw material for grammatical analysis; the hostility talk as per the PI 652 opening sentence is to its meaning/use aspects; as paradox is to faces; as hostility is to psychological-or-mind-state/expression aspects; the case of understanding context translates to grammatical understanding i.e. of the hostility talk as an identity-as-paradox case, locating in the threefold language game of sentence + meaning/use cases; here, no guessing or interpreting obtains since each of the three members of the grammar warrant one another in that they live with immediacy in one another cf. per analogy, ladder + up/down aspects; where interpretation, like guess, does obtain lends to analysis only as that of being a paradox case, the faces of which are verb/noun senses.

Games: paradox + faces; per PI 43, word (sentence) + meaning/use cases; hostility talk +state-of-mind/expression cases; interpretation, guess + verb/

noun senses; per analogies, ladder + up/down aspects, drabbit + duck/rabbit faces.

653. Imagine this case: I tell someone that I walked a certain route, going by a map which I had prepared beforehand. Thereupon I show him the map, and it consists of lines on a piece of paper; but I cannot explain how these lines come to be a map of my route, I cannot tell him any rule for interpreting the map. Yet I did follow the drawing with all the characteristic tokens of reading a map. I might call such a drawing a 'private' map; or the phenomenon that I have described, "following a private map". (But this expression would, of course, be very easy to misunderstand.)

Could I now say: "I read off my having then meant to do such-and-such, as if from a map, although there is no map"? That, however, means nothing but: **I am now inclined to** *say "I read the intention of acting thus in certain states of mind which I remember".*

To rehearse. The (PI 201) thesis of the *Investigations* is that identity is paradox, called the rule, as neither of opposite cases + existing as both qua either.

Comment. Per PI 653 grammar qua law: where the map-maker/route-walker cases are taken as distinct paradox-face cases, there is no connection between the two; where there is the person as both of these cases, there is the paradox case as the coincidence (the connecting case) of the both aspects; assorted language games exemplifying distinction and coincidence are as follows.

Games: paradox + faces; coincidence + distinction; intention + intending/intended cases; person + map-maker/route-follower cases; person + mind-state/body-behaviour cases; certain journey + mental-map/physical-enactment cases i.e. private/public cases; interpretation + interpreting/interpreted cases; per PI 43, word + meaning/use cases; remembrance + remembering-to/remembered-to cases; per analogies, ladder + up/down aspects, drabbit + duck/rabbit faces.

654. Our mistake is to look for an explanation where we ought to regard the facts as 'proto-phenomena'. That is, where we ought to say: **this is the language-game that is being played.**

To rehearse. The (PI 201) thesis of the *Investigations* is that identity is paradox, called the rule, as neither of opposite cases + existing as both qua either.

Comment. Per PI 654 grammar qua law: rather than philosophy explaining reality it describes reality – and in terms of a threefold grammar, a threefold language game, of paradox + faces; this is to see the grammar as the proto-phenomenal case.

Games: identity-as-paradox + identical faces cf. the drabbit paradox; description + verb-sense/noun-sense cases; per analogies, ladder + up/down aspects, drabbit + duck/rabbit faces.

655. The point is not to explain a language-game by means of our experiences, but to take account of a language-game.

To rehearse. The (PI 201) thesis of the *Investigations* is that identity is paradox, called the rule, as neither of opposite cases + existing as both qua either.

Comment. Per PI 655 grammar qua law: the threefold case of identity is the grammar case of identity, the language-game case of identity; it is to be described, not explained; it is not sprung from experience, hence is not of itself an empirical case (which empirical case is the raw material for grammatical analysis); it comprises the threefold grammar case of identity-as-paradox + identical fasces – cf. per analogy, drabbit + duck/rabbit faces – as the threefold case of reality + mind-state/experience cases.

Games: paradox + faces; per PI 43, word + meaning/use – logical/empirical – cases; description + mind-state/experience cases; per analogies, ladder + up/down aspects, drabbit + duck/rabbit face

*656. What is the **purpose** of telling someone that previously I had such-and-such a wish? – Regard the language-game as the **primary thing**. And regard the feelings, and so forth, as a way of looking at, interpreting, the language-game!*

One might ask: how did human beings ever come to make the kind of linguistic utterance which we call "reporting a past wish" or "a past intention"?

To rehearse. The (PI 201) thesis of the *Investigations* is that identity is paradox, called the rule, as neither of opposite cases + existing as both qua either.

Comment. Per PI 656 grammar qua law: talk of a past experience (a wish, a memory, an intention) is talk in part of a threefold language game or identity-grammar; one interprets i.e. understands the language game to be threefold as paradox + faces as, say, language + thinking/feeling cases; the grammar is primary, as the entirety of its three distinct yet interrelated members; if to seek the point or purpose or origin of the language game is the issue, the seeking is in vain for the language game has no point or purpose or origin but, rather, is the warrant for these cases; to seek for explanation is the empirical way; this way is the raw material for grammatical analysis; the grammar – the language game – is primary; the grammar just is.

Games (case of grammar, language games, primary cases): identity-as-paradox + identical fasces – cf. per analogy, drabbit + duck/rabbit faces; per PI 43, word + meaning/use cases; language + thinking/feeling cases; life + language/action cases; per analogies, ladder + up/down aspects, drabbit + duck/rabbit faces.

657. Suppose this sort of utterance always took the form "I said to myself, 'if only I could stay longer!'" The purpose of such a report might be to acquaint someone with my reactions. (Compare the grammar of "mean" and "vouloir dire".)

To rehearse. The (PI 201) thesis of the *Investigations* is that identity is paradox, called the rule, as neither of opposite cases + existing as both qua either.

Comment. Per PI 657 grammar qua law: taking it from PI 656 that identity grammar allows not of explanation but of description, each of the three members of the threefold grammar or language game is given its point, purpose, warrant, by the other two members being the case in that all three live in one another as inseparables cf. per analogy, ladder + up/down aspects; where the case is of word-use as paradoxically word-meaning, the purpose of the speaking case is paradoxically its meaning case (and vice versa) i.e. the purpose of the public case is paradoxically the private case (and vice versa).

Games: paradox + faces; per PI 43, word + meaning/use cases; language + private/public – cf. self-talk/report – cases; per analogies, ladder + up/down aspects, drabbit + duck/rabbit faces.

658. *Suppose we always expressed the fact that a man had an intention by saying "He as it were said to himself 'I will ..."* – *That is the picture. And now I want to know: how does one employ the expression "as it were to say something to oneself"? For it doesn't mean: to say something to oneself.*

To rehearse. The (PI 201) thesis of the *Investigations* is that identity is paradox, called the rule, as neither of opposite cases + existing as both qua either.

Comment. Per PI 658 grammar qua law: picture talk is identity-as-paradox talk; intention is to intending/intended cases; as paradox is to faces; as talk is to self-related/others-related case i.e. as language is to private/public cases; to say that a case is – as it were – another case, is to say that a case is – paradoxically (hence, neither consistently nor contradictorily – another case; here, the meaning case is not paradoxically the word case – it is paradoxically the expression case.

Games: paradox + faces; intention + intending/intended cases; language + private/public cases; talk + self/others related cases; per analogies, ladder + up/down aspects, drabbit + duck/rabbit faces.

*659. Why do I want to tell him about an intention too, over and above telling him what I did? – Not because the intention too was something going on at that time. But because I want to tell him something about **myself**, which goes beyond what happened at that time.*

I reveal to him something of myself when I tell him what I was going to do. – Not, however, on grounds of self-observation, but by way of a reaction (it might also be called an intuition).

To rehearse. The (PI 201) thesis of the *Investigations* is that identity is paradox, called the rule, as neither of opposite cases + existing as both qua either.

Comment. Per PI 659 grammar qua law: paradox is to faces; as person is to intention/enactment – cf. intuition/enactment, myself/my-behaviour – cases; per grammatical threefold case, each of its three members is grammatically necessarily qua inseparably the case without any but all three together being grammatically sufficiently the case cf. per analogue, ladder + up/down aspects.

Games: paradox + faces; self + inner/outer cases; person + intention/action cases cf. intuiting/expression cases cf. thinking/doing cases; per analogies, ladder + up/down aspects, drabbit + duck/rabbit faces.

660. The grammar of the expression "I was then going to say …" is related to that of the expression "I could then have gone on".

In the one case I remember an intention, in the other I remember having understood.

To rehearse. The (PI 201) thesis of the *Investigations* is that identity is paradox, called the rule, as neither of opposite cases + existing as both qua either.

Comment. Per PI 660 grammar qua law: the text presents itself in two paragraphs; the first treats with distinct paradox-face cases (alternative intention/having-understood cases), the second with the paradox case (memory, remembrance) as the coincidence of those distinct cases.

Games: paradox + faces; coincidence + distinct cases; remembrance + intention/having-understood cases; per analogy, ladder + up/down aspects, drabbit + duck/rabbit faces.

*661. I remember having meant **him**. Am I remembering a process or a state? – When did it begin, how did it continue; and so on?*

To rehearse. The (PI 201) thesis of the *Investigations* is that identity is paradox, called the rule, as neither of opposite cases + existing as both qua either.

Comment. Per PI 661 grammar qua law: paradox is to faces; as remembrance is to subjective-state/objective-him – mental-process/external-happening, cases cf. per PI 43, meaning/expression cases.

Games: paradox + faces; remembering + internal/ external aspects; per analogies, ladder + up/down aspects, drabbit + duck/rabbit faces.

*662. In an only slightly different situation, instead of silently beckoning, he would have said to someone "Tell N. to come to me". One may now say that the words "I wanted N. to come to me" describe the state of my mind at that time; and again one may **not say** so.*

To rehearse. The (PI 201) thesis of the *Investigations* is that identity is paradox, called the rule, as neither of opposite cases + existing as both qua either.

Comment. Per PI 662 grammar qua law: from PI 43, the meaning of a word is its use; as, per PI 662, the mind-state aspect of the sentence ("I wanted N. to come to me") is its expression aspect (gestural or verbal i.e. not-said or said) as well as not an expression aspect in it being a meaning aspect.

Games: paradox + faces; word (language) + meaning/use – cf. state/ expression – cases; per analogies, ladder + up/down aspects, drabbit + duck/rabbit faces.

663. If I say "I meant him" very likely a picture comes to my mind, perhaps of how I looked at him, etc.; but the picture is only like an illustration to a story. From it alone it would mostly be impossible to conclude anything at all; only when one knows the story does one know the significance of the picture.

To rehearse. The (PI 201) thesis of the *Investigations* is that identity is paradox, called the rule, as neither of opposite cases + existing as both qua either.

Comment. Per PI 663 grammar qua law: the empirical-sense picture talk translates grammatically as follows; picture talk is identity-as-paradox talk; whole-story-talk is threefold-grammar-talk; paradox alone is insufficiently the story qua the threefold grammar – language game – of paradox + faces.

Games: paradox + faces; picture + told-out cases; per analogies, ladder + up/down aspects, drabbit + duck/rabbit faces.

664. In the use of words, one might distinguish 'surface grammar' from 'depth grammar'. What immediately impresses itself upon us about the use of a word is the way it is used in the sentence structure, the part of its use – one might say – that can be taken in by the ear. – And now compare the depth grammar, say of the verb "to mean", with what its surface grammar would lead us to presume. No wonder one finds it difficult to know one's way about.

To rehearse. The (PI 201) thesis of the *Investigations* is that identity is paradox, called the rule, as neither of opposite cases + existing as both qua either.

Comment. Per PI 664 grammar qua law: taking it that the language-depth case is to the language-surface case; as the word-meaning case is to the word-use case (as per PI 43); as a paradox-face case is to its corresponding other face; the meaning of the 'to mean' case is its use: here, it is not that a word means something in depth, and at the surface; rather, it is that, of the word, its meaning is to its use, as its depth case is to its surface case, as a word-hearing case is to (say) a word-heard case.

Games: paradox + faces; wording ('to mean') + meaning/use cases; language + depth/surface aspect; per analogies, ladder + up/down aspects, drabbit + duck/rabbit faces.

*665. Imagine someone pointing to his cheek with a grimace of pain and saying "abracadabra!" – We ask, "What do you mean?" And he answers, "I meant toothache." – You at once think to yourself: how can one '**mean** toothache' by that word? Or, what did to **mean** pain by that word **amount** to? And yet, in a different context, you would have asserted that the mental activity of **meaning** such-and-such was just what was most important in using language.*

But how come? – can't I say "By 'abracadabra', I mean toothache"? Of course I can; but this is a definition, not a description of what goes on in me when I utter the word.

To rehearse. The (PI 201) thesis of the *Investigations* is that identity is paradox, called the rule, as neither of opposite cases + existing as both qua either.

Comment. Per PI 665 grammar qua law: like distinct paradox-face cases, the abracadabra/toothache cases are distinct cases; however, whereas the paradox-face cases are coincidentally the paradox case, the abracadabra/toothache cases are not equivalent cases in the shared human language case; the abracadabra case is a subjective definition whereas the toothache case is an objective (shared, common) case featuring in a describable language-game case.

Games: paradox + faces; per PI 43, word + meaning/use cases; per analogies, ladder + up/down aspects, drabbit + duck/rabbit faces.

666. Imagine that you were in pain and were simultaneously hearing a piano being tuned in the next room. You say "It'll soon stop". It surely makes quite a difference whether you mean the pain or the piano-tuning! – Of course; but what does this difference consist in? I admit, in many cases some direction of attention will correspond to your meaning one thing or another, just as a look often does, or a gesture, or a way of shutting one's eyes which might be called "looking into oneself".

To rehearse. The (PI 201) thesis of the *Investigations* is that identity is paradox, called the rule, as neither of opposite cases + existing as both qua either.

Comment. Per PI 666 grammar qua law: paradox case is to paradox-face cases; as the cessation-talk case is to the pain/tuning cases; the cessation-talk case – whether as a pain-talk case or a tuning-talk case – is a talk case, the meaning of which is paradoxically its utterance; the pain/tuning paradox-face cases as distinct cases are different cases, also, as a coincidence qua paradox case, they are the cessation-talk case cf. the way-up/way-down ladder-aspects which are distinct aspects yet are one another in being the ladder case.

Games: paradox + faces; cessation-talk + pain/tuning cases; attention-direction + inward/outward cases; cessation-talk (re: pain or tuning) + meaning/utterance cases.; per analogies, ladder + up/down aspects, drabbit + duck/rabbit faces.

667. Imagine someone simulating pain, and then saying "It'll get better soon". Can't one say that he means the pain even though he is not concentrating his attention on any pain? – And what about when I finally say "It's stopped now"?

To rehearse. The (PI 201) thesis of the *Investigations* is that identity is paradox, called the rule, as neither of opposite cases + existing as both qua either.

Comment. Per PI 667 grammar qua law: simulation is to *"It'll get better soon"/"It's stopped now"* cases; as paradox is to faces; as pain case is to non-attending-to/non-attended-to cases; here, empirical-sense talk is irrelevant other than it serving as raw material for conversion to grammatical talk.

Games: paradox + faces; simulation + *"It'll get better soon"/"It's stopped now"* cases; pain case + non-attending-to/non-attended-to cases; per analogies, ladder + up/down aspects, drabbit + duck/rabbit faces.

668. But can't one also lie in this way: one says "It'll stop soon", and means pain – but when asked "What did you mean?", one answers "The noise in the next room"? In this sort of case, one perhaps says: "I was going to answer …, but thought better of it and answered …"

To rehearse. The (PI 201) thesis of the *Investigations* is that identity is paradox, called the rule, as neither of opposite cases + existing as both qua either.

Comment. Per PI 668 grammar qua law: paradox is to faces; as per PI 43, word (the cessation-talk – re: pain or noise) is to meaning/use cases; as cessation-talk is to truth/lie cases; here, to mean the pain case but state the noise case – to say one thing but mean another thing – is, as it were, to tell a white lie in that the opposite cases as seemingly contradictories, are paradoxically one another.

Games: paradox + faces; word + meaning/use cases; cessation talk + pain/noise cases; per analogies, ladder + up/down aspects, drabbit + duck/rabbit faces.

*669. When speaking, one can refer to an object by pointing at it. Here pointing is a part of the language-game. And now it seems to us as if one spoke **of** a sensation by directing one's attention to it. But where is the analogy? It evidently lies in the fact that one can point at a thing by **looking** or **listening**.*

*But in certain circumstances, even **pointing** at the object one is talking about may be quite inessential to the language-game, to one's thought.*

To rehearse. The (PI 201) thesis of the *Investigations* is that identity is paradox, called the rule, as neither of opposite cases + existing as both qua either.

Comment. Per PI 669 grammar qua law: pointing outwardly in whatever way, like directing attention inwardly, is to verb/noun senses; as paradox is to faces; as, per PI 43, word is to meaning/use – essential/non-essential cf. meaning/not-meaning – aspects.

Games: paradox + faces; word + meaning/use – cf. thinking/speaking, essential/inessential, mental-process/sensation, verb-sense/noun-sense – cases; per analogies, ladder + up/down aspects, drabbit + duck/rabbit faces.

670. Imagine that you were telephoning someone, and you said to him, "This table is too tall", and pointed at the table. What is the role of pointing here? Can I say: I **mean** the table in question by pointing at it? What is this pointing for, or these words, or whatever else may accompany them?

To rehearse. The (PI 201) thesis of the *Investigations* is that identity is paradox, called the rule, as neither of opposite cases + existing as both qua either.

Comment. Per PI 670 grammar qua law, whether a person is seen pointing or inferred to be pointing, and whether the pointing is gestural, or by looking, or by aiming the mind at the pointed-to object: pointing is to verb-noun senses; as paradox is to faces; per PI 43, the purpose or point qua meaning of a word is its use; in the absence of any of the three dimensions of the point + verb/nun senses grammar the ungrammatical (unlawful, going against the rule) case obtains; the pointing case as the threefold grammar, like every language game, serves the purpose of bespeaking identity – its lawfulness – as paradox.

Games: paradox + faces; pointing + pointing-to/pointed-at aspects; per analogies, ladder + up/down aspects, drabbit + duck/rabbit faces.

*671. And what do I point at by the inner activity of listening? At the sound that comes to my ears, and at the silence when I hear **nothing**?*

*Listening, as it were, **searches for** an auditory impression, and so can't point at it, but only at the **place** where it is searching for it.*

To rehearse. The (PI 201) thesis of the *Investigations* is that identity is paradox, called the rule, as neither of opposite cases + existing as both qua either.

Comment. Per PI 671 grammar qua law: inner activity is to outer behaviour; as a listening-for is to listened-for; as searching-for is to searched-for; as hearing is to heard; as sound-finding is to found-sound; as silence-finding is to found-silence; as paradox face is to corresponding other paradox face; as pointing-at (or pointing-to) is to pointed-at (pointed-to).

Games: paradox +faces; listening cf. hearing cf. searching cf. pointing cf. sound-seeking cf. silence-finding + verb/noun senses; per PI 43, word + meaning/use cases; per analogies, ladder + up/down aspects, drabbit + duck/rabbit faces.

672. If the receptive attitude is called a kind of 'pointing' at something – then it isn't at the impression we get in that way.

To rehearse. The (PI 201) thesis of the *Investigations* is that identity is paradox, called the rule, as neither of opposite cases + existing as both qua either.

Comment. Per PI 672 grammar qua law: paradox is to faces; as receptivity cf. sensation or impression is to receiving/received – pointing-at/pointed-at, sensing/sensed, impressing/impressed – cases; as per PI 43, word + meaning/use cases.

Games: paradox + faces (and variants, as per Comment); per analogies, ladder + up/down aspects, drabbit + duck/rabbit faces.

673. A mental attitude doesn't 'accompany' words in the sense in which a gesture accompanies them. (As a man can travel alone, and yet be accompanied by my good wishes; or as a room can be empty, and yet flooded with light.)

To rehearse. The (PI 201) thesis of the *Investigations* is that identity is paradox, called the rule, as neither of opposite cases + existing as both qua either.

Comment. Per PI 673 grammar qua law: paradox is to faces; as accompaniment is to verb/noun aspects; per each case of paired opposites as distinct paradox-face cases, each is not the other; the empirical sense of accompaniment, implying side-by-side dualism, translates grammatically as accompaniment qua coincidence cf. the way-up/way-down aspects of a ladder; a word-meaning (cf. mental attitude) accompanies a word-use (cf. gesture) differently in that the meaning/use (mentality/gesture) cases are distinct paradox faces, yet coincide as the word qua paradox case.

Games: paradox + faces; coincidence + distinct cases; accompaniment + verb/noun cases; per PI 43, word + meaning/use – cf. mental-attitude/ gesture – cases; person + mental-attitude/natural-expression cases; traveller + alone/well-wished cases; room + empty/light-filled case; per analogies, ladder + up/down aspects, drabbit + duck/rabbit faces.

674. Does one say, for example, "I didn't really mean my pain just now; my mind wasn't on it enough for that?" Do I ask myself, say, "What did I mean by this word just now? My attention was divided between my pain and the noise"?

To rehearse. The (PI 201) thesis of the *Investigations* is that identity is paradox, called the rule, as neither of opposite cases + existing as both qua either.

Comment. Per PI 674 grammar qua law: the empirical-sense talk grammatically translates as follows: paradox is to faces; as statement is to pain/noise cases; as per PI 43, word (re: pain or noise) is to meaning/use cases.

Games: paradox + faces; attention + divided aspects; word + meaning/use cases; per analogies, ladder + up/down aspects, drabbit + duck/rabbit face.

675. "Tell me, what was going on in you when you uttered the words ...?" — The answer to this is not "I was meaning ...":

To rehearse. The (PI 201) thesis of the *Investigations* is that identity is paradox, called the rule, as neither of opposite cases + existing as both qua either.

Comment. Per PI 675 grammar qua law: going-on-in-head case is to utterance case; as distinct paradox face is to its counterpart distinct face; as per PI 143, word is to meaning/use cases; as word is to not-one-another cases; as per analogy, ladder is to up/down aspects as distinct aspects.

Games: paradox + distinct faces; wordage qua coincidence + distinct meaning/utterance case; per analogies, ladder + up/down aspects, drabbit + duck/rabbit faces.

676. "I meant **this** by that word" is a statement which is used differently from one about an affection of the mind.

To rehearse. The (PI 201) thesis of the *Investigations* is that identity is paradox, called the rule, as neither of opposite cases + existing as both qua either.

Comment. Per PI 676 grammar qua law: empirical-sense talk translates to grammatical talk as follows: **this** talk is identity-as-paradox talk; paradox is to faces; as per PI 43, word is to meaning/use – cf. mental-affliction/ expression – cases; it is not that I/meaning are paradox faces; rather, it is that paired paradox faces are the I/myself, also the meaning/use, cases.

Games: paradox + faces; **this** qua person + this/this – mind/body – cases; language (word) + meaning/use cases; per analogies, ladder + up/down aspects, drabbit + duck/rabbit faces.

677. On the other hand: "When you were swearing just now, did you really mean it?" This amounts to something like: "Were you really angry?" — And the answer

may be given on the basis of introspection, and is often some such thing as "I didn't mean it very seriously", "I meant it half jokingly", and so on. There are differences of degree here. And one does indeed also say, "I was half thinking of him when I said that".

To rehearse. The (PI 201) thesis of the *Investigations* is that identity is paradox, called the rule, as neither of opposite cases + existing as both qua either.

Comment. Per PI 677 grammar qua law: the empirical-sense (say, introspection-sense) talk is raw-material talk for grammatical treatment as follows: it is not grammatically that one can half mean or doubly mean a wording; rather, grammatically, it is that, per PI 43, the meaning aspect of a word qua paradox (cf. an ambiguity) case is its use aspect.

Games: paradox + faces; ambiguity + double senses; word + meaning/use – feeling/expression, half/half, serious/joking – cases; per analogies, ladder + up/down aspects, drabbit + duck/rabbit faces.

678. What does this meaning (the pain, or the piano-tuning) consist in? No answer comes – for the answers which at first sight suggest themselves are of no use. – "And yet at the time I **meant** the one thing and not the other." Yes – now you have only repeated with emphasis something which no one has contradicted anyway.

To rehearse. The (PI 201) thesis of the *Investigations* is that identity is paradox, called the rule, as neither of opposite cases + existing as both qua either.

Comment. Per PI 678 grammar qua law: of the pain/noise cases, to word-mean one rather than the other is not to mean it definitively, implying the two cases as contradictories, but is to word-mean – as paradoxically word-use – either the one (say, pain) or the other (noise).

Games: paradox + faces; word (whether pain or noise) + meaning/use cases; per PI 304, neither (Nothing or Something) + both (Nothing and Something; per analogies, ladder + up/down aspects, drabbit + duck/rabbit faces.

679. *"But can you doubt that you meant **this**?" – No; but neither can I be certain of it, know it.*

To rehearse. The (PI 201) thesis of the *Investigations* is that identity is paradox, called the rule, as neither of opposite cases + existing as both qua either.

Comment. Per PI 679 grammar qua law: paradox is to faces; as neither face is to faces; as **this** qua neither certainty nor doubt is to both certainty/doubt cases qua this/this cases.

Games: paradox + faces; neither aspect + both aspects; per PI 43, word (certainty, doubt) + meaning/use cases; per analogies, ladder + up/down aspects, drabbit + duck/rabbit faces.

680. *When you tell me that you cursed and meant N. as you did so, it is all one to me whether you looked at a picture of him, or imagined him, uttered his name, or whatever. The inferences from this fact that interest me have nothing to do with these things. On the other hand, someone might explain to me that cursing was **effective** only when one had a clear image of the man or spoke his name out loud. But one wouldn't say, "It depends on how the man who is cursing **means** his victim".*

To rehearse. The (PI 201) thesis of the *Investigations* is that identity is paradox, called the rule, as neither of opposite cases + existing as both qua either.

Comment. Per PI 680 grammar qua law: from PI 43, to mean a curse is to use it; here, in whatever empirical-sense way one means it or whatever strategies are involved, the case – grammatically – is that word-meaning is paradoxically the word-use; just as the ladder's way-up aspect is warranted solely by the ladder and the way-down aspect, so word-meaning is warranted solely by the word and its use; per the curse case qua paradox case as its meaning/behaviour cases qua paradox faces, these cases are distinct hence irrelevant to one another yet also coincide as the curses case thus having everything to do with one another.

Games: paradox + faces; word (say, curse) + meaning/use – cf. verb/noun, cursing-N/cursed-N – aspects; per analogies, ladder + up/down aspects, drabbit + duck/rabbit faces.

*681. Nor, of course, does one ask: "Are you sure that you cursed **him**, that the link with him was established?"*

Then this link is presumably very easy to establish, if one can be so sure of it, can know that it doesn't miss its target! – Well, can it happen to me that I intend to write to one person and in fact write to another? And how might that occur?

To rehearse. The (PI 201) thesis of the *Investigations* is that identity is paradox, called the rule, as neither of opposite cases + existing as both qua either.

Comment. Per PI 681 grammar qua law: cursing a particular him, establishing a particular link, hitting or intending a particular target, is paradoxically the particular case cursed, established, hit or intended; whatever the language game, paired opposites qua faces or aspects happen qua exist as paradoxically one another.

Games: paradox + faces; curse, link, target + verb/noun senses; per PI 43, word + meaning/use cases; per analogies, ladder + up/down aspects, drabbit + duck/rabbit faces.

*682. "You said, 'It'll stop soon'. – Were you thinking of the noise or of your pain?" If he answers, "I was thinking of the piano-tuning" – is he stating that the link existed, or is he making it by means of these words? – Can't I say **both**? If what he said was true, didn't the link exist – and is he not for all that making one which did not exist?*

To rehearse. The (PI 201) thesis of the *Investigations* is that identity is paradox, called the rule, as neither of opposite cases + existing as both qua either.

Comment. Per PI 682 grammar qua law: the cessation talk is to stating/stated – cf. making/made, stating/made, making/stated – cases; as paradox is to faces; as per PI 43, word is to meaning/use cases; as link is to link-cases.

Games: paradox + faces (and parallels, as per the Comment); per analogies, ladder + up/down aspects, drabbit + duck/rabbit faces.

683. I draw a head. You ask, "Whom is that supposed to represent?" – I: "It's supposed to be N." – You: "But it doesn't look like him; if anything, it's rather like M." – When I said it represented N., was I making a connection, or reporting one? And what connection was there?

To rehearse. The (PI 201) thesis of the *Investigations* is that identity is paradox, called the rule, as neither of opposite cases + existing as both qua either.

Comment. Per PI 683 grammar qua law: the drawing talk is to reporting/reported – cf. making/made, making/reported, reporting/made – cases; as paradox is to faces; as per PI 43, word is to meaning/use cases; as link is to link-cases; as representation is to verb/noun senses; as connection is to connected cases.

Games: paradox + faces (and parallels, as per the Comment); per analogies, ladder + up/down aspects, drabbit + duck/rabbit faces.

*684. What is there in favour of saying that my words describe an existing connection? Well, they refer to various things which didn't materialize only with the words; they say, for example, that I **would have** given a particular answer then, if I had been asked. And even if this is only conditional, still it does say something about the past.*

To rehearse. The (PI 201) thesis of the *Investigations* is that identity is paradox, called the rule, as neither of opposite cases + existing as both qua either.

Comment. Per PI 684 grammar qua law: a wording as a paradox case qua description case describes – out-pictures – its meaning/use existents qua paradox faces; this is so, whatever the wording's logical sense as (say) conditional, or its empirical sense as (say) referenced to the past; the three members of the threefold word + meaning/use case are grammatically connected in that each is a distinct case yet lives in the other two cases cf. per analogy, ladder + up/down aspects.

Games: paradox + faces; per PI 43, word + meaning/use cases; per analogies, ladder + up/down aspects, drabbit + duck/rabbit faces.

685. *"Look for A" does not mean "Look for B"; but I may do just the same thing in obeying the two orders.*

To say that something different must happen in the two cases would be like saying that the sentences "Today is my birthday" and "My birthday is on April 26th" must refer to different days, because their sense is not the same.

To rehearse. The (PI 201) thesis of the *Investigations* is that identity is paradox, called the rule, as neither of opposite cases + existing as both qua either.

Comment. Per PI 685 grammar qua law: as the paradox case is to its faces; so, the look-for case is to its A/B cases; so, the birthday talk is to its day/date cases; so, unity is to difference; so, coincidence is to distinct cases.

Games: paradox + faces; unity + difference; per PI 43, word + meaning/expression cases; per PI 215, sameness + same/same cases; coincidence + distinct cases; look-for + A/B cases; birthday + day/date cases; per analogies, ladder + up/down aspects, drabbit + duck/rabbit faces.

686. *"Of course I meant B; I didn't think of A at all!"*

"I wanted B to come to me, so as to ..." – *All this points to a wider context.*

To rehearse. The (PI 201) thesis of the *Investigations* is that identity is paradox, called the rule, as neither of opposite cases + existing as both qua either.

Comment. Per PI 686 grammar qua law: as the threefold grammar qua wider context; herein, per PI 43, word-meaning is to word-use qua not word-meaning; as B is to A; as paradox face is to counterpart face.

Games: paradox + faces; word + meaning/use – meaning/not-meaning, B/A – cases; per analogies, ladder + (say) up/down aspects, drabbit + (say) duck/rabbit faces.

687. *Instead of "I meant him", one can, of course, sometimes say, "I thought of him"; sometimes even "Yes, we were speaking of him". So, ask yourself what 'speaking of him' consists in!*

To rehearse. The (PI 201) thesis of the *Investigations* is that identity is paradox, called the rule, as neither of opposite cases + existing as both qua either.

Comment. Per PI 687 grammar qua law: paradox is to faces; as, per PI 43, of-him wordage is to meaning/use – cf. thinking/speaking – aspects.

Games: paradox + faces; wordage (of-him) + meaning/use – meaning/meant, say, thinking/speaking – cases; per analogies, ladder + up/down aspects, drabbit + duck/rabbit faces.

688. *In certain circumstances, one can say, "As I was speaking, I felt I was saying it **to you**". But I wouldn't say this if I were in any case talking with you.*

To rehearse. The (PI 201) thesis of the *Investigations* is that identity is paradox, called the rule, as neither of opposite cases + existing as both qua either.

Comment. Per PI 688 grammar qua law: circumstances talk is threefold-grammar-context talk; paradox is to faces; as to-you wordage is to meaning/use – cf. feeling/speaking, thinking/speaking, indirect/direct – cases.

Games: paradox + faces; from PI 43, wordage (to-you) + meaning/use – cf. indirect/direct (and parallels) – aspects; per analogies, ladder + up/down aspects, drabbit + duck/rabbit faces.

689. *"I am thinking of N." "I am speaking of N."*

*How do I speak **of** him? I say, for instance, "I must go and see N. today" – But surely that is not enough! After all, when I say "N.", I might mean various people of this name. – "Then there must surely be a further link between my words and N., for otherwise I would **still** not have meant HIM."*

*Certainly such a link exists. Only not as you imagine it: namely, by means of a mental **mechanism**.*

(One compares "meaning him" with "aiming at him".)

To rehearse. The (PI 201) thesis of the *Investigations* is that identity is paradox, called the rule, as neither of opposite cases + existing as both qua either.

Comment. Per PI 689 grammar qua law: paradox is to faces; as per PI 43, wordage (N, HIM, of him, of N) is to meaning/use cases.

Gamesa: paradox + faces; wordage + meaning/use – cf. thinking/speaking, mental/behavioural, aiming-at/aimed-at – cases; per analogies, ladder + up/down aspects, drabbit + duck/rabbit faces.

690. *What if I at one time make an apparently innocent remark and accompany it with a furtive sidelong glance at someone; and at another time, looking straight ahead, speak openly of somebody present, mentioning his name – am I really thinking **specially** about him when I use his name?*

To rehearse. The (PI 201) thesis of the *Investigations* is that identity is paradox, called the rule, as neither of opposite cases + existing as both qua either.

Comment. Per PI 690 grammar qua law: whether or not a person spoken of is present in the room, or named, or given a furtive sidelong glance, the spoken-of wordage (in light of PI 43) is to its meaning/use cases; as paradox is to its faces; from which, a meaning case qua a paradox face is specifically referenced to its expression case qua counterpart paradox face cf. per analogy, ladder-ascent aspect referenced specifically to – as being paradoxically – ladder-descent aspect.

Games: paradox + faces; spoken-of wordage + meaning/use cases; name + naming/named – cf. verb-sense/noun-sense – cases; per analogies, ladder + up/down aspects, drabbit + duck/rabbit faces.

*691. When I make myself a sketch of N.'s face from memory, I can surely be said to **mean** him by my drawing. But which of the processes taking place while I draw (or before or afterwards) could I say is meaning him?*

For one would, of course, like to say: when he meant him, he aimed at him. But how does someone do that, when he calls the other person's face to mind?

I mean, how does he call HIM to mind?

How does he call him?

To rehearse. The (PI 201) thesis of the *Investigations* is that identity is paradox, called the rule, as neither of opposite cases + existing as both qua either.

Comment. Per PI 691 grammar qua law: sketch case or reembrace case (N's face, HIM) is to verb/noun senses; as paradox is to faces; as per PI 43, word is to meaning/use cases; as aim-at is to aiming-at/aimed-at cases.

Games: paradox + faces (and variants, as per the Comment); per analogies, ladder + up/down aspects, drabbit + duck/rabbit faces.

692. Is it correct for someone to say: "When I gave you this rule, I meant that in this case you should ..."? Even if he did not think of this case at all as he gave the rule? Of course it is correct. For "to mean it" just did not mean: to think of it. But now the question is: How are we to judge whether someone meant such-and-such? – That he has, for example, mastered a particular technique in arithmetic and algebra, and taught someone else the expansion of a series in the usual way, is such a criterion.

To rehearse. The (PI 201) thesis of the *Investigations* is that identity is paradox, called the rule, as neither of opposite cases + existing as both qua either.

Comment. Per PI 692 grammar qua law: meaning such-and-and-such is to such-and-such expressed; as the face of a paradox is the counterpart face; here, one judges (warrants) such-and-such as meant if it is paradoxically told out or gesturally shown.

Games: paradox + faces; per PI 43, word (rule cf. subject matter) + meaning/use – cf. teaching/learning – aspects; per analogies, ladder + up/down aspects, drabbit + duck/rabbit faces.

693. "When I teach someone the construction of the series ..., I surely mean him to write ... at the hundredth place." – Quite right; you mean it. And evidently without necessarily even thinking of it. This shows you how different the grammar of the verb "to mean something" is from that of the verb "to think". And nothing is more wrong-headed than to call meaning something a mental activity! Unless, that is, one is setting out to produce confusion. (Similarly, one might speak of an activity of butter when it rises in price; and if no problems are produced by this, it is harmless.)

To rehearse. The (PI 201) thesis of the *Investigations* is that identity is paradox, called the rule, as neither of opposite cases + existing as both qua either.

Comment. Per PI 693 grammar qua law: thinking is to speaking; as, per PI 43, meaning is to use; as paradox-face case is to counterpart paradox-face case; here, PI 693 makes the point that grammatical meaning is not psychological thinking qua mental process but grammatical meaning is grammatical thinking in that these grammatical cases feature in variant language games, each bespeaking identity as paradox; put another way – it is not that a person's psychology non-exits, considered empirically; it is that, considered grammatically, psychology is irrelevant other that as raw material for grammatical treatment.

Games: paradox + faces; per PI 43, word + meaning/use – cf. thinking/speaking, mental-process/behaviour, logical/empirical – cases; per analogies, ladder + up/down aspects, drabbit + duck/rabbit faces.

BIBLIOGRAPHY

Wittgenstein. L. (1953). *Philosophical Investigations*. Trans. Anscombe. G.E.M. Blackwell.

Wittgenstein. L. (2000). *Philosophical Investigations*. Trans. G.E.M. Anscombe. P.M.S. Hacker and Joachim Schulte. Blackwell.

ABOUT THE AUTHOR

Bart Anthony Keegan, Ph.D., lives quietly in London pursuing his foremost interest: the philosophy of suffering. During his sojourns in England and Australia, he studied divinity and philosophy and began to question the meaning of life, the sense that theologians and philosophers made of it. This interest gradually focused on how to think about anything at all and the logic that is used as the tool of thinking. Bart met up with Anselm's proof for the existence of God and this changed entirely the direction of his interest. In that moment, he began to question if the way we think is in need of radical change from the root: the axioms of thought themselves.

The Diary of Atonement, *Poems & Prose of Atonement*, and *Identity as Paradox* are the fruit of Bart's questioning: They offer up as their thesis that each identity–person or thing–in the story of the world is an atonement of opposites: a paradox, from which, Bart came to understand that suffering, as sorrow, together with its opposite such as glory qua that which is glorious are cases as paradoxically one another, where their paradox case as their common identity case is neither one of them but both of them at once, and this (borrowing from Anselm) as that than which nothing greater can be conceived–identity-as-paradox as, so to call it, creativity as such. Each identity in the story of the world is a creativity, presenting either wholly negatively, wholly positively, or by turns each of these opposites. By which, that which is called the problem of evil–here called the problem of suffering–is accounted for as warranted by the justice of creativity as such, the fruits of which thereby are the cases of good and evil, glory and suffering, rejoicing and sorrow—the head-and-tail faces, so to speak, of the coin of untold measure that is identity as paradox.

Bart invites discussion regarding his work:
trabkeegan@talktalk.net

ABOUT THE DESIGNER

Elizabeth Beeton is a jill of all trades and mistress of none. Her life is mundane, made up of the usual things many humans experience: marriage, kids, ailing parents, aging, failing health, church, in-laws, outlaws, and scrabbling for a living.

She lives in Kansas City, Missouri, USA, writes novels, and is the owner of **B10 Mediaworx**, an author publishing services company. She designs print books, ebooks, and book covers. She publishes her own novels under the B10 Mediaworx imprint, and literature in a niche religious genre under the Peculiar Pages imprint. They don't make any money, but they are works that deserve a place in the Library of Congress. She builds and maintains her own websites.

She has a bachelor's in English, creative writing and journalism, from the University of Missouri at Kansas City.

She also reads, organizes her office endlessly, and tinkers on her computer (sometimes to ill effect). She's a fair-weather Kansas City Chiefs and Royals fan, half-arsed planner, avid cross stitcher, dilettante crafter, and aspiring odalisque. She regularly thumbs her nose at her to-do list as if it has any authority over her at all. Her life's goal is to finish all the craft projects she has ever begun. *All* of them.

b10mediaworx.com